ALAIN ELKANN

INTERVIEWS

Tel.: 212-989-6769 Fax: 212-647-0005 www.assouline.com ISBN: 9781614286325

Art director: Camille Dubois. Editor: Taylor Viens. Printed in China.

ALAIN ELKANN

INTERVIEWS

ASSOULINE

CONTENTS

ALAIN ELKANN

WRITER

Who did you first interview?

The first interview I conducted was a very long interview with the Italian writer Alberto Moravia and it ended up as a book. The title is *Life of Moravia* (*Vita di Moravia*) and the book has been translated in thirty-five languages. It came out just after he died in 1990, and it became a sort of moral will and a biography of Alberto Moravia.

Who did your interview next?

I had a call from Tele Monte Carlo, a private television company that later became La7. They asked me to interview Umberto Eco and the interview took place at the Belgian University of Louvain.

Why did you decide to continue with the interviews?

For a fiction writer like me, interviews became a very interesting new genre which didn't interfere with my fiction writing. Conducting interviews has been like going to prolonged university, because each interview is like having a private lesson from an interesting person on a different subject.

How would you describe your interviews?

My purpose is to let people be free to say what they feel and what they want. I let people speak, because the reader wants to know about the person you are interviewing and not about the interviewer. You must never forget that you are not doing the interview for yourself, but for your readers. You should never take things for granted, and sometimes obvious questions are important to be asked.

Do you prepare all your questions in advance?

I don't think that it always works to prepare all the questions in an interview, which is ultimately like a dialogue. Sometimes the person goes in a different direction and it would be a mistake to insist on your questions.

How does an interview progress?

An interview has the same pace as a short story, and it has to have a beginning and an end. You can't say everything in an interview. It's like a photograph, when you capture a moment of someone's life.

What do you want to know about the person you interview?

I like the "métier." If I interview an architect I want to know about his conception of architecture. If I interview a designer I want to know what they have to say about fashion and their own style. I suggest to the person I interview to explain concepts that may seem complicated in a simple way. I try to make my interviews as simple as possible, as readable as possible.

How do you decide who you are going to interview?

There is no specific rule; I always try to be as eclectic as possible in my choices, as you can see in this book. I have interviewed immortal stars like Sophia Loren, Marcello Mastroianni, Brigitte Bardot, and Catherine Deneuve, just to name some; Nobel Prize writers like the Russian poet Joseph Brodsky or the Peruvian writer Mario Vargas Llosa; designers like Vivienne Westwood, Giorgio Armani, Miuccia Prada, Gianni Versace, or Zac Posen; art dealers like Anthony d'Offay and Old Masters dealer Marco Voena, or a contemporary group of artists like Mark Grotjahn, Sterling Ruby, Urs Fischer, and Dan Colen.

How do you prepare for your interviews?

First, you have to study the subject, you have to know the person you are going to interview. Often what is good is to know a little detail which is not so obvious and which surprises the person you interview, and therefore they open up.

Is it true that, since 1989, you have done an interview every week?

Sometimes I did more than one, because I was also working in T.V. It is a way of life. I have done thousands. It's a strange work. It's a way of socializing, studying and communicating. It is also very stimulating to discover new people and new subjects.

Do you have a favorite interview?

This question is like asking who is your favorite child, or what your favorite book is! The answer is, "It's the one I haven't yet done but the one I hope to do in the future."

Do you have any regrets?

Yes, I would have liked to interview Pablo Picasso, Charlie Chaplin, James Joyce,

Ernest Hemingway, Winston Churchill, Virginia Woolf, Princess Diana, Elvis Presley, Mother Teresa, Albert Einstein, or Dr. Schweitzer. . . .

Is there an interview you particularly care about?

Yes, the one with Robert Silvers, who recently passed away. He was the greatest editor in the world and this is terribly important because I don't believe there is a really good writer without an editor.

How did you learn the craft of making an interview?

I took the *Paris Review* interviews called "Writers at Work" as a model. My examples in the art of being clear and precise are writers like Ernest Hemingway, Truman Capote, Alberto Moravia, and Raymond Carver.

What kind of people do you like to interview?

You don't always have to interview a very well-known person. Readers can come to know someone who is equally interesting but maybe less in the spotlight. My choice was never for the mainstream, but for what I thought was interesting.

Do you still enjoy conducting interviews?

Yes, and what I enjoy now is to see a book coming out with so many facets. In the span of thirty or forty years these people are the protagonists in their own fields.

How would you describe this interview book?

It's like a book of photography made of words. You can read an interview per day or, if you read the whole book you can have fun, because it's like a novel with many characters. Or you can keep it in your library and it can be used as a reference book.

What is the defining quality of your interviews?

My view is a nonspecialist view. I report exactly what people say. My technique is to write all the interviews longhand. Probably I am pedantic, as I sometimes ask the person I interview to repeat what they say. There should be no doubt about their answers.

Interview by David Hornsby
London
May 2017

~

YOU MUST NEVER FORGET
THAT YOU ARE NOT DOING THE INTERVIEW
FOR YOURSELF, BUT FOR YOUR

readers.

DAVID ADJAYE

ARCHITECT

The leading architect David Adjaye OBE RA set up his first office in 1994, where his ingenious use of materials and his sculptural ability established him as an architect with an artist's sensibility and vision. Adjaye Associates now has four international offices, with projects throughout the world. He is the John C. Portman Design Critic in Architecture at Harvard University and designed the National Museum of African American History and Culture.

Would you say that the architecture of today is very different from the architecture of the past?

We live in a very different age, so the way in which we procure architecture has changed. It is much morc concentrated and focused, using the digital age to marshal experiences from different offices.

What makes buildings of today so different?

When we talk about the evolution of modernism we have to understand what happened in the twentieth century, the invention of the elevator, air conditioning, and the glass wall. . . . We can make a new kind of architecture, so we can accommodate the explosion of urbanism and people moving to the city in a way which we could not have done with the techniques of the past.

What is the difference between the architecture of the twentieth and twenty-first centuries?

The twentieth century was about our understanding of the industrialization of the way in which we make buildings. We talked about material industrialization, panelizing, and glass was something you could produce in hundreds of sheets. Architecture responded by being in awe of that and celebrating it. The twenty-first century has given us the tools to marshal, customize, and focus, with this incredible production that we never had before. This is a massive shift.

What is happening now?

My generation believe that with the dawn of the digital age we have the tools to take advantage of what has happened. We are no longer in awe. We are obsessed with what a building means, how we can tailor it to a community. It's not about shapes or forms, but reading the city, reading the people. My generation bespoke the industrialization process. With computers we can generate efficiencies in all the forms. We can create the narrative with materials. I can create pixelated glass, send it to a computer, and obtain what I want at a reasonable cost. The city has now become very complicated and dynamic.

Skyscrapers were perceived as the symbols of modernity. Is it still like that?

Skyscrapers are an important symbol, but my generation don't believe in that for the future. The answers are no longer singular, they are complicated. The vertical is not the only answer to density.

Is this what you teach to your students at Harvard?

It is one of the things. We teach the techniques of adding, modifying, and reinventing. These are the tools of dealing with the old city.

What else do you teach?

The understanding of cities, and that the city is the ultimate inspiration of architecture. The answers are in the city itself, if you look hard enough.

Which cities do you use for your case studies?

Cities from every continent that have produced interesting responses to the idea of the city. All regions have their models. We no longer see the world as a singular modern experiment, but as multiple models, and we need to be sensitive to what their trajectories are about. Architecture should be responding, and of the place.

How do you state your own style?

My generation is not interested in our own style as proposed in the past to create a signature. We are interested in process, intellectual curiosity, and response. So we hope you see these three things in every project, and then you recognize the architect by the way in which they respond to the problems. We refute the reduction of architecture to a series of motifs.

What is the difference between building for private use and building for institutions?

Building a private house for my clients has been about the exploration of retreats from the density of the city, creating refuges for individuals, couples, and families, so they have a different world. The public work is to explore the dissolving of institutional walls, to make them more like an infrastructure for citizens, offering accessibility and openness to the widest audience. These buildings offer an open language, to allow an ease of use and uptake. That is the project of the public realm of architecture right now.

If I understand you well, you are paying a great deal of attention to the needs of people?

When I designed the new libraries in East London, people thought that libraries were private institutions for other people. Our job was for them to realize that libraries are like a resource, like water, to turn on and off; a sort of democratization of knowledge, through openness and accessibility.

Which of your many projects do you like the most?

I love them all! I am lucky that I never did a project that I did not want to do. I find that it is empathy and intellectual sympathy with the person I am working with that is critical for the success of making architecture.

How can you work on different continents at the same time, with different inspirations?

The wonderful thing about architecture is that it is slow. It allows time to research, learn, infiltrate, experience, to role-play in many cultures and communities, which gives invaluable information about how to work in different contexts. I have to relearn every day, to question what I already know, and respond.

From history we remember the pyramids in Egypt, the Colosseum in Rome, the Parthenon in Athens, the Eiffel Tower in Paris, the Empire State Building in New York. Do you want to build and leave to posterity a symbol like these?

It is a kind of misguided inspiration to aim your architecture on leaving a symbol of your age. If you look at the pyramids, it is an evolution, until they reach their perfection. It is not about making what is symbolic of an age. We focus on citizens and utility. I am fifty and Renzo Piano for example is eighty. When he did the Centre Pompidou in Paris [also known as the Beaubourg], they thought it was awful. History decides what is good and not good, not architects. Architecture has transformed itself in the past twenty years. It's so fundamentally different that it's mind-blowing.

Is architecture a good career for young people to follow?

It is not a boom career and it is not flooded with people, it is a specialized world. There is an increase in the amount of architecture, because there are more people and there's a need. The architect of today is a technical organizer, more like a conductor than an artist, building teams and making meaning out of it.

What about aesthetics?

Aesthetics are very important, but have changed in the way they manifest. It's still about beauty, but we seek that beauty in many different ways.

And villages?

Our notion of habitation is an evolved form of villages. The village helps in forms, or organization and density, but its own motif is pretty much complete. The major task now is the unprecedented level of influx of people into cities. This is the problem that needs to be cracked.

Is this a great moment to be an architect?

It is a great moment. The technology means we can work with planetary architecture for the first time, and be responsible all over the world.

Why do you have your base in London?

London's geographic position helps, as I choose to go to site, wherever it is.

When you build, what is your major goal?

The fulfillment of the happiness of the people who use it.

London
June 17, 2016

~

AHARON APPELFELD

NOVELIST

I meet Aharon Appelfeld, as I always do when I am in Jerusalem, at the Ticho House, the cafe where he goes twice a week to write longhand on a white sheet of paper with his biro pen.

I ask him what he is writing at the moment:

I published, a few months ago, a children's book that was rather successful. It is the story of two children living in the woods during the war. Now I am rewriting in Hebrew a book that I published many years ago in America. It is the story of a man who goes home after his liberation from the concentration camp. Going home, he tries to understand what happened. His mother was crazy about Bach music and loved churches. His father was a quiet man, living in a small town, fighting against provinciality. But on his way back he meets a woman who loved his father before he married his mother. . .

How many books have you written?

Forty-two books, and somehow they are like one book. It is always my enlarged eye on my parents, my origin, my experience.

Your books were considered strange in Israel for many years.

If we put it in a mild way, they were considered anti-Israeli, because I did not speak about them. But now people are understanding that their real roots are in Europe; and the Sephardic Jews have their roots in the Orient. Therefore, they are coming to my books. I receive many letters where they say, "Our parents were Holocaust survivors; they never spoke about it, we never asked them, they never told us. Now we understand what we have lost and your books became our family."

Do you still believe that literature has some importance?

Yes, because literature is humanity. Through literature we touch the real things. The real physical things of human being.

What is fiction?

The inner life of human beings. It is not the chronological thing that happened to you.

What about the importance of storytelling in fiction?

It is the deep dialogue with yourself and with your surroundings.

There is music in literature?

Yes, it is very important. I cannot imagine a good piece of fiction without musicality.

Is Hebrew a good language for musicality?

Yes, if you use the language in a proper way: choice of words, punctuation, rhythm.

Are you a slow writer?

I am checking and rechecking, several times, every page. I write, for instance, a page in the morning; at night I reread the same page, and in the following morning again; and all this before I print it.

By doing so don't you lose the momentum of the plot?

No, because if you are running after the plot the text will remain poor. In other words the sentence and the paragraph should always remain autonomous. Every sentence should be important, as well as every paragraph. The plot is important but has no value without a rich text.

Which writers would you use as an example to explain this?

Kafka is a good example. There are many prominent writers that I like, such as Thomas Mann, Dostoyevsky, Tolstoy—but they are not on the same scale of Kafka.

Why?

First of all, seriousness. There are writers who are totally devoted to their work and Kafka is one of them. Dostoyevsky was devoted to two things: writing and gambling. Tolstoy in his late years wanted to become a religious preacher and that ruined his writing. Mann had a sceptical mind: with his rationality he could not reach the origin of the mystery.

Today do we still have totally devoted writers like Kafka?

I am close to Philip Roth, Malamud, Bellow. They were committed writers, but in a different scale.

What makes a great writer?

The capacity to understand human beings and to be close to them. Of course there is also talent. I don't like, and never understood, pathological writers who hate Jews or all kinds of people.

Like Céline?

Yes. He is a very interesting writer, more than interesting. But I am also amazed to see that writers like Dostoyevsky, who could understand the soul of a simple peasant as much as the soul of a degenerate aristocrat, when it comes to Jewish people, for him all of them have a long nose and their pockets full of money.

Why do you consider Hemingway a great writer?

He was devoted to his weaknesses. I admire him because of his factual and dry style and he is never imposing on the reader. He understood himself.

And among Jewish writers, who do you admire?

Kafka because he is very interesting. He was predicting what was going to happen to him, to us. He wrote a story, *In the Penal Colony*, where he had foreseen what was going to happen twenty years before the Holocaust.

What is the mission of a writer?

A writer should not think about a mission, he should be occupied with the sentences or the plot of the story he is writing—this is his mission. He should know that he is not going to change the world, and he should be modest.

But is fiction art?

Of course, in good hands.

Jerusalem
October 16, 2013

~

Through literature we touch the real things.

The real physical things of human being.

GIORGIO ARMANI

FASHION DESIGNER

Giorgio Armani is in good spirits, wearing long dark-blue Bermuda shorts and a dark-brown T-shirt. He is tanned and resting at his home on the island of Pantelleria, an oasis of true luxury, very quiet, and with a light breeze. It's seven o'clock in the evening and, in the shade of old palm trees that the designer bought into his property from an aristocratic Sicilian family, it is time for tea and biscuits purchased at a local *pasticceria*. We are situated on a bluff overlooking the sea, and at about 9:30 we will dine at another spot on the property, which is made up of lots of houses joined together by small paths that are lit after sunset by very many candles in simple black lanterns.

Giorgio Armani, you have routinely spent the month of August on Pantelleria. What is the reason for your thirty years of loyalty?

I'm a creature of habit. I love rediscovering what I have started, and here in this place I have started a great deal. At first glance it seemed to be a difficult island: I had always imagined an island as a place with white beaches, and instead—this is one big rock. My first impression was not one of easy living, and there was nothing that was particularly attractive about this place. In those years everyone talked about going to Saint-Tropez, where you could mingle with the jet-set people or go dancing at balls. Here, however, there was not even electric light.

But you have stuck with it?

Yes, the island has maintained its fascination, but nowadays it also has new facilities. The promontory where we are now is very beautiful, and Sergio Galeotti and I decided we would make a home for ourselves here. From year to year I have added something: First of all I created the space where the swimming pool is, then this oasis with the palm trees, and then the other houses.

What is so special about this place?

Every year I come here with many friends. . . . I could show you a history of twenty-five years through photographs of the summers. The place itself does not alter, it is the people who change. I have tried to show the greatest respect to the nature of the place. I have dispensed with designer objects and there are just a few pieces I bought in the markets of Morocco. The colors are my quintessential grayscale, beige. As if they were made up of bright colors, strong and then filtered through nature, the sun, the wind. Then this house is a bit like a large boat, everyone has their independence, but there are certain rites to be followed, like there are on a boat. Before sunset, candles are lit everywhere. Everything is well organized, and the guests light candles everywhere. Everything is on schedule and my guests are familiar with some basic rules. For example, breakfast is taken in the morning with everybody together between the hours of nine and ten o'clock. In Milan I mostly see work colleagues, while here I feel free to let myself go, even to become rather romantic; I like to open up here, I like to hear other people tell their own nostalgic stories. In the city you cannot do this, there's not enough time.

What kinds of relationships do you have with your friends?

I am demanding and possessive. I give a great deal to my friends and I like to receive their loyalty and empathy in return. I do not want to exchange material things, I've been blessed by good fortune and that is not what matters. I want there to be a sense of understanding—in short, what I really enjoy is that they make me an absolute priority. Spend twenty days with Armani and don't go anywhere else. Armani wants you and you must come!

And who are those who you want?

First of all, my family members, for instance my sister Rosanna, my nieces, Silvana and Roberta, and my nephew, Andrea, and their chums, as well my sister Rosanna's little dog. Then there are the people I work with, like Leo and Graham and others. I have chosen to live without surprises. It is as if there is a love affair that becomes reinforced. I do not like playboy holidays where one goes in hope of adventure. Here we do not stay up too late at night because it is a crime to lose any hours from the coming day.

Do you have lots of people around so that you don't get lonely?

No, because when I am alone it affords me long moments of contemplation. I think that to be alone means to think about all the good things that one has, about how the day is coming when none of this will any longer be ours. Life passes, mine is a life dedicated to my work, which I have confused with real life. My luxury is to say what I think. It is according to my own taste to discard a paradigm that does not fit into the world of Armani. And in the same way to discard whatever it may be that I do not like to have in my life.

What is it about today's world that strikes you?

Today what is considered desirable has become so because it has been proposed by the media. And furthermore fashion also suffers, at the moment when you put a bag with a dress that has nothing to do with it. Fashion must go hand in hand with being right-minded, that's what counts, and I am looking for poise and composure, equilibrium, both in material things and also in relationships.

In October the Guggenheim Museum in New York will put about four hundred of your garments on display.

Yes, selected from my archive, some are on loans made by the general public or by famous people. I realized how in the history of my work there are certain fixed points that return continuously. And it looks interesting, you see how the same theme can be interpreted in different styles according to the time. Black and white, for example, you can change the shape or the length, but it is always coming back into fashion. I try to distance myself from them, but I find myself always coming back. And what this comes to mean is that the Asian way of dressing is the most logical and the most comfortable. My objective is to make clothes that form an integral part of the body of a man and of a woman.

And what about being elegant?

At one time when we were talking about being elegant it meant only one thing, the most formal clothes: a black suit with a string of pearls for her, a double-breasted blue suit for him. Nowadays what is meant by being stylish is wearing what harmonizes with the atmosphere that one is experiencing at that moment of time.

How would one be stylish on Pantelleria?

With loose fitting cotton slacks, knee-length or calf-length shorts, and with loose knitwear running over the body with muted colors, such as lavender blue, green, jade, orange-red, or colors that appear aged and mature.

But Armani, are you not the man in dark blue?

I am speaking about other people. It is true that for years I have been recognized as the man in the dark blue T-shirt, but there is that moment of awakening and becoming conscious of something, that you can also be in another way without betraying your principles. And so on Pantelleria I have experimented with my colors as I mentioned before, and with a certain success. He laughs.

You are about to open a large space in Milan in Via Manzoni. How will it be?

For me, having worked as an assistant in a department store in the sixties, I have always been fascinated by the diverse and anonymous buying public, and this is a big gamble. Ever since then I have liked the idea of having a small store where one sells only what one likes, without having to say, "This is not beautiful, but it sells." This is four thousand, five hundred square meters of space in which I am selling Emporio Armani, Armani Jeans, Armani/Casa—a new brand—and there is also going to be a Japanese restaurant, Nobu, a restaurant for young people that I hope will become a meeting place; as well as Sony, who will have a location there. For me it is a dream which has become reality.

Do you want to wake up a sleeping Milan?

To think I would be waking a sleeping Milan would be presumptuous. But strangely, in Milan there is a reluctance to adapt to new ways of life, and all new meeting places are places that are not immediately greatly frequented. Perhaps by doing so much I can insist that Milan really is able to change and certainly my space is something altogether new.

A drug store in Paris, a shop on Madison Avenue in New York and another in SoHo, you never stop. The question is almost redundant, but are there no breaks in this work?

There is a requirement for continuous updating which results from there being an extremely lively and active competition. Then, with the logic of today, one puts together a store that looks futuristic and after three years it has become outdated. Nothing lasts longer than a decade.

Everyone wants to buy what you make, do you feel under siege?

No, I feel gratified. When I hear prominent people talk about Giorgio Armani's great success in the past five years and his amazing company it is a compliment that fills me with pride. My life has been a mad rush, which has required the employment of all my physical energy, but I have become close to people who have given me a lot back, above all by accepting me as I am with all my contradictions.

You are still rebelling against the idea of being a prisoner of your own personality, and, if I understand correctly, you just want to be yourself?

Yes, but as I have said, I have remained true to myself. Thirty years ago I saw Pantelleria with the same love and with the same eyes. Of course, since then I have seen the whole world, but I have never gone away from here.

Do you want a private life?

Laughing again. More than anything else in life. I read about people who have economic power, who buy houses, who organize megaparties to gratify themselves. I have done this for the sake of my work, but to me all that is of little importance. When people see me, they recognize that what they have in front of them is a person who is perhaps rich, perhaps powerful in his field, who is recognized for his work in the world, but who has remained a normal human being with his own faults. It repays me well not to have taken advantage of the kind of envied lifestyle, which is also very conducive to becoming a misfit.

Even when it comes to Milan?

Yes, because that is my reality.

Do you consider yourself an essentially loyal person?

Yes, I think loyalty is one of my points of reference.

Pantelleria
August 20, 2000

~

Nothing
LASTS
L
O
N
G
E
R
THAN A DECADE.

PROSPER ASSOULINE

PUBLISHER

Prosper Assouline and his wife, Martine, have a large, open plan office on the twenty-seventh floor of a Park Avenue building. From their windows you can see the Chrysler Building, the Empire State Building, and Grand Central Station. I go into Prosper's studio, where he has a very large desk and brass lamps over the desk. The view is spectacular. We sit down, he is smiling and I ask him:

You work in luxury, style, and culture, but are you a book publisher at heart?

Absolutely. We do a lot of other things around the book, but, like the hamburger, without the beef there is nothing. The book is the center.

Are the books that you prepare and publish works of beauty?

Yes, all made in our kitchen in New York. We have an office in Paris, but everything is made here in New York. We are publishers, but not printers and distributors. Our pleasure is to make the layout and the text.

Does being a publisher of luxury books give you much pleasure?

We are proud, because it is intense.

How many books do you publish?

Fifty to sixty books a year. We have published one thousand five hundred books in total until now, and I think that is a lot.

What kind of books?

Everything about style, looking into style. We made a book with the recipes of Jackson Pollock, *Dinner with Jackson Pollock*, in which we talked about art and food. It was a huge bestseller.

What do you consider a bestseller with this kind of book?

For us, when we sell more than twenty-five thousand copies, it is really very good.

We sell in twenty-two shops around the world, and in selected bookstores and lifestyle stores. We have been publishing for twenty-two years.

Where did you start?

We had no idea about the business, at the beginning it was just an act of love. My wife, Martine, and I dearly love the hotel La Colombe d'Or in Saint-Paul-de-Vence. At the time I was the art director and publisher of magazines. We were in love with the place and we did a book on it, not about celebrity but about lifestyle. For us this place is the ultimate luxury, where we can eat simple tomatoes surrounded by a Picasso or a Léger.

How did you become Assouline?

When we decided to create a small series on couturiers, Mémoire de la Mode, from the present and the past. There were no books on couturiers at the time. We felt that fashion was at the right moment, so we created a collection of four books every six months, starting with Azzedine Alaïa, Chanel, Vionnet, and Dior. We were in Paris in Place Vendôme for twenty years, selling high quality for a low price, and we published the books like a magazine, four issues every three months. Then we translated them into twelve languages and went all over the world. We sold millions of them.

Then what happened?

I started to take it seriously. We opened an office in New York because we wanted to become international, and Assouline became a brand.

What kind of a brand?

Exactly what we still do today. All of our books tell a story, like a movie, and we wanted to have the spirit of our brand. Our stores, the first one was in rue Bonaparte in Paris, are in the same color that we use today. A sort of Moroccan red, it is warm like leather, and one has the feeling and the smell of a library. You can sit, have tea, and you can buy everything. In other words, our stores are the continuity of our private apartment. We mix different styles, we don't use decorators because we don't want to have an imposed style.

The world of books has changed, so how do you position yourself today?

What changes is the channel of distribution. Bookstores sadly are closing, country by country, more and more. This is a big change for most publishers, because they don't have the channel of distribution. We had the chance to understand this and we now have a very important website, and it is now our most important store. We have our own stores and we created our own distribution; we have our own sales force.

[illegible] do you sell the most?

The US is our number-one country, but we find there is a niche for our books in most countries of the world.

We could say yours are luxury books; do you think there will always be a niche for luxury?

If you stay in your field and you protect your brand. For me the most important people in a dinner party are not the people you invite, but the ones you decide not to invite. In other words we want to be coherent about who we are and what we are publishing. We receive hundreds of projects and proposals, and we refuse so many every day. We cannot publish everything, just what is good for the brand.

How do you decide what to publish?

It is obvious for us, it comes naturally. I decide everything with my wife alone. We have five collections and each one is like a family, and has something to say, and has to grow naturally.

What are the books that over the years became your classics, and that you feel most proud to have published?

In each collection I will give you one book. First we have The Ultimate Collection; each page is made by hand. We want to give the sensation that each is a personal album. The latest one in The Ultimate Collection is *The Impossible Collection of Wine*, in which we took the most talented sommelier in the world to choose the best bottles of the last century. It is not only beautiful; it is educational. Secondly, we have The Icons Collection; the one I am most proud of was the first one, the illustrated biography of Lee Radziwill. Then a collection named Classics Collection, the latest one is *The Italian Dream*. It is one of my favorite books, like a movie, four hundred pages in which Gelasio Gaetani d'Aragona Lovatelli tells the grand tour of Italy through wine, and it is not only about wine but also about families and style. Then we have a collection named Legends, and for me the best book in this collection is *Paris in the 1920s with Kiki de Montparnasse*. It is really a pretext to discover that moment of the history of art in Paris with Kiki. We also reprint nonstop. We have books we are still printing after twenty years.

What is next?

To survive. To grow exactly in the same direction, and to make a few more stores like the Piccadilly one in London, a concept store on culture. The next one is going to be in Dubai, then New York, and then China.

Can we ultimately say that you have no doubt about the importance of books?
No, we must never forget that we come from the book. My first memory is a little Haggadah that my father gave me when I was five years old, illustrated in only one color, green. I am very proud to be able to say that we became a family business, because our two children now work with us. One is in charge of marketing and digital, and the other is in charge of development in Europe.

New York
November 6, 2016

~

WE DO A LOT OF OTHER THINGS AROUND THE BOOK, BUT, LIKE THE HAMBURGER, WITHOUT THE BEEF THERE IS NOTHING. THE BOOK IS THE CENTER.

RICHARD AVEDON

PHOTOGRAPHER

Richard Avedon is a small man. His face is sunken in and he hides behind his white mane of hair and large tortoiseshell glasses. He is dressed in black velvet and has shiny shoes. He's in the middle of the Sala delle Cariatidi in the Palazzo Reale in Milan explaining how an image of his is to be hung. Together we walk through the rooms of his exhibition (to be inaugurated on January 17, 1995 and running through 5 March, with Kodak and Versace as sponsors). The show is called *Evidence* (1944–1994). He asks for a coffee, a bottle of mineral water, and a piece of *gianduiotto* (a chocolate-and-hazelnut candy from Piedmont). He says:

This building has a wonderful history. It was built in the eighteenth century, bombed in the last war, renovated then, and again twenty years ago, and it's still incredibly chaotic. In the ballroom, I've hung photographs of people dancing from the nineteen-sixties. There will be music by Gluck and Vivaldi in the background. So the ghost of the eighteenth century will be able to have a conversation with Twiggy, Jean Shrimpton, Penelope Tree, and Verushka. This is the prelude. The beginning of another room will be dedicated to 1945 fashions in Paris—photographs of Dovima with the elephants, Suzy Parker, Marlene Dietrich, and Marella Agnelli. The rest is fashion.

What is fashion for you?

I've tried to get rid of the artificiality of women seen as ideas, and to transform them into real women who go into shops, walk down the street, and cry on the underground.

The show isn't just about fashion.

It's a combination of images from Italy and the United States, from the streets of New York and Harlem. I was influenced by the neorealism of Antonioni, Rossellini, and Fellini, and I took pictures of street performers in Rome and Palermo. Then there are some portraits I did of actors like Chaplin, musicians, writers, intellectuals, and directors like Ford, and Renoir. And portraits of Eisenhower and Kissinger.

In one room there are four photographs taken during the Vietnam years.

The first is *Factory with Andy Warhol*. It represents the sexual revolution of that time period. The second is Middle Class, which features the Ginsberg family. The third has to do with the people that wanted the war—The Mission Council—who were the administrators of the war in Saigon. The fourth represents the movement against the war, with *The Chicago Seven*.

What about the images of the working class?

In the following rooms there are portraits of the working class out west during the Reagan years, when he said that the country was seeing great prosperity. It wasn't true, there was widespread unemployment. Mines were closing, things were really bad in agriculture and for sheep farmers as well. People didn't have work and had to move around to look for work. They were the drifters. I have photographs at the Palazzo Reale taken in an insane asylum in southern Texas, and pictures of napalm victims in Vietnam. The finale comes from the Volpi Ball in Venice on New Year's Eve in 1989, when the Berlin Wall fell. There you see the end of aristocracy and of communism. Finally, there's a little room of portraits of my father in the last days of his life.

How does it feel to see this retrospective of yours?

The photographs have taken on a life of their own. I feel as though I'm organizing an exhibition of many other photographers.

Do you like your own photographs?

If I didn't, I wouldn't show them.

What's the difference between 1944 and 1994?

Fifty years of experience. The difference between a young man and one who is at the end of his life.

Have you changed a lot?

I feel alive when I take photographs. But my photographs always leave me feeling defeated. I am never able to put everything I know into them.

What do you know?

My influences are literary. I haven't learned from other photographers.

Has your technique changed?

It has developed. I look for similarities between people that seem like opposites. I went to Washington one day to photograph Henry Kissinger. He told me, "Be kind." I would have liked to have asked him what he meant by that. Should I have made Kissinger younger, taller, or thinner?

What's it like working for *The New Yorker* or for Versace?

Sometimes I am in agreement with *The New Yorker*, and sometimes I am not. When I work for Versace, my work is creating an image that defines their advertising campaign. It's different if I photograph a woman for myself.

What kind of plans do you have?

I've become a publicity machine and am no longer an artist. The part of me that gives interviews and talks about the creative process is the complete opposite of me as a photographer. I've become my own widow. When the shows are over, I'm not going to give any more interviews. I will go away and read and think up a new job.

You've been accused of playing both sides. An artist on one hand and a publicity machine on the other.

These accusations against photographers who work in advertising are attacks from jealous people lacking in imagination. Some photographers go to the foundations and beg to hold an exhibition or go off and marry rich women. Or worse yet, they become martyrs with a following. This is because they don't know how to make money. I don't beg foundations or the government for money. I earn my living working with magazines and by doing advertising campaigns.

What types of women appeal to you?

Generous, intelligent women with a sense of humor and the ability to make me laugh. Women with a strong character.

Do you have a Jewish background?

The photographs of my father, Jacob Israel Avedon, speak a lot to my Jewishness. My Jewishness can be seen in my humanitarian interests. I've never put the focus on Jewish guilt the way Woody Allen has. Being Jewish is one of the things I'm most proud of in my life because I inherited a passion for intellectual culture and family values.

What about your children? Are you close to John?

He's a writer. He's finishing a book with the Dalai Lama, with whom he traveled for five years. We are very close. We talk and laugh about work.

Are you anxious about the future?
No. I would like to have more time. I am entering into my final act, and my hero is Matisse, because he completely reinvented himself in old age. That is my dream.

Milan
January 13, 1995

~

But my photographs always leave me feeling defeated.

I am never able to put everything I know into them.

I FEEL ALIVE
WHEN I TAKE PHOTOGRAPHS.

BRIGITTE BARDOT

ACTRESS

The French actress, who has been an idol for two generations, tells about her life in this interview, from her childhood on the outskirts of Paris, to how she became a cinema star, all the way to her years out of the spotlight in Saint-Tropez.
On September 28, 1994, Brigitte Bardot turned sixty years old. Here she is spirited and blunt, and she talks about her career and her campaign to defend animals. Brigitte Bardot is direct, and she has no regrets about her career as an actress. She says that she has never felt particularly beautiful. She has always preferred sweetness to sex. While she has no intention of talking about her son, who is now an adult, she does speak enthusiastically of her campaign to save the seals as part of her work leading the foundation that bears her name. These have been memorable campaigns that have also seen practical results, such as less ruthless techniques by poachers in the Great North.
Brigitte Bardot is another legend that, unfortunately, is getting older. She (politely) dislikes Sophia Loren, who is the same age. Bardot was not happy about the advertising campaign the Italian movie star did for a company that makes furs, and says she could never be friends with that type of woman.

You will soon turn sixty. Does this upset you?
No, it's what comes after fifty-nine!

What are some of your fondest memories?
Holding a baby seal in my arms on an ice floe.

You don't have fond memories of your acting career?
My career as an actress is part of a whole other world by now.

How did you make your debut?
I made my debut like all of the other actresses just starting out. . . .

SUCCESS IS UNPREDICTABLE

AND FRAGILE.

What do you remember about meeting Roger Vadim?
I remember that I was just starting out and he was already a famous director.

What was your life like at the time? Did it change a lot?
Yes, in those years, in the mid-nineteen-fifties, everything changed. Debuting in the cinema changed my existence.

How much did your beauty have to do with this change?
To tell you the truth, I don't feel all that exceptional. That's how it always has been, and that hasn't changed.

Did you expect to have so much success?
No. Success is unpredictable and fragile.

What films do you feel most attached to?
The Truth [*La Verité* 1960], . . . *And God Created Woman* [*Et Dieu . . . crea le femme*, 1956] and *The Bear and the Doll* [*L'Ours et la poupée*, 1970].

You met de Gaulle. What memories do you have of him?
Vivid memories really. He was a person that really stood out.

When did you discover Saint-Tropez? And why, after having lived there for so long, did you decide to leave your homes there?
I discovered it many years ago. Unfortunately, I am not like a snail or a turtle, and I can't take my houses with me when I move.

When and why did you decide to leave your acting career behind? Do you have any regrets, or the desire to start again?
I have no regrets. If I wanted to keep acting, I would have never left the cinema.

Who were the most important directors for you?
Clouzot, Vadim, Autant-Lara, and Michel Deville.

What about actors?
I couldn't care less about actors.

When did you begin taking an interest in animals?
I always have and always will.

Tell me about your work, your commitment to animals?

It is a battle. A fight against cruelty, stupidity, and the indifference of humans. It's animals against man, a furious fight meant to better the conditions of animals in the world, to open people's eyes, to fight their selfishness, and to protect the weakest from the most destructive forces.

You have criticized Sophia Loren for advertising fur. Do you know her personally?

No. I don't frequent these types of women who wear fur and advertise it.

Your husband is a member of the Front National party. Are you on the far right?

I am a woman that defends animals, right, left, and in the center. Animals aren't political.

What do you remember about Rome and Capri, from when you filmed *Contempt* [*Le Mépris*, 1963], with Godard?

I remember Godard. And I remember him the way he's always been. A unique person.

Do you remember Alberto Moravia?

Certainly, and I read his books.

And what about Jacques Prévert?

And who could forget a character like that?

What do you think of Mitterrand's statements on your being a supporter of Vichy's pro-Nazi government?

I never talk politics.

Are love and sex very important to you?

I prefer passion and sweetness.

You have often been seen at night in clubs playing the guitar, barefoot. Is having a good time important to you?

Yes, but I never force myself to dance or sing.

You were married to German playboy Gunter Sachs. Perhaps you liked the idea of being the wife of a very rich man?

I have never put a gun to anyone's head to obligate him to marry me.

Is money important to you?
I prefer love.

How do you live today?
The way I like.

Do you realize you are a legend?
No but, luckily, you have reminded me. . . .

Have you changed a lot in the last few years?
Yes. I have gotten older.

What do you think of the cinema today?
It doesn't interest me.

What are your main concerns?
Animals.

What about your flaws?
I have flawed qualities and quality flaws.

Are you generous?
I believe so.

Do you have any unfinished dreams?
Yes, when I am startled awake.

When people ask you what kind of gifts you'd like to receive, what do you say?
To love animals, help out my foundation, don't eat horsemeat, and stop wearing fur.

France

September 21, 1994

~

I HAVE NO REGRETS.

IF I WANTED

TO KEEP ACTING,

I WOULD HAVE NEVER

LEFT

THE CINEMA.

ROBERTO BENIGNI

ACTOR

Roberto Benigni won the Oscar for Best Actor for his role in *Life Is Beautiful* [*La vita è bella*, 1997]. He was the first actor to win an Oscar for a performance in a foreign-language film since Sophia Loren had won for *Two Women* almost forty years before. His film received seven Academy Award nominations and won Best Foreign Language Film, Best Music, and Original Dramatic Score. Roberto Benigni famously received his awards in exuberant style.

They are saying your film is a masterpiece. Do you agree?

I like this film a lot. I made something that is really, really simple. I am very grateful for those that speak well of my film. For those that say that it is a masterpiece, well, if I had their addresses, I'd send each and every one ten kilos of the sweetest apples. But the critic [Goffredo] Fofi has issues with the film. He says that the first part is more beautiful than the second part, which deals with concentration camps. If he has an issue with the film, that is still satisfying, because Fofi has a brilliant mind. He is a very generous person. Every time I read something he's written, I die of laughter.

Why does he prefer the first part of the film?

It's nice that he has a preference, but the film is a single entity. One part can't exist without the other. It's the same person. The same thing. The situation changes in the second part.

Are you and your wife as in love in real life as you are in the film?

Ah, *amore*! When I think about Nicoletta, I leap, leap with joy like I am in the fields going from one valley to the next. I lie on the grass satisfied. This, perhaps, is an artistic interpretation, but it's true in life as well.

Did you woo her the way you did in the film?

Excuse me, but here we are entering into territory that is full of all kinds of wonderful things, but they are things each of us delicately and jealously keep for ourselves. I can, however, tell you that from the first scene of the film, Nicoletta Braschi looked at my character with such a powerful feeling of love that I couldn't help but be overwhelmed with emotion. She's a memorable actress.

Are you a clown?

I would really like to be one. I'd kiss anyone who called me one if this were really the case. The clown is the greatest expression of someone who brings well wishes. Being a clown is bliss. It's like describing a cloud at a quarter past three in the afternoon.

They say you are a crafty little devil. Is that true?

Oh God no. No. I don't like people who are cunning. Not at all. Who is that sly fox that called me a crafty little devil?

Your character in *Life is Beautiful*—the Jewish man Guido Orefice—who is he?

He's a Jewish man who has assimilated. I tried to create a character who was a Jewish man during the Italian racial laws, which was a truly scary, indescribable, and despicable time. But he's not a practicing Jew or a serious Jew. He's a kind, honest, and gentle Jew. I wanted to highlight the immeasurable injustice that took the Jews to a frightening and repugnant inferno. *Why did they pick on him?* I asked myself.

Do you feel a bit Jewish?

When asked if he was Jewish, Chaplin was said to respond, "I'm afraid I don't have that honor."

OPTIMISTS ARE AMAZING PEOPLE BECAUSE IT IS DIFFICULT TO BE OPTIMISTIC, AND IT'S LESS REWARDING THAN BEING THE OPPOSITE.

Was Chaplin a maestro for you?

He's a maestro for pizza makers, barbers, woodworkers, and even for the Elkanns. If he hadn't been, so many things wouldn't have come to be.

They say you have very strong political leanings.

Well isn't that a big surprise! I say that I am open about the people I love, the actors I choose, and everyone knows who my partner is. Each of us is proud of his or her choices, even to name the restaurants where we go to eat. Why should I hide my political leanings? I put more trust in some than others. What is the problem with that?

What did those on the right say about your film?

At the beginning, they said negative things. Then a journalist—Renato Farina—said amazing things. I'd like to thank him publicly.

Do you place a lot of importance on criticism?

I place a lot of importance on affections, and without affections, we are dead. I am sad if someone doesn't like my film. A clown will die without laughs or emotions.

Did you expect so much success?

I really hoped they would love the film. Especially because this doesn't have the same impact as a comical film full of easy laughs. It's a kind of a unique film.

What did Rabbi Toaff say to you? [Chief Rabbi of Rome from 1951–2002]

He's such a gentle man. He saw the film, and he had his arm, which was in a cast, up to his neck. He was really moved, and he hugged me and told me "Bravo." He's a person with an enviable sense of joy, an extraordinary person, and he was so incredibly warm to me. He truly touched me.

What about the little boy?

Nicoletta chose that little boy. Out of two thousand, she said, "That's him." And we didn't look for any others.

Are Italians racist?

No. But every country has its issues. Believe me, eradicating racism is difficult. It takes a lot of time. It's a terrifying thing, but I don't think that Italians are truly racist.

What do you hate the most?

The thing that terrifies me the most is when a human being is stripped of his dignity. Seeing someone stripped of his dignity is the thing I hate the most.

Do you think we are going through a down period?

No. It's extraordinary. Perhaps I say it a bit foolishly, but it seems like an era that is full of amazing things, with great contradictions.

Do you laugh a lot in real life as well?

Pope John XXIII said that a day without a smile is a lost day.

Are you really so optimistic?

I like the practice of optimism. Optimists are amazing people because it is difficult to be optimistic, and it's less rewarding than being the opposite. Byron was a great poet. He was attractive, rich, and pessimistic. I was born ugly, small, and I'm not a great poet, but I am an optimist.

How do you handle such great success?

The amazing thing is that people love me, and I love those that love me.

Do you like being interviewed?

Yes. When I'm interviewed, I ask myself, *Why are they asking me this thing?* Then I would like to interview my interviewer.

What about Fellini's *Interview* [*Intervista*, 1987]?

Look, any Fellini film is extraordinary. One goes in with two thousand lire worth of things in his head and comes out with eighteen thousand lire worth, at worst.

And what about for you, Benigni?

I would like for it to be the same.

Rome

January 4, 1998

~

ROBERTO BOLLE

BALLET DANCER

Your tour started in the gardens of the Royal Palace in Turin. How was this for you?

I am doing some gala evenings along with Alessandra Ferri with pas de deux selections from classic and modern pieces. This allows the audience to better see the talents of the lead dancers. They are all couples from the ballet companies in Hamburg, London, Paris, and Amsterdam.

Are you sad that Alessandra Ferri is retiring?

I am very sad because we have an artistic bond and a rare complicity between artists. She is very good, and it's a pity that she's leaving in such splendid shape. But I admire her and appreciate her precisely because she's leaving the stage at her peak. She wants to leave an indelible memory of herself.

How did it feel being in Turin again after the inaugural ceremony of the Olympics?

I have to say that I was very happy. The Olympics was a truly one-of-a-kind and unforgettable experience, an emotion I will never forget.

Is dancing in royal gardens, amphitheaters, or stadiums different than dancing in a theater?

Yes. It is very different. It is much more exciting. Open-air theaters or gorgeous natural architectural settings have a harmony that goes well with the harmony of dance, and for dancers, these places have a greater energy than that of the theater.

Even if the theaters you frequent are the Mariinsky, La Scala, or the Royal Opera House?

Of course the historic theaters have a different magic than modern ones, and they help the artist with his art.

Which theater feels most like yours?
Without a doubt, La Scala. I grew up there. Though I've danced in many great theaters, I have a certain affection for La Scala.

Future plans?
London at the Royal Ballet and then I will do *Swan Lake* at La Scala in December. Last month I debuted at the Metropolitan with a reception that exceeded expectations.

Who were your models as dancers?
I took inspiration from various artists, such as Nureyev and Baryshnikov. I took different teachings from each one.

Who was the biggest "maestro" for you?
I would have liked to have worked with Nureyev and Baryshnikov, but it wasn't possible. I met Nureyev when I was fifteen years old, but unfortunately, I was too young and he died shortly thereafter.

What does it mean to be a dancer?
It means being an artist who interprets roles and actions with his body. You experience the emotions and the music in your body, which is like an instrument that communicates with the audience.

How do you stay in shape?
I train five or six hours per day. At times it is very difficult.

Is there a lot of narcissism?
Yes. There is narcissism. Because you are constantly in front of a mirror, but it's a tool for our work, and I don't think that dancers are much more narcissistic than anyone else.

You are from Casale Monferrato. What kind of relationship do you have with the Piedmont region?
Actually I've become a bit Milanese, but I'm proud of my roots. Piedmont is an amazing place. I feel at home in Milan, but it helps to have lived in the countryside and to have known a different way of seeing things and people.

Do you feel like a citizen of the world today?
Yes. I have no problem adjusting in the cities where I go. I felt at home in New York for a month, and then I spent two weeks in Hamburg. Every place enriches me in differently.

Do you travel light?

I would like to, but I have a very large suitcase only for dance, training, shows, and all the rest. At least two suitcases if all goes well.

Is it possible for you to have a normal life outside of dancing?

No. Dance is my passion, and I live according to this.

Are politics and sport parts of your life?

Certainly. Outside of dance, I have been a UNICEF ambassador for eight years working on causes having to do with childhood.

Do you work every day?

Always. I go on holiday once a year. I go to the sea. I swim, I go scuba diving, and I relax.

After Alessandra Ferri's retirement, have you already decided who will be your next dance partner?

There are many good ballerinas, but there is no other great, complete artist like her.

When did you realize you had this talent?

Dance was a passion of mine from the time I was a child. When I entered La Scala, I realized that it could become my future.

When will you stop?

Difficult question. I don't know. It depends on my body and my ability to stay in shape.

Do you pay a lot of attention to your health?

Yes. Of course. I try to take care of my body, which is my instrument, so that it is in the best physical shape possible.

Has the world of ballet changed from the times of the Russian ballet dancers?

Yes, very much. The aesthetic and athletic abilities of dancers have increased quite a lot. And ballet dancers are closer to gymnasts compared to ballet dancers from the last century.

Turin
July 22, 2007

~

I TRY TO TAKE CARE OF

my body,

WHICH IS

my instrument,

SO THAT IT IS IN
THE BEST PHYSICAL SHAPE POSSIBLE.

JOSEPH BRODSKY

POET

The 1987 winner of the Nobel Prize for Literature, one of the greatest living poets, author of *A Stop in the Desert* and *Roman Elegies*, has just arrived in Rome. I meet the Jewish Russian writer in the bar of his hotel. He drinks tea and smokes, chewing on the filter of his Kent cigarette. I ask him:

Joseph, how do you see the revival of anti-Semitism in Europe?

This is what happens when society feels less politically and economically secure. In Germany it coincided with the period following the Weimar Republic. And Russia has never been secure economically. Anti-Semitism is a phenomenon.

What do you think of skinheads?

It's National Socialism. There has never been Nazism anywhere else: only in Germany. Personally, I do not think that it will ever really come back again. I don't know how to judge the degree of seriousness of these recent instances of anti-Semitism in Germany and Italy. But the fact that some groups are overwhelmingly made up of young people tells you that anti-Semitism has not yet been completely destroyed.

What were the particular characteristics of the anti-Semitism that you experienced when you lived in Russia?

It was of the time, and also within political campaigns. The state authorized it. As long as the state itself is not anti-Semitic, the situation is not so very serious. I think the state in Italy already has laws against racism and these laws must be applied. Maybe these laws should be rewritten and made even stronger.

Does anti-Semitism exist in America?

No, Americans have too many other things on their mind. America is multicultural. There isn't any one minority or majority that is dominant. The only racial prejudice in the U.S. that as you know is still present is the one against black people, but there are harsh laws to counter it, notwithstanding the inertia of the populace.

What characteristics does anti-Semitism have in Russia these days?

They have these attitudes, first and foremost.

Does this frighten you?

I am happy to live in America now. I'm happy with my life. Frankly, I do not think that all this talk about anti-Semitism in Europe is of any great importance for Europeans. I am more concerned about their economic conditions and the blood which flows in Yugoslavia. Even Jews, I believe, need to identify their own priorities. My own priority, the one that burns inside me and troubles my conscience, is the people who are dying every day in Yugoslavia.

How can anti-Semitism be eradicated?

It's another racial prejudice; above all else it is a prejudice. People have such prejudices, and they are nurtured by dissatisfaction with the reality of their situations. The real problems come to the surface when someone turns prejudice into a system. You cannot completely eradicate anti-Semitism. Maybe you can replace it with another prejudice; but do not ask me what, because I would not know how to answer. Maybe if people could express their dissatisfaction with their situation through institutional channels, and I am not just talking about elections, they would become more free of these racial prejudices.

Why do you still live in exile?

I don't think of it as exile. That's too melodramatic. I am not a victim and I do not like to be thought of as one. It has become fashionable, a status symbol, to be a victim. There are many people who don't have anything else to say except that they are victims.

Would you include Jews in this category?

Jews are not the only victims. They do not have the prerogative on suffering. During the last war six million Jews died in concentration camps, but twenty million Russians also died.

Why don't you go back to Russia?

It's very simple. If I went back to Russia I would find myself in a privileged position. Politics is not at the heart of this: I would have money in my pocket, while many people do not have any. I used to be like everyone else, now I would be exceptional. Today I have this halo round my head and I would be loved and adored. I do not think I deserve that love, and even if I did deserve it, I always find such positive feelings very hard to endure. It is much easier to be detested than beloved.

In America do they love you or hate you?
They ignore me and they leave me alone. And that is worth more than anything else.

But are you not curious about returning to live in your own country, now that it has begun its reconstruction?
There is reconstruction, but I have other things to do. I know that Russia, in one way or another, will make it. Russia is a country with a wonderful cultural and linguistic heritage and will produce great literature, if only for statistical reasons. The only aspect of Russia that interests me is its literature. Its culture, its literature in particular, does not depend on its political situation as many would have you believe. It depends on intellectual genius arising from its cultural heritage. And in Russia there is a lot of both one and the other.

And in the West? Are the differences decreasing between the Western countries and the countries of the East, countries all around the world?
Out of literature and language, it is language that does not combine. The East and West are merging, they come together in the "counterculture" or in "anticulture," and I consider politics part of this counterculture.

Do you believe in a United Europe?
It is a pernicious idea and Italians should be the first to recognize that. To make a Deutsche Mark or an ECU you need to belittle the value of a "siesta," you need to work like crazy while giving up your own identity. What I do not like about the concept of a United Europe is the supremacy of the Protestant North over the Catholic South.

So what happens now? Can this be turned around?
It is possible not to go forward in that direction.

Are you a nationalist?
Every nation has its cultural heritage. But European unity would be a disaster for the literary heritage of the European countries. Today, the best literature is produced in the former colonies, more so than in the motherlands. "The center cannot hold," as the poet Yeats says.

The same happens in Russia?
It originates from the provinces of the Empire. At one time poetry originated in Moscow and Saint Petersburg, now it originates from every distant province.

What are you going to do during your time in Italy?

I want to understand why Europeans are being so stupid as to propose unity for Europe.

Would you like to come back to live in Europe?

I would like to spend more time in Rome and in Italy, because I love your country.

But Italy is shot through with political, economic, and psychological crisis. . . .

It's all to do with "original sin." If one does not believe in it, it is a crisis; if one believes in it, it is not.

Why?

Because without the concept of original sin, one can fantasize about the goodness of the human being and design utopias. You can be, in other words, a Jean Jacques Rousseau. If you believe in original sin, you know that man has the capacity for both things: goodness and badness. This means that man is evil and not only good. If you believe in "original sin" you can set about constructing a society built on different premises: you are looking for a way to make a good society for bad people. I highly recommend to all those Italians who think that their country is in a crisis to go to a library and find an edition of *The Federalist Papers*. This treatise is a major commentary on the principles that gave birth to the American Constitution. These documents should be translated and handed out in every civilized country in the world.

What ideas do you have about the future of America?

I have lived outside the democratic system long enough not to be really annoyed when my candidate doesn't win the election. The American system cannot be completely blown away into thin air by a single individual.

What is your relationship with Solzhenitsyn?

I have run into him. I respect him as a writer, but not as a "political brain." He is the Russian version of a Rousseau. He does not believe in original sin despite his Orthodox faith.

Rome
December 1, 1992

~

TINA BROWN

JOURNALIST

I arrive at Lincoln Center in New York for the fifth Women in the World public meeting. The theater is full, as it would be for an opera premiere. This is a two and a half day event at Lincoln Center where extraordinary women from all over the world express their views, their concerns, their aims. It is about the news as seen through the eyes of a woman.
Diane von Fürstenberg, Tina Brown, and the American Ambassador to the United Nations Samantha Power (the youngest Ambassador ever), are talking about the event with pride. At the UN the night before, for the fifth year The Diane von Fürstenberg Award was given to some exceptional women for their work, their courage to fight for survival. "Women capable of turning struggle into leadership," says Diane von Fürstenberg.
Tina Brown interviews Ambassador Power, who was a journalist and winner of the Pulitzer Prize. They talk about Uganda, Syria, the gay question in Africa; about terrorism, Ukraine, and Central Africa.

Did you leave active journalism to devote yourself entirely to "The Women of the World?"

I did. I think that today's journalism is a theatrical journalism, combining storytelling and curiosity with live events. Today, people don't want to read about Rwanda, Syria, India, it is all about shiny objects.

How has it gone this year?

We had Ruslana, Ukraine's pop singer and a leader of the Kiev protests, on the first night. We had Hillary Clinton and Christine Lagarde, very powerful and exciting women. Every year we try to have some of the most inspiring women in the world, from Syrian refugees to a panel of women from Egypt, Tunisia, Yemen, and Iraq. We also had the presence of former President Jimmy Carter, who talked on his new book about women.

Do you think that there is more solidarity among women than men?

Men are used to having the stage. Women still do not have the opportunity.

What is your activity today?

I am developing "Women of the World" in different places: Los Angeles, Chicago, India, Brazil, London; of course on a smaller scale.

Who is supporting you?

We get money from big sponsors like Bank of America, AT&T, Coca-Cola. . . .

You only go on stage?

We had five hundred and ten million Twitter impressions. Social media is enormous.

Do you miss conventional journalism?

I love magazines, but there are only two or three places left. It has become a difficult profession. I loved it when I was the editor of *The New Yorker* and the *Daily Beast*.

Do you consider yourself a feminist?

I am interested in the global movement, but I don't want to be defined as "feminist." I love these women and I love to bring them to the stage.

Do you think that women are stronger now?

There are more women than men in colleges nowadays, but they still do not have the same salary and there is still a lot of violence towards them. But countries where women are repressed have economies that don't do well.

But now there are many women in key posts, even in the economic world?

Yes, it is one of the reasons why they want to lift up women in Japan. As I have said, repressing women is bad for the economy.

But women have come so far. . . .

Yes, but there is still a long way to go. There are not enough women in politics in Washington. If there had been more, maybe we would not have had a war in Iraq.

Which other woman would you like to invite for next year?

I would love to have Angela Merkel. She has got Europe in the palm of her hand. . . .

New York
April 9, 2014

~

PIERRE CARDIN

FASHION DESIGNER

Pierre Cardin arrives in a dark green Jaguar driven by a chauffeur dressed in an impeccable blue uniform. The fashion designer gets out wearing a blue jacket with gold buttons, a shirt with large checks and a white collar, white pants, and small glasses ringed in black. His office is a large, disorderly room full of photographs, designs, and memories.

How much of the Italian side of you remains?

I owe my success to France and the recognition of my talent to France, but I am still Italian at heart and in terms of taste.

Where were your parents from?

Venice. I came to France at age two. After spending his childhood in the countryside, my father sought refuge in France at age sixty because he had lost everything in the war. I went to live in Vichy. I lived there through the war years from 1940 to 1945, and then I came to Paris where I began to work in fashion in the very famous Paquin fashion house.

What was Vichy like during the war?

I worked with the Red Cross. I worked with poor people that had problems and were looking for help. I was twenty years old, and I got through things. I was arrested by the Germans in Moulin while I was trying to get to Paris. Fortunately, I wasn't Jewish and they didn't deport me. After the war, I didn't feel like continuing to be a Red Cross worker. A fortune teller—a sixty-five-year-old woman in Vichy—read my cards and told me that I would be successful, exceptionally successful, and that my name would be known as far away as Australia. I thought she was crazy because, at that time, I didn't have anything. I asked her for a name in Paris so I could get started with a fashion house. When I arrived in Paris, I remember that it was early morning, and I was in the rue Royal, going to the house of the person whose name she had given me. I stopped a man on the street to ask him where the house was, and he was the person I was going to see. I showed up at Paquin, and there I met Cocteau, Bérard, and Jean Marais. They were making costumes for the film *Beauty and the Beast* [*La Belle et la bête,* 1946].

Has your life changed a lot since then?

No. Nothing has changed despite my success. Of course today I have much more money. I am well known. But I live in the same way.

How do you see the world?

I've already been around the world twenty-seven times. The world seems really small to me. I no longer see the world as being the same size as I did forty years ago. I travel with a small suitcase. I keep it with me. I used to travel for fun, but now fun and work are all mixed together and thus I travel mostly for work. I remember seeing Mrs. Gandhi and her son in India. I met Mother Teresa. I knew the Communist countries well, even though I went there with a capitalist image. I found this contrast interesting.

What are your thoughts about fashion?

I learned from Dior. One shouldn't show too much. For me elegance is about concealing. Today they show everything. The body is like a liquid that takes the shape of the vase. Today it's all about the body. For me, showing too much of somebody is not at all exciting. It's not all about sex and the body.

What do you think about Prada and Gucci?

They are commercial brands. Gucci is a leather maker that made suitcases. I found success without money. I made it on talent alone. That's how I made my name. The banks didn't create me. I am the only owner of my brand.

Are things good or bad in fashion?

Bad. People look too much to Hollywood stars and fashion magazines for inspiration. It's a baroque interpretation, but young people today are like that. But I would like to be young today as well.

Paris
June 12, 1998

~

MAURIZIO CATTELAN

ARTIST

You are one of the most famous Italian artists alive today. Why do you choose not to have a studio in one place?

Art doesn't come as much from inspiration as it does from the obsessions and fears that we all face every day. I have never been able to escape from the world around me, close myself up in a space, sit down at a desk and say, "I am an artist. I must create." Having a studio might be relaxing. I could choose to not go sometimes, to call in sick. However, art is, above all, a way of looking at reality. There are no Sundays or days off. You can never take a holiday from yourself.

How do you work and how do you create your pieces?

Every minute of the day, and every situation is work. Perhaps this is why there is no "where" as much as there is a "through" or a "thanks to." I have always thought that work was like going to the gym. The more effort you put in, the bigger your muscles get and the more your joints get stronger. Doctors say that ligaments are much more important for athletes than muscle mass because they allow the body to make the most of its physical capabilities. Art works in the same way perhaps, except I feel less like an athlete and more like one of those Sunday runners that is often out of breath and risks keeling over every time.

One of your works that shows Pope John Paul II lying on the ground was a success but stirred up controversy. Have you ever had contact with the Vatican?

The Royal Academy in London, where I showed that piece, received a letter from the Vatican, which expressed surprise at how the religious themes were treated so inadequately in that show. My work was perhaps truly inadequate because it didn't talk about the historic person or public figure as much as about the precariousness of power, of defeat, and of failure, which are always lying in wait. And all men are equal when faced with fear.

Why do you spend so much time in New York?

I spent many years in other places before coming to New York. After having spent twenty-five years in Padua, I moved to Forlì, which at the time seemed to me like a mirage of an active universe where things were happening. Today Forlì still seems like a unique place, but more for the fact that you can eat an excellent *piadina* [a type of Italian flatbread] with prosciutto there. I'm not passing any kind of judgment. I'm the last person who should be passing judgment. But I am aware that living in New York is truly a special thing, because it's like an open-air office that works twenty-four hours a day.

What does it mean to be an artist today?

Someone once defined me as a concept worker. This is perhaps the only definition that helps me provide an answer to these kinds of questions. Perhaps being an artist only means looking at and reflecting reality, trying to expose details that would otherwise go unobserved. Artists are the antennas of the present, whatever present they may find themselves in.

Who are your teachers?

I did many jobs before becoming an artist, and I found art through trial and error. When I started, art fascinated me because it seemed like an alternative to salaried work, a way to rewrite the rules so as to not be somebody else's employee. Marcel Duchamp always said, "I prefer breathing to working." I don't think I have teachers, but I do have many "schoolmates" with whom I can try to find the answers to the math homework.

What kinds of projects are you working on?

The Berlin Biennale, which I curated along with Massimiliano Gioni and Ali Subotnick, is the only project I have worked on and challenged myself with in the last twenty months. Having gone to the other side this time—working in a group and organizing something as opposed to being organized—has changed things. It's as if everything works in a different way all of a sudden without the certainties you thought you had created. But, at the end of the day, we are both the victims and the tormentors. It only depends on the role we find ourselves playing in a certain moment.

Who are the most interesting Italian artists, in your opinion?

In Italy there's a network of very active and very interesting artists that isn't just made up of young people. For some reason, there are people who suddenly disappear, and we should go find them and bring them back. When art works, it has no expiration date.

AND ALL

MEN

ARE

=

WHEN FACED WITH

FEAR.

Don't you think prices for art have become excessive?

If prices are so high, it is never the artists' fault. It's because of a system in which the auction houses, for example, manage to figure out the economic tastes of the market. The market is constantly selling a mirage, a perspective that has very little to do with the works and that has more to do with the enormous amount of money moving through it, going up and down. The real problem is that this system transforms the world of collectors. The best art collections are always the result of risky wagers about the future and intrepid acts of courage, never a focus on the safe horse.

Do you ever fear losing your talent?

I've been afraid since day one, and I will always be afraid. But I don't fear losing my talent as much as failing or being exposed. You can't lose something you don't have.

What would you have wanted to do if you hadn't become an artist?

For me, art has always been the answer to a problem. It has never been a finish line to cross or an objective to pursue. If one day I realize that art no longer satisfies my needs, perhaps I will go back to looking for a new path that will complete me.

There are many new museums and contemporary art foundations in Italy today. What do you think about this?

There are many extraordinary experiences in Italy. Turin is a perfect example of the synergy between the public and private sectors. In just a few years, the city—with an excellent museum program and an ambitious group of collectors—has become one of the hubs for contemporary art in Italy, and plays an active role in the international debate. It has the same energy as places that are very different, like Miami, for example. Perhaps if all of the gallery foundations, public museums, and private museums worked toward a specific common objective, then Italy could truly do a lot for contemporary art. As always, the most interesting things happen, or can happen, only when there are many people in the same room.

New York
June 4, 2006

~

CICCIOLINA

PORN STAR

In June 1994, the Hungarian-Italian porn star, politician, and singer Ilona Staller (also known as Cicciolina) accused her husband, the American artist Jeff Koons, of treating her very harshly. When I spoke to her, she was on the run with her two-year-old son, Ludwig, having left Genoa for Trieste. On the phone, her voice sounded quite calm; she did not seem agitated at all. She had "kidnapped" Ludwig the week before in violation of a U.S. court order in New York, where he was living with his father. The day before we spoke, Staller had taken to the microphones on Teleroma 56, a cable-television program broadcast in Lazio, the region around Rome. She appealed to then Justice Minister Alfredo Biondi, juvenile court judges in Italy, and the Italian Parliament, for help, stating, "until the Italian laws that protect Italian citizens like my son are made to be respected. I am in Trieste, but I don't feel safe. Minister Biondi needs to help me. My husband is going to kill me. He keeps threatening me."

Ilona, what is happening?

Believe me, the situation I'm in is not easy. My husband in the United States is a powerful man because he has a lot of money, and in the United States—more so than in Italy—you can buy anything.

Are you in Italy now?

Yes. But he has hired important lawyers in Italy as well. He wants the child right away. This is why he threatened me again yesterday on the telephone, telling me, "You will see!" These words frighten me, knowing the type of man he is.

Where are you at the moment?

Near Trieste. Actually, in Trieste. I was in Genoa before, but it's not true that I was staying in the home of a porn star. Maybe someone is trying to get publicity by saying that. Today my friends are only lawyers. I no longer have time to see anyone. I no longer have a life until this matter is resolved. As I told you, my husband is a powerful man.

Okay, but who gives you money?

I still have an account open in the Parliament bank. I am going through my assets. My husband no longer gives me a dime. So I have to pay with my own money. It's true that I eat like a bird, but everything is so expensive in New York. I have to take taxis to get around the city.

What about the child?

He's Italian-American, and therefore he's protected in Italy. My husband hates Italy, and hates that my son is here.

Do you hate your husband?

No. I don't hate him, but he's threatening me. I thought he was an intelligent person considering that he is educated and is cultured. But obviously culture isn't enough. He is an impossible man.

What does he want from you?

Our child, but as a way of showing how powerful he is and not because he really cares about him. It's that he can't stand to lose.

Is he jealous? Does he still love you?

No. I don't know. He wants the child to keep him away from his mother. But the child should stay with both of us, and he only wants him for him.

In the meantime, you aren't working at all anymore?

No. What do you expect me to do while I'm here on the run? And I want it to be clear that I am no longer a porn star. I would like to do television interviews and shows. I have a sparkling wit and am very funny when I want to be.

When do you think this situation with you, your husband, and your child will end?

Soon, I hope. It's time for it to end, but first and foremost, I hope that my husband doesn't want to kill me, because he's a psychopath and capable of anything!

Trieste
June 16, 1994

~

BENJAMIN CLEMENTINE

MUSICIAN & POET

Benjamin Clementine is a Mercury Prize-winning pianist, poet, singer, and songwriter. He was recently featured on the cover of *T: The New York Times Style Magazine*.

Benjamin, when did you discover that you were a poet and a musician?

When I went to Paris eight years ago I was nineteen. I had already read a lot of poetry by [William] Blake. I was going to the town library and taking any book of English literature from the shelves. I was running away from school just to read books.

How has your family influenced you?

We are five siblings, and we all played instruments for a hobby. I started playing drums, and when my brother bought a piano I started to play the piano. When my parents divorced I went to Camden and I was in a homeless place. I tried to live with my father, who remarried after the divorce, and it didn't work. I went to live with my mother and it didn't work either. I met a guy who made me live in his flat. Then I found a job in a retail shop, but I was not happy so I went to Paris.

What did you do there?

It was an adventure. I just thought about the day. I never spoke to anyone. I was sleeping in the street. I tried to work for a few days in a kitchen, but then I left. I was writing about life, but I have lost my writing of the time.

What about music?

After six months doing nothing in Paris I started singing in front of the Sacré-Cœur or in the train. I met people who invited me to sing in a bar. I went to stay in a hostel for twenty euros a night. I made enough money to buy a guitar and I started playing. For about two or three years I was writing my own music, but I was singing famous songs. Then I bought a keyboard and really started composing.

Who discovered you?

I met a lot of people. In Paris people have a big ego, but you cannot rely on them. Many people let me down, until I met one person on the street and he said he had a studio. I went there to record music, and one of his friends had a record label and wanted me to sign a contract. I said no. I could not trust anyone at the time. I told him he could be my manager. I went to play in hotels, birthday parties, stations, and then we went to the Cannes Festival and I was playing with a band, my own band, in a hotel. In the middle of the show I realized that people did not care. So I left. I stopped playing and went to another bar with my manager. There was a piano at the back and I played on the piano. It was one a.m. and I played until five a.m. It was magical. People were taken, and the owner of the bar followed and found us, and he wanted to make a record label to record my songs.

And so, what happened?

I was still playing in a bar and in trains, and I recorded three songs that were sent to the radio stations in France, and then *France Inter* wanted to interview me and decided to play my songs. We made a video with one of my songs, "Cornerstone," and after six months Jools Holland saw the video and his production team invited me to audition for them, and I got in to play with Paul McCartney and it was quite something. The next day I went back to Paris and played in the train again.

Is Paris your city?

Yes, that is where I became a man.

But New York is quite similar to Paris?

Just bigger.

Have you moved to America?

I moved to New York. I don't think New York is America; it is the world. It is like Paris without Parisians. It is multicultural.

Do you still consider yourself British?

Yes, of course. I am very proud of my nationality. English is my first language, but now I am known as the Englishman from Paris.

Is Paris in your songs?

Of course. If you look at one of my videos called "London" the video is shot in Paris because I am longing for London in Paris. I am from London, and whatever happens, you never deny where you are from. But of course footprints of Paris are carved on my heart.

How would you describe, if you can, your music and your songs?

I think for me the greatest musical artists that ever lived never sang, but spoke. This is my opinion about people like Bob Dylan, or Léo Ferré, or Johnny Cash. They are not singers like Pavarotti. I am striving to be one of them, and the way I am doing this is to try looking up to them. I am looking at these great artists like one would look at his father. Their music spoke, that is the difference.

What are you trying to do?

I am creative and I am still searching to find my ground. I don't think I will find a particular thing to do. My passion is for art and for people, a passion to trigger the part of the human being that has been ignored. We all ignore ourselves sometimes, and try to pretend nothing has happened. But things need to be dug deep, and we have to appreciate everything we have. This is where my passion lies.

Has your life changed?

My life has not changed, my surroundings have. I don't play in the train, but I am doing the same thing, playing for people.

What are you doing next in America?

I have three more shows. I come back in June for a tour around America. My music is not just for Europe, but for all human beings.

Is success in America very important?

Of course, but success is an illusion. I can say that I was successful playing in the streets in Paris. Fame is not success. Gold and money is not success. Success is finding the principles of what you are inspired to do. Once you find the principles, the consequences vary.

Is freedom your first and strongest value?

No, it is joy. Joy is hard to get for some people. If I was not joyful I would not be in America today; I would have been dead by now. I have been depressed for so long. In Paris I had nothing, no family, nothing; but I was joyful. And I found music, and it made me live for another day. So I said let's keep on doing it.

Do you believe in talent?

I believe in ingenuity; I don't believe in talent. The reason why I make music is because I shared the gamble, because of my experience. No one taught me how to play the piano. The reason why I play is because I am passionate, excited, and curious. Some people go to school to learn music and how music is done. I have nothing against that, but for me it is a little bit like going to school to learn how we can let the sun shine.

Ingenuity is something we are all born with, and it is up to us to discover what we can do with it; it grows by experiences. We need time, but we live in a world where time is not on our side, apparently. In order to get stuck into what we can do we must take our time. We need dedication, and practice.

Do you work very hard?

I work as much as I can work. My ability is determined by how and what I feel. I play the piano whenever I feel like it. I try to let it come as naturally as possible. I always follow my feelings and I don't believe in mistakes, because I believe that error leads to portals of new discovery. This is what I have been doing all my life. When I make a mistake it helps me to move to a different place.

What is the contact you make with the people who come to listen to you?

They are beautiful people, from young to very old. I don't know what people want in music. It is up to each person to discover. Some people are OK with listening to one person. Other people listen to a lot of different music.

And what about you?

I play more music than I listen to. I only listen to a few. I listen to classical music. I love Debussy, Chopin, Ravel, Satie.

What are you looking for?

I can say it in one sentence and that is, "I want anyone to feel that they, too, are somebody." I have seen all sorts of people and we all do the same things and worry about the same things. The luxury of my life is being able to see and mingle with all kinds of people. You just have to do what you love, and there will be consequences and you have to be ready to pay the full price. I want to keep the mentality that I have nothing to lose. My music speaks for itself, and it is me. I have learned too many tricks to think that I own something. It is very important to feel, as I said, that one has nothing to lose. When I create music, it is not just for me. I am glad that, even in my lowest moments in life, I still did not depend on drugs and alcohol, because I know it is an easy route for some people to forget their sorrows.

Do you perceive your life to be a journey?

It is a completed journey, done a long time ago; and I won. I know that I still have a lot to learn, and I am humbled by my past experiences.

New York
February 13, 2016

~

DAN COLEN

ARTIST

Daniel Colen is an artist based in New York. His work consists of painted sculptures appropriating low-cultural ephemera, graffiti-inspired paintings of text executed in paint, and installations. His *Purgatory* paintings are on show at the Massimo de Carlo Gallery in Milan until June 14th, 2017. I interviewed him in his new studio in Red Hook, Brooklyn, which is on two very large floors of a red brick building that is just on the water.

Dan, your new works represent deserts, stones, cactuses, loneliness, light. How come you make these landscapes when you are here, in front of Manhattan?

I split my time and studio practice between New York City and my farm in Columbia County. Access to the wilderness has become very important to me. I've spent a lot of time driving and hiking all over America, Mexico, South America, and Europe, and I find the experience of being immersed in nature very inspiring. That said, the city has always been and continues to be very important to me. After my first show at Rivington Arms in 2003, showing photorealist paintings of interior spaces, I had an inspiration to make landscape paintings, but instead pursued a different need, to break out of the confines of 2-D and the picture plane of painting. I began making sculpture and working with less traditional materials, so these landscape paintings have been a long time coming.

What did you do?

I made two architectural pieces—both almost like ruins: one was my friend Dash's wall; and the other, titled *Hugs, Drugs and Bugs*, looked like a large wooden crate, its structure inspired by Jeff Wall's *Vampires' Picnic*. These works led me to the boulder sculpture series that I showed at the Whitney Biennial in 2006.

When did the *Bubblegum* paintings come?

The *Bubblegum* and *Birdshit* paintings came directly out of these boulders.

How did you decide to do this?

The papier-mâché boulders I was making at the time were covered in trompe-l'oeil birdshit, as well as bubblegum and spray paint. The birdshit and bubblegum both immediately seemed worthy of their own focused explorations. This began a longer fascination I'm still connected to: the idea that a painting is both an image and an object.

Is your work figurative or abstract?

I began trying to juggle pursuing figuration and abstraction simultaneously in the work. Maybe tightrope-walking is a better metaphor; I was trying to stay on the edge of a fence, so I was always one step away from a very blatant display of both forms of representation. This dovetailed very naturally with my interests in trompe-l'oeil. Setting out to place equal value on content (picture, narrative, theme), process, and material became a guiding principal in studio. I see the new landscape paintings as the culmination of all these investigations.

Were these works successful?

The *Birdshit* and *Bubblegum* paintings were very important for my development. I witnessed them truly transcend my original goals. The material took over. Both groups of paintings began as straightforward conceptually based works and transformed into sincere, lyrical abstractions.

When did you invent the famous *Candle* paintings?

In 2004, soon after my first show. The image is of a candle that has just gone out. The space in the painting is depicted as still being illuminated by some light emanating from the wick of the candle. It occurs to me as a divine light—like the burning bush: a place to commune with God. It was a still from Pinocchio: Geppetto's work table, the place where a craftsman brought an inanimate object to life. It all seemed very fitting. I originally intended a series of different images, all of which gave me a similar feeling of a divine transmitter.

Were you also influenced by Vermeer?

I made a painting of a detail from a Vermeer painting. It was of the glass globe that hung from the ceiling in his painting *The Allegory of Faith*. I loved how simply and precisely Vermeer painted the globe and ribbon—the paint marks are so evident as material and tool, but the image is also so vivid. This unfortunately proved less fertile of a subject for me, and so I set off on making a series of candle paintings. I added smoke in the shape of words—each one had a different word or expression. Each painting has as its source the same image, but from a different edition of the book. These editions,

It occurs to me as a divine light—

like the burning bush:

a place to commune with God.

made decades apart and presumably with different printing presses that gave them this wide variety of colors and resolution, is something that allowed each painting its own character. I understand my candle paintings as highly mediated—my touch was informed by a trail of other crafts and touches: animators cell, photographer, book printer . . . and then finally oil paint.

How many works do you do on the same subject?

It really varies from each body of work. Sometimes just a few, maybe a dozen paintings as with the *Candles* or the board paintings, or sometimes several dozen as with the *Birdshit* and *Bubblegums*. This is an outcome from open exploration and finding new pockets of potential in the series that I didn't know existed from the outset.

Do you paint by yourself?

I began painting alone in a room, but ever since my senior project in art school and the increasing pressure of deadlines I have worked with the help of friends when finalizing my projects. I'm always working with new techniques, which can really make progress slow and hard. I needed help to finish up my first show as well—once the candle paintings became too large for me to accomplish the wet-into-wet technique that I used to make them, I began needing more hands.

What about your sculptures?

The early sculptures also played a role in developing a more consistent relationship with assistants. Their role in my practice has developed over the years; I maintain very intimate dialogues with many of them and enjoy their insights and the progress they allow for. My work has opened up because of these relationships, and the more my practice evolves the more people I come in contact with that help me realize my ideas. I find all these relationships very fulfilling. I'm always juggling working with master craftsmen and apprenticeships; I find both dialogues very compelling and helpful in moving the work forward.

Since when did yours become a success story?

I'm not sure I can really say, it's hard to pinpoint that moment. The Whitney Biennial in 2006 seemed important, as did a group show called *Bridge Freezes Before Road* that Neville Wakefield curated at Gladstone Gallery a few months before that. Another thing that stands out is my first show at Gagosian—I'm not sure you can even call it a show, it happened before I met Larry. I hung four altered found paintings in the four bathrooms on twenty-forth street. It opened at the same time as a David Smith show in the main space. At the time I couldn't imagine a more epic show.

Your work has become quite expensive. Has money changed your life?

Biggie Smalls said it best, "Mo' money, mo' problems." Honestly, I'm very grateful for all my successes and try to use that gratitude as a driving force. The biggest impact the money has had is that it has allowed me to pursue my art with fewer and fewer distractions in more and more precise ways.

Did success trouble you?

Success can be troubling at times. The feeling of letting go of a work around my first few shows was difficult—experiencing a work that I'm intimately connected to leave my studio and turn into a consumer object was challenging, but I adjusted to that. Mostly I'm grateful for my success. It allows my studio practice to develop in a totally unobstructed way. Well, not really, but I've had a lot of freedom to follow my development in a very natural way. I have a lot of gratitude for this.

What about now?

I'm at an interesting moment in which I'm taking stock of the studio I've created. As I said, it happened in a very natural way. I'm now seeing things in retrospect that might work better if I arrange them a little differently. I'm trying to reorganize so less things can distract me from the art making.

How did you move on since the *Candles* and *Bubblegum*? Where are you now?

I am very focused on three new bodies of oil paintings, all landscapes. It has been a long time since I have put such a focus on oil painting, which is very exciting. I've also been developing an ambitious performance-based project over the last few years. Fine tuning the script has been a very slow process, but I'll hopefully start working on rehearsals with actors and objects in the next few months.

You will show your new *Purgatory* paintings in Milan at Massimo De Carlo Gallery. What are they?

I think of these paintings as objects just as much as images. John McCracken would say he sculpted with color, and that idea, as well as his sculptures in general, has really informed these paintings; both the surface and the paint getting built up in a very precise way. These paintings are basically made through a highly ordered build-up of transparent oil glazes. Unlocking the right formula for each work takes a lot of trial and error. They could be seen as paintings of skies, but the abstract atmosphere Rothko builds up seems more relevant to me—the idea that a painting can be a place to have a spiritual experience is very important to me.

Desert is another series that is not completed and that hangs in your studio. The contrast between walls, meaning dark, and the light, seems to be very important, like a search for light and the pursuit of freedom. Is it so?

The *Desert* paintings are kind of the flip side of the same coin as the *Purgatory* paintings. They are about what is impenetrable, about dirt, rock, and earth—they are meant to be impenetrable themselves. They are about hope in the hopelessness, or the infinity at a dead end. The paint is pure; I use no mediums; as opposed to the *Purgatory* paintings, which are mostly sprayed, and so I think of them as air and the *Desert* paintings as earth. I build up very thin, very flat layers, and although the imagery is so blatant, this searching is a very romantic and abstract experience. One mark clues you into the next, the paint is more important to the development than the source image. That said, the source has helped shape these works. Each image is from Wile E. Coyote cartoons, and they depict the places where he has failed, where he has been destroyed and defeated by the Road Runner. Which also is the same place where he is resurrected, only to concoct another mischievous plan that will inevitably end in his own demise.

Does it take you a long time to start and finish a painting?

Yes, painting for me is very slow and searching. I am looking to discover something in the process, in the making, that I did not know at the outset.

Do you produce a lot of work?

The amount of work I make varies. At the moment everything with both my painting and sculpture is developing very slowly, so I will probably produce a much smaller body of work in the next few years than I have in the last few.

Do you have any masters?

I love art, and I love looking at art. I try to see as much as possible in person, and I am constantly looking at books. As I've mentioned the inspiration for these new paintings is varied—McCracken and Rothko are important, so are Brice Marden, Mark Grotjahn and Agnes Martin. I've been looking at a lot of landscape and spiritualist painters: Georgia O'Keefe, Arthur Dove, Agnes Pelton, Barnett Newman, Courbet, and Claude Lorrain. The German Romantics, the Pre-Raphaelites, the Hudson River School, and Ed Ruscha have also always been important to how I think about painting.

And with sculpture?

My sculpture and performance work draw from similar inspirations, but I'd say Nauman is very important. I have been looking at Pierre Huyghe and Urs Fischer a lot lately. Everything creeps into the work; Leos Carax movies, Stephen Reich, Beckett, Sam Shepard, Buster Keaton, The Three Stooges . . . .

Do you draw or take notes?

My sketchbooks play a big role in my practice. I write and I draw—I go through times in which most of my progress is happening in my notebooks and other times where the only way forward is working with the actual material.

Do you like to draw?

My training was in drawing, so it is very important to me. But at this stage I really only use it to think, brainstorm, and plan.

Brooklyn
2017

~

PAOLO COLOMBO

ARTIST & CURATOR

You started your life as an artist and exposed your work at Mario Tazzoli's Galleria "Galatea" in Milan in 1974. Then you stopped painting for many years, and worked as curator and director of various museums and art institutions—in the United States, Switzerland, Italy, and Turkey. Now, since a few years, you still work as a curator, but you also went back to your own work of artist. How come? Would you define yourself as an eclectic figure?

No, not really eclectic because we are in the same field of art, but by nature I have always liked to look at something from both sides. Curiously the introduction to the catalogue of my first exhibition at Galatea was written by an artist whose work I love, Fausto Melotti. Melotti himself stopped his work as an artist for many years, while he had a family with small children. In retrospect it would seem that I followed his footprints, as I also stopped my practice of art while my family and son were young.

Therefore you became a curatorial figure in the U.S.?

At that time I was in Chicago, and as art and artists were the only thing I knew it was natural to work within the art system. I started as a research assistant at the Museum of Contemporary Art in Chicago, and from there I went on to Philadelphia at the Tyler School of Art.

Then you moved back to Europe. Why?

I was appointed director of the Centre d'Art Contemporain Genève, where I stayed for ten years.

What was your job about?

It was both curatorial and administrative. I have had the opportunity to work with many artists at the outset of their career, in Philadelphia with Robert Gober and Carroll Dunham, in Geneva with Kiki Smith, Pipilotti Rist, Ugo Rondinone, and Juan Muñoz.

Why did you move to Istanbul, where you still work today?
At first, in 1998–99, to curate the sixth Istanbul Biennale, where I had the opportunity to work for the first time with William Kentridge and Francis Alÿs. One month before the opening of the Biennale, Istanbul was hit by a seven point four earthquake, which affected the exhibition in more than one way. The show was dedicated to a great singer from the 1920s, Antonis "Dalgas" Diamantidis.

How come you moved on to become the first curator of the MAXXI, the new contemporary art museum built by Zaha Hadid in Rome?
I was appointed by Giovanna Melandri, then minister of culture. I had a particularly nice time there, with exhibitions by Francis Alÿs and Ed Ruscha, both experiences that I remember most fondly.

Did you work with Ed Ruscha again after that?
Yes, recently in 2015 at the Pinacoteca Giovanni and Marella Agnelli in Turin. We put together an ideal collection of works from the public museums in Turin (my home town), relating to the main themes in Ruscha's work.

art
responds
to
a
demanding
yet
very
generous
muse.

Like?

Automobiles, cinema, and crime.

You have worked in various places, but established your home in Athens. How come?

It is the city I love the most. I have always loved it. I worked there as a young artist between 1977 and 1981. I have always loved Greek culture, especially its modern poetry and its popular music tradition between the 1920s and the 1950s. It is an extraordinary subculture, an urban blues formed from the union of Turkish and Greek music following the exchange of population between the two countries in 1922. "Dalgas" was one of the extraordinary musicians that is part of this tradition.

And it is in Athens that you have started your personal work as an artist again. Why, after twenty-five years? What happened?

I just picked up a pencil and my old box of watercolors, which I still have, and started as if not one day had gone by. I have only used watercolor and paper during my whole life because I think it is easily transportable and because it is a technique that does not allow for corrections.

You said that you are from Turin, the city of the Arte Povera. Are you one of these artists?

The answer is no, because my practice is strictly intimate. It demands to be seen one-on-one, like one would read a book, and it is fundamentally lyrical. But in fact I did work with a number of artists from Arte Povera, I had a wonderful time, and have much admiration for them.

You said that you use the technique of watercolor because it is easy to travel. You live in Athens, but most of your time you travel. . . .

I work one week per month at the Istanbul Museum of Modern Art, where I curate exhibitions and advise the collection.

Why did you go back to Istanbul?

I was hired after I left MAXXI in Rome, at the beginning to curate an exhibition on the relation between Turkish and Greek shadow theater, avant-garde film animation in the 1920s in Poland and Germany and eight contemporary artists. The exhibition was called *In Praise of Shadows.* This led to other projects that included young Turkish artists and other artists from the region, from the Caucasus to the Balkans to the Middle East.

Do you know these countries well?

Never enough, but I have a particular affinity with Georgia, extreme eastern border of the classical world where Jason Golden Fleece. There I encountered the work of two creators w favorite artists ever in the world. One is the filmmaker Sergei Parajar dead. I saw massive doses of his films in Tblisi, and the other, the most ary puppeteer in the world, Rezo Gabriadze.

You seem interested in a world that is sadly in the news for reasons other than art. But in your experience art seems to be very lively there, far from the main centers like New York and London. . . .

Art thrives away from the static of the center. It has a purpose that is not determined by reasons of success, fame, and the pot of gold at the end of the rainbow. Today we forget that Goethe wrote Dr. Faustus in the midst of the Napoleonic wars. Art responds to a demanding yet very generous muse.

What are you going to do next, will you be painting in Athens?

Art and more art for me: an exhibition with Qbox Gallery in Athens, and I am curating an exhibition with Rosemarie Trockel—another ideal collection from museums in Turin—for the Pinacoteca Giovanni and Marella Agnelli in November of this year; and I am cocurating the Iraqi pavilion for the 2017 Venice Biennale with Dr. Tamara Chalabi.

Athens
June 19, 2016

~

CATHERINE DENEUVE

ACTRESS

Catherine Deneuve is working on a film set in Paris. She sounds a bit annoyed on the phone. She hesitates and asks how I got her phone number. She is suspicious. "It's not possible. If you want to do an interview, talk to my press office." Before she hangs up, I am able to say, "I wanted to ask you a word about, or a memory of, your friend Yves Saint Laurent." The actress's demeanor suddenly changes. Her voice broken with sorrow, she pauses a long time to reflect. She then responds emotionally:

I would like to point out one thing in particular. He is a person that can't be replaced. He was an extraordinary, truly extraordinary man.

Would you say he was a genius?

He most certainly had genius in him. He was extraordinary in his work, different from anyone else.

What kind of relationship did you have?

He was a loyal friend, a partner, so close that I opened my heart to him. I was very attached to him. The least I can say is that I am deeply sorry.

He called you "Catherine, my sweetness." Was the feeling mutual?

He said I was the most adorable, protective friend. He adored me, and I adored him.

Did you consider yourself a sort of "Mrs. Saint Laurent?"

I would send him bunches of white flowers at home. He adored that flower.

What does Saint Laurent's death mean for the world of fashion?

It's an overwhelming loss. He represented a style, a world, and an era. Truly something that can't be replaced.

Does he leave any heirs?
Talent can't be inherited at all. It is something unique, which in this case, belonged only to him.

Are there other designers that come close to his talent?
No, nobody.

Was he the only great one in fashion? Nobody else is comparable?
The two greats were Chanel and Saint Laurent.

What did Saint Laurent's greatness consist of?
Yves wasn't just a designer. He was a creator.

With these words, when she seems to have forgotten that she said she didn't want to talk, she is once again politely cold.

I beg of you to excuse me, but I really must go. I am in a meeting. I don't yet feel like talking about Yves. That's enough.

Paris
June 3, 2008

~

TALENT

can't

BE INHERITED AT ALL.

MARGUERITE DURAS

NOVELIST

Marguerite Duras's book, *The North China Lover* (originally published in France in 1991 as *L'Amant de la Chine du Nord,* by Gallimard*),* became a literary sensation for two reasons. The first reason was that Duras left Les Éditions de Minuit, which had published *The Lover* in 1984. That book won the Prix Goncourt and sold more than a million copies. The second reason was that the new book tells the exact same story as *The Lover* and with the same characters—the writer's mother, her mean older brother, the younger brother who died too soon, and, most of all, the Chinese lover, a rich man of twenty-seven who took her virginity when she was fifteen and a half. He was her lover for more than eighteen months.
This interview was conducted in Paris during June, 1991. At the time, Marguerite Duras was still worn out from a recent operation, but she's enthusiastic about her new literary effort.

Why did you feel the need to rewrite the same story you already told in *The Lover?*

Did you like the new book? You must have read the preface, where I explain that after learning of the death of my Chinese lover in 1990, I felt the need to write the same story in another way.

This book reads more like a novel. It seems like you talk a lot more about your younger brother, Paulo, than about your mother. In *The Lover* your mother didn't really know your Chinese lover. In the new book, you reveal that they saw one another. That they talked and liked one another, and it seemed almost as if your mother was fond of him.

My mother considered him almost like a son. I wrote the script four times for Jean Jacques Annaud, who is shooting a film inspired by *The Lover.* But I don't like the film Annaud is making. It's too commercial, and very different from my kind of cinema. I no longer like other people's cinema. So I very happily wrote *The North China Lover.* It's a novel that is like a film. *The Lover* was more like a chronicle than a novel, and the character Thanh, our houseboy, was missing. Thanh was an amazing person, and I loved him so very much. I had a strong impulse to write this new story. My adolescence in Indochina, an unforgettable and extraordinary place; my mother who had me when she was already in her forties; my younger brother, Paulo, who died in 1942 and who was my favorite; that monster of an older brother, Pierre, who was a mean, lying thief. My mother favored him in such a terrible way, and, in any case, they were both terrible. My mother favored him because he was a gigolo. He complimented her and stole from her. He left with our inheritance, and I never saw him again. But the protagonist of both books is the Chinese lover.

Didn't you mythologize your father?

I didn't know him. He died when I was five. Myths are Greek, and my mother and my brother, Pierre, were the tragedy. I loved my younger brother like crazy, and actually, in my new book, I talk about how we had an incestuous relationship.

You describe the Chinese lover the same way in both books, but many details are different. Which version is the truth?

The truth is in both books. But in the new novel I describe things better with more details. My fear of blood when he took my virginity. I describe how I took his hand and put it on my genitals when he picked me up for the first time in his big black car, a legendary Morris Léon Bollée. Rewriting the same story in a bit of a different way with the same characters is a curious, almost one-of-a-kind literary event. They say that I'm the most free of French lady novelists. Perhaps it is my readers who have allowed me

They've always told me that I was a really free spirit from the time I was a little girl.

HE TOLD ME WHAT I WROTE ON THE LAST PAGE OF THE LOVER. THAT NOTHING HAD CHANGED. THAT HE STILL LOVED ME, AND HE WOULD NEVER STOP LOVING ME, AND THAT HE WOULD LOVE ME UNTIL THE DAY HE DIED. NOW HE IS DEAD, AND I COULD CONTINUE REWRITING THE SAME STORY.

to express myself so freely. When speaking about *The North China Lover* a journalist said, "This isn't just your memory. It's our memory." In this new novel, you sense my fear of death even more. The fear that my Chinese lover—who was a libertine, a layabout, and smoked opium—might kill me because he didn't want another man to have me. They've always told me that I was a really free spirit from the time I was a little girl. I was free because my mother was miserable and poor—she had to sell the jewels I'd received from my father in order to buy food. My mother didn't care that I was prostituting myself. She only loved Pierre anyway.

You had already described Pierre very well in *The Lover.*

Yes. He disgusted me. I hated him, and he still torments me to this day even though I don't know where either he or my mother is buried. Obviously they are buried near one another. My mother's love for Pierre was disgusting.

Why did you change publishers?

I will never go back to Éditions de Minuit. They wanted to cut fifty pages of the book after having kept it for nine weeks.

In your new book, you talk about how, at age fifteen, you told your Chinese lover that you would write a book about the relationship you were in.

Yes. At age ten, I was already writing poetry. As I write in both *The Lover* and *The North China Lover,* when my Chinese lover came to Paris after the war and called me—and he was married with kids at that point—he already knew that I was a writer, because he had read a book of mine.

Did he really telephone you?

Yes. And he told me what I wrote on the last page of *The Lover.* That nothing had changed. That he still loved me, and he would never stop loving me, and that he would love me until the day he died. Now he is dead, and I could continue rewriting the same story.

Paris
June 13, 1991

~

UMBERTO ECO

PHILOSOPHER

Umberto Eco, many people know where you are, but you prefer not to disclose the location. How will you spend your summer?

Here in my country house as usual, where last year I was finishing writing *The Mysterious Flame of Queen Loana*. All of my books were started and finished in the countryside. *Foucault's Pendulum* took eight years. I wrote it on holiday, at Christmas, at Easter, and in the summer. Let me repeat something I've said many times. I finished *The Name of the Rose* on January 5th, which is my birthday. So, out of superstition, I decided that I needed to finish the second book on January 5th. Actually I was finishing up around January 2nd, but then I let things drag out a bit and was able to finish on January 5th. The third book went the same way, though the fourth book, *Baudolino*, was finished at the end of July, and I thought to myself, "Something is not right. It is known that novels go on autopilot toward the end, and therefore it's a truly unstoppable process. Honestly, I eventually put my mind at ease, because my grandson Emanuele was born a few days later. I finished *Loana*, my latest book, between the end of August and the beginning of September. This year, my calendar is open in August, and this perhaps worries me a bit. Of course, I have to prepare for some lectures, and in the mornings I go into town with the pharmacist to have an aperitif before lunch."

So what type of August will it be?

Carefree, leisurely reading, things that aren't obligatory. Perhaps it will be more productive for this exact reason. Perhaps I will reread—who knows—some great philosophical work.

What is your favorite kind of reading material?

I am not methodical. For quite a few decades now, I have had a sort of "moral impediment" in the sense that I only read fiction at night before going to sleep. Reading during the day would be like taking time away from more important works. Sure, there have been exceptions. Two years ago, for example, I was ill for a week, and I reread Thomas Mann's *The Magic Mountain* in the afternoon. Years ago I had pneumonia, and I ended up in the hospital where I reread *War and Peace*. I have to be ill to read fiction in daylight.

Does that mean that fiction is only entertainment for you?

No. It is that I am a philosopher and a semiotician by profession.

But don't you also consider yourself a novelist?

That doesn't mean anything because even when I translate Nerval or write an essay on Joyce, I work day and night. During the day when I read a book, I can't stop myself from letting some little word force me to get up and go consult another book. If you do this with fiction, it is less of a pleasure and you are less likely to let yourself go with the narrative flow without interrupting it. You can only do this in bed. You can't even do this on the beach because there will always be someone to disturb you. To read fiction well one needs solitude, night, a bedside lamp, and continuity.

Do you have a proper library in the countryside, like you do in Milan?

Not like in Milan, but because I send all of the double copies and a lot of other things to the country, I have twenty thousand books that cover me for emergencies. If I receive two Moravia books or two Hemingway books, I always send the second copy to the countryside.

What do you do in your library?

Walk from one shelf to another . . . In my library, it's not necessary to look for a specific book knowing exactly what you want as is, unfortunately, the case in our libraries where one needs to meticulously fill out forms to take out two books maximum. I think about the American libraries where the reader has direct access to the books. Someone looks at A and then goes to B and C and the D that he had overlooked or forgotten. And that's where the grand adventure begins.

What adventure?

Discovering books, the relationship with books. If you have twenty thousand books, adventure isn't guaranteed, but if, as in my case in Milan, you have thirty thousand books, the adventure is inevitably there.

And so one ends up wasting time—even if in a useful way—in a library?

It is not a waste of time, because then there is a result. One wastes time, for example, playing golf. Bernard Shaw reportedly said, "It isn't necessary to be stupid to play golf, but it helps." In the library, I would say that it's not necessary to be intelligent, but it helps.

You have had many obsessions, for example, far-off seas, Sherlock Holmes, Dumas, Joyce, Saint Thomas. . . . What is your obsession now?

The best obsessions are the ones that return. Unless one decides to go looking for the philosopher's stone the day after tomorrow. The obsessions stopped in adolescence. In actuality, life is about pleasing your father even after he is dead. Realizing as an adult the things you dreamed about doing.

And what did your father want you to do?

He wanted me to become a lawyer. We lived in a small town and so that was the profession that stood out the most. But when I was young, he watched me very carefully as I wrote novellas or drew comic strips. He was a clerical worker, but he was proud when my first book came out, and I know he read the whole thing at night.

Was your father able to enjoy your success?

No, but he saw that my second book was reviewed by Eugenio Montale in the *Corriere della Sera*, and he was pleased. A great poet reviewing me in a great newspaper.

Do your children have the same relationship with you that you had with your father? Do they also come to the country?

All generations are different from one another. Yes, of course, the family comes and then mid-month, friends arrive. And then the night-time concerts and all kinds of madness starts.

What kind of madness?

For example, wonderful theatrical improvisations. Unfortunately we had to stop when the greatest comedian among us—Emilio Tadini—died.

Well, what do you do?

We make up dialogues between drunkards from Milan or we make fake radio shows. The friends are always the same.

Is this all part of your latest book?

Certainly, because they sang songs from the 1930s and 1940s, so I knew them all by heart.

Is one always a product of his own generation?

I would say so. Luciano Berio was always with us, but he didn't make experimental music. He would bang away at the piano, playing Genovese songs from his childhood.

Is it nice to go through life like a young man?

I take it as a compliment when they tell me I'm like a goliard [a wandering student in medieval Europe given to writing ribald, satirical Latin verse]. In any case, I've taken inspiration from the greatest goliards, from Rabelais to Joyce. . . .

Would you also like to write a humorous novel?

I believe I've already written one without realizing it. One of my foreign editors always says she laughs like crazy when she reads my books, even when everyone dies.

Laughter is very important to you, isn't it?

Not split-your-sides laughter, but a smile. Not taking yourself too seriously and not taking others too seriously. This has already been written in the book of Ecclesiastes.

Near Urbino
July 15, 2004

~

TRACEY EMIN

ARTIST

Tracey Emin is in her London studio. She says:

I bought this building in 2010. I live two minutes from here in a really old house that was built in 1729. This once used to be an artists' area, it was pretty derelict for a long time. I bought the small house next door and I will knock it down and David Chipperfield will help me build a new house which will join onto the studio. When I am old, even if I can't walk I still want to be able to work, I can live next door to the studio and my studio staff can look after me. You have to think about this stuff now—later I will be too old. It is my way of ensuring that I can carry on working.

So, is it London forever?

No. I spend my time in New York, the South of France, Miami. Yes, it is my base, because I am British, and because it's home.

Where do you feel more creative?

On the airplane. My creativity is more to do with an emotional resource and it has more to do with what I am, not where I am.

So why do you move about so much?

One reason is because I can. I enjoy the spirit of it. I never ever get bored, so it's not because of boredom. I like different seasons, different weather. Each place has such a different character and feeling. It can spark something off in me.

Since 1995, when you first exhibited your famous work *Everyone I Have Ever Slept With 1963-1995*, have many things changed in your life?

Yes, unbelievably.

And also in you?

They have. I would never make that work now. It was twenty-one years ago that I made it and a lot should change in twenty-one years to a person, internally and externally.

You have said that for instance you are not interested in sex anymore, but in love. What does it mean?

When I was younger I was confused, I divided them too much and because of that I would confuse sex for love, which was wrong.

So you didn't give up sex?

I did. I can have actually a relationship with someone without sex because I really love them and that love can override all the animal qualities.

Like you have with your brother?

No, I don't mean a platonic relationship. The easiest way to explain things is that I would rather be alone than feel unloved. I like my solitude. If I keep on moving it is because moving means essentially I am alone. I don't move with my family. I think to be an artist you need solitude because you need some purity of thought, some clarity. I protect that within myself and within my work. Now that I am getting older it matters a lot to protect it within myself.

What are you protecting yourself from?

From losing my creativity, losing my love of art, losing my spirituality, losing all the things you have to nurture as you deal with more and more of the outside world.

Success is an enemy?

Success is fantastic. My most successful thing that I have done is to keep working. I know a lot of artists that still work, but they are jaded or they are cynical and they don't have the same kind of belief that they did when they were younger.

But you are still obsessed by you?

She laughs. Yes. I still use me, I still work with me!

You think others care?

I care, and others care about the emotional resonance in my work. My last exhibition that took place at White Cube this autumn was titled *The Last Great Adventure Is You*. Nearly all of the work was about loss. Loss of heart, loss of life, of youth, of being beautiful. Being fifty-two, not twenty-five. Other people identified with this and art should not be difficult, art should give you something, there should be a dialogue. Forty-five thousand people went to see my exhibition in five weeks in a commercial gallery. The majority of them were people between the age of fifteen and twenty.

You have said several times, in particular about a famous artist like Louise Bourgeois, that women artists are not as appreciated as men. Is that true?
It is changing and it is purely history and time that dictate this. In a hundred years' time everything could be completely different.

Were there fewer women artists in the past?
Yes, now there are many more women artists and so with time we'll see.

At one time male artists, from Tiziano to Picasso, from Courbet to Matisse, were obsessed by naked women. You are doing that with yourself?
Yes. I am my own model. When you look at Picasso I am sure he used his own body as a model, all the women are square like he was. My favorite artists are Edvard Munch and Egon Schiele, they used themselves constantly in their work. So did Rembrandt and van Gogh.

In the case of Schiele, is it a bit of the nonsexual love you were talking about?
No. He is dead. But I did write a thing recently about being able to continue love even when someone dies. You can love the dead.

This happened to you?
No, but I think there is such a thing as the living dead, that when someone goes somewhere else you can continue to love without having the love returned and that feels like death.

Unrequited love and aging seem to be your fears?
I am not scared of dying, funnily enough. I never thought I was going to live for a long time when I was young, but now I have changed my mind. Which means I am much happier than I was. I see a future . . . .

What kind of a future do you see?
A good future. Working, painting, making sculptures, gardening. I used to grow every vegetable on the roof of my old studio and I loved it. Now I want to do it again, here and in France.

You like money, sports cars, nice houses, and you vote Conservative. Why?
I voted Conservative because it appeared at the time they were going to take care of the arts and I like David Cameron, the Prime Minister, as well because I think he is kind. They didn't make all the big cuts which they could have. Even if there's no money, I said please don't cut money for the arts, because the arts are really important.

Is England a good country for artists?
In Holland artists were given money every month by the government and at the end

of the year they had to give back a painting. The Dutch government had more bad art than they knew what to do with. The scheme did not work to produce good art. In Britain, if you are a good artist it means you are good.

What has changed in your art?

I have gone back to my beginning. Everything I do is with my hands.

Do you try many different media?

I always worked in different media, always. Bronze is new. I have only been working in bronze for three years and learning how to do it.

What are your ambitions?

To keep working and for my work to be protected, so it has some kind of legacy. That's it.

Do you think we are living in an interesting period for art?

Yes, on many different levels. I think for one thing we are living in a time of fear. There's also this feeling that time is moving so fast, really fast. The job of the artist is to actually make time stand still, to give a moment so the viewer can reflect internally and visually externally and have a response. Art is like a wall. You stop and it talks to you. Art is not competing with technology, machinery, spaceships. Art is something else. So it's a really interesting time for the artist at the moment, a very difficult time. I am talking about the artist in the biggest sense that it could be.

Do you feel different from when you started?

When I started I was innocent.

Have you lost your innocence?

There is a little bit of innocence left, a tiny bit.

And it is this innocence that is left which keeps you an artist?

Art was like my lover, even when I tried to run away or get away from it, art always came back to me and saved me. Art never left me. It is a bit like faith, or some people say God or something, this entity of art never abandons me, it looks after me financially as well as spiritually, socially, but most importantly I have to remain morally secure.

London
December 11, 2014

~

LOULOU DE LA FALAISE

FASHION DESIGNER

Loulou de la Falaise, with her international pedigree, epitomized the archetype of the Parisian lady. I loved her elegance, her imaginativeness, her brilliant creativity, and her incorrigible nonconformity. She also had the great good fortune to work with Yves Saint Laurent.

Loulou (Louise de La Falaise Klossowski de Rola) is a stylish and energetic woman, reminiscent of an Irish Setter or a pure-blooded racehorse. She is a celebrity, a goddess of inspiration, who lives the life of an adventuress, a life in which she is adroitly able to unite the present with the past. To her intimate confidants she is the most faithful friend imaginable. She followed several different paths, including marriage at an early age to an Irish lord succeeded by some bohemian years as a New Yorker in the world of pop art and Andy Warhol, until Yves Saint Laurent invited her to come and work with him. So this is why Loulou has made Paris her city of choice.

As is well known among those who know, a somewhat tribal atmosphere prevails at the Maison Saint Laurent, so it can hardly be considered surprising that Anna, Loulou's one-year-old daughter, who is the goddaughter of Yves, along with Thaddée, her husband, an author and a refined man of sophisticated accomplishments, play a singular role among the enchantments of the *hôtel particulier* on the avenue Marceau. Every evening Thaddée arrives to fetch Loulou in the company of Anna, the one and only baby who is admitted to the salon and who crawls around on all fours in the inner sanctum of the master. And indeed the latter, being very Catholic, has made her a gift of his glittering antique crucifixes, and these have become her playthings.

Loulou's apartment is on the rue des Plantes in the Fourteenth Arrondissement. It is exceptionally capacious; two enormous rooms (similar to artists' studios), decked out with mezzanines, intercommunicate. The first is the domain of Anna, the second of Loulou and Thaddée, who proclaim that the entire decoration of their apartment is altogether the effect of chance. Every object seems to be somehow suspended in grandeur; one's first impression is that it all looks like the temporary staging for a touring festival, but then somehow the provisional concludes by becoming definitive. White curtains evoke billowing clouds, an azure-blue carpet captures the sky, the lime greens (Loulou's grandmother was Russian) recall leafy trees in woods, and an immense bed, a gift from her mother, Maxime de la Falaise, is out on patrol as a sofa in the living room, sailing like a boat in the middle of the sea; a batik reinforces this impression.

The first activity that Loulou undertakes on her return home in the evenings is a change of clothes, and she slips effortlessly into one of the opulent dressing gowns that her forever-friend Fernando Sanchez designs for her. The earlier part of her evenings she passes in and out of nightclubs; later on she can be found with her familiars in their homes. The Klossowskis allocate their weekends to Sens, 120 kilometers from Paris, where they have taken a property with their close friends Leonello and Maria Brandolini; the Brandolinis also have a daughter, Xenia, who is the same age as Anna. Customarily their autumn holidays, and additionally their Easter and summer breaks, are enjoyed at Montecalvello, a vast château located in the province of Viterbo which the painter Balthus, the father of Thaddée, acquired at the time when he was the director of the Académie de France in Rome.

By any standards, therefore, Anna has an exceptional mother, but Loulou does not seem to think that her life is in any way out of the ordinary:

"This is how my family is: the women have always played a hugely significant role. I am thinking of my mother, who now lives in New York, and of my grandmother, a ravishing woman of exceptional elegance: both have always treated life as an odyssey, always living freely, as if by magic, as if they were gypsies; and with a superb taste for enjoying themselves and for light-heartedness, and all without ever losing their sensibility for the truly important values in life."

Paris

1986

Originally published in *Vogue Paris*

MIA FARROW

ACTRESS

Mia Farrow is in Venice for the first time as a Goodwill Ambassador for UNICEF. She looks rejuvenated. Her hair is long and loose and she's wearing an antique pink T-shirt, black pants, and sandals. Accompanying her is her son Seamus, the child she had with Woody Allen, who is considered to be a young genius. At age fifteen he became the youngest student ever to graduate from Bard College, and was admitted to Yale Law School at age sixteen. At Yale, he is to study human rights law. Mia Farrow is a kind, poetic woman with a strong sense of determination; just the way we've come to know her in films like *Rosemary's Baby* [1968] or in the many films directed by her ex-husband, Woody Allen.

Mia Farrow, how long have you been a UNICEF Ambassador?

Since 1999.

How did you begin working with the organization?

I was asked to help in the fight against polio. I think they chose me because I had polio when I was nine years old, but thank God I got through it without any consequences. One of my adoptive children, a little boy from Calcutta, also had polio.

And how is he today?

Unfortunately, he is in a wheelchair. But he is getting much better care now than he was before.

You have lots of children. How many do you have exactly?

I have fourteen. Ten of whom I adopted from war zones. Some are already grown and work and are married. One is a lawyer, another one is a teacher, another one is a psychologist, and another is the director of a school. In addition to all of these children, I have three grandchildren as well.

Are all your children the same for you, whether they were adopted or not?

Yes, of course. For me, they are all exactly the same.

So would you recommend that people adopt more?

No, I wouldn't push anyone to take that path. It seems obvious to me because I adore children, and I can take care of them. I have a beautiful house in New York. I am very lucky and have enough money, and therefore it is right for me to adopt these kids in desperate situations. Now, for example, one of my adoptive children is blind and needs a lot of care and really needs me. I began working at age eighteen, and so today I can work less and dedicate myself to this. Certainly, I occasionally work in the theater, on television shows, or in films.

What does your commitment to children involve?

For example, now I am in Venice for an evening event raising money to send to the health crisis in Ossetia. I've also been to Nigeria, Angola, Somalia, and Sarajevo. Now I hope to go to Sudan.

What do you do during these trips?

I look around as much as possible. I try to understand what UNICEF does and what the aims are. I especially listen to the people who speak to me about their needs. I try to best represent UNICEF and to help the organization reach its objectives. UNICEF is able to do things that many political leaders aren't able to do. When I return to the United States, I speak with the media. I try to tell about the things I've learned in the best way possible. People listen to me because they trust me.

What is the worst situation you've seen?

In Angola, right after a fragile peace agreement after twenty-seven years of conflict. A place where there are millions of mines that haven't been defused, where the infrastructure has been destroyed and where nobody knows anything about anyone else. Everyone is looking for someone, and a third of the population is in refugee camps. I saw too many children die in Angola, and it was truly a distressing situation.

Have you adopted children from there as well?

From Angola, no. However, I remember having seen a man who looked at my son Seamus's belt and told me that he had had the same belt, and that he had had to eat it. People were eating anything—roots, seeds. And then there is the frightening problem of the mines, which are everywhere and out of control.

Were you scared?

I have to say that I was only in certain areas, which can only be reached by airplane.

Can you tell me more about this work?

UNICEF is extraordinary, and it allows one to do great work. To vaccinate children and bring food and blankets. To help those in need. Here in Venice, for example, now we are raising money to send to Beslan, where that horrible tragedy happened.

How many people has UNICEF saved?

It would be impossible to quantify.

Why do you bring your children with you?

Because Seamus is sixteen years old, and we need young people who can speak with other young people.

As a UNICEF ambassador, how much money have you been able to raise?

It is hard to give a number, but I know that when I did a show on CNN people were calling into a toll-free number and the donations really went up. As I said before, because I am fortunate to have many people that put their trust in me, many people respond to my appeals.

What kind of relationship have you maintained with the cinema?

I love films. I have always liked the cinema very much. But now that I don't have any big parts planned, I'm acting in *Fran's Bed*, which is playing on Broadway. The show is going very well, and I am very happy about this. When one has worked for many years in the cinema and wants to have a long career, one needs to know how to wait for the right role. Furthermore, one also needs to know how to do other things, and not let the cinema take up all of one's time. I am lucky because I love many different things, and I especially love getting together with my children and grandchildren. I have to say that my life is truly full right now.

New York
September 9, 2004

~

I LOOK AROUND AS MUCH AS POSSIBLE.

JULIAN FELLOWES

WRITER & DIRECTOR

Did you think Downton Abbey would be such a success?

No. The received truth at the time of the film *Gosford Park* [2011] was that the audience had gone. It was one of those fabulously inaccurate prophecies that show business tends to specialize in. I've read in the papers that we took *Downton Abbey* to the BBC and got turned down. It's all untrue; it was pretty smooth going actually at ITV.

You were an actor. As an actor did you imagine you were going to be a writer?

After drama school I wrote a couple of historical—what we used to call bodice ripper—novels. They weren't of any merit, but I had stuck my toe in the water. I didn't write again until I'd been acting for quite a long period and began to think I needed a second string.

Were you a good actor?

I was beta-plus successful. I was a running character in a very popular series called *Monarch of the Glen* [2000–2005], I was in a Bond movie, I was in a movie with Catherine Deneuve. I had a lucky break in *For The Greater Good* [1991], a mini-series for Danny Boyle. It wasn't bad, but life decided otherwise.

As an actor, does it help your screenwriting?

Yes, I think that when you are an actor you develop a good instinct for what is sayable and what is not sayable. When an actor has a problem with a speech, their solution may not be the right solution but they are almost always right that there is a problem.

You became an Oscar winning screenwriter and a Lord?

I think we are who we are. You have a bit more money and you are a bit more attractive to hostesses if you're in the news. My friends are the same as the friends I had before I'd written anything. I think we go in for long friendships in England; that's a national characteristic.

Did you want to become famous and rich?

Fame is a funny business. Fame may be the spur when you're young, but I think when you

FAME IS A *funny* BUSINESS.

are older it's the price more than the spur. I think if most people could have the success and the rewards in their careers without the fame they would probably choose that.

Have you always been interested in the class system?

I wouldn't say always. My favorite piece of my own work is *Separate Lies* [2005], and that is about self-knowledge. For me the key virtue is self-knowledge. I think if we have a real understanding of who we are, then we are able to withstand life's buffeting. What makes you vulnerable is lying to yourself.

Is class a very English thing?

I think it's everywhere, sometimes in disguise but everywhere. It's a question of judging people for what they are and not who they are. That strange sensation of being disliked by people who don't know you, I had that as a Catholic when I was young. I do examine that theme, in Downton I have had black characters, Jewish characters.

At this very moment prejudice and racism are coming back massively in Europe.

The danger area is that casual unthought-out slight prejudice that creeps in. The English upper and middle classes were no less guilty than anyone else. As a child of the fifties and sixties you really did think that anti-Semitism was probably finished, the idea of desecrating graves and attacking synagogues just seemed to be over, to have gone like smallpox. The recurrence of the disease is fantastically depressing.

How did you build your many characters and did you build them with the actors?

When you are writing a series it's not like a film, because you write for the performances. You can see that this actor is funny or this one is moving and you deliberately concoct situations to play to their strengths. If an actor says to me could I have more of this or less of that it's always worth listening, as they are inside the character.

Do you love all your characters?

I think what we got right is that we don't give either side any more weight than the other, no more moral weight or intelligence. The love affair between Anna and Mr. Bates has the same dramatic weight as the love affair between Mary and Matthew.

How do you manage to create all these characters?

I think you know all sorts of people and you just do it. Sometimes when you read it over you see a false note and say, "Oh she wouldn't have said that or used those words," and then my wife reads it over and she says, "I don't think Mrs. Patmore the cook would have said that," and she's usually right, and then after that it goes to the producers and it's only then that anyone else sees it.

Which are the most popular figures?

Everyone likes Maggie Smith as the Dowager, but they all have their following.

As an actor, once you are a lord or a butler, you can be typecast. Don't they get typecast?

Not Maggie Smith, she is already famous for herself. Hugh Bonneville is also pretty famous in England and so is Elizabeth McGovern.

Is Lord Grantham a loser, as he lost his wife's money?

I don't think he's a loser at all, he is one of the lucky ones, because his estate is going to get through. There were many families that could not embrace the changes and survive that period. I think it's an American concept that you never look depressed, that nothing ever goes wrong. . . . In Europe it's not considered to be a loser to say one has had a terrible year, because we all have a terrible year at one time or another.

So you make them very human, and there are ambiguous characters like Thomas the gay footman and Bates the valet of Lord Grantham?

Yes, Thomas is in one sense the least generous, but on the other hand being homosexual at that time was very tough. They were still prosecuting homosexuals into my teens. Some people thought it was wrong, my parents thought it was wrong. I grew up in the atmosphere that this was the wrong thing to be doing so I am sympathetic to their plight.

And Bates?

He never reveals his feelings. He doesn't need a mass of friends, he doesn't need reassurance, he doesn't need to tell everyone his troubles. I am fascinated by those people. He doesn't need forgiveness. He needs his wife Anna to love him and as long as she loves him then that's enough.

And what about Anna?

His wife is a kind of enabler, generous, kind, perfectly social, easy to get on with, but she knows her husband is none of those things so she has to be the bridge between him and the rest. She normalizes her husband for you, even though her husband is not normal.

And Carson the butler?

He is more of a believer in the old order than any of the family. He believes much more passionately in the class system than either of the Granthams. He just feels that when the boat starts to rock it will all fall apart, so every last detail must be maintained for as long as it can be.

And Mrs. Hughes the housekeeper?

She represents the majority of people in domestic service. For her it's a job. She's not unhappy. When the system comes to an end she won't be particularly bothered and will use her skills in some other way and move on.

Even Mrs. Patmore the cook?

She has a marketable skill. She became a very important character and a lot of that was to do with Lesley Nicol who plays her, because she's very funny.

And what about Mary?

She's quite tough. The thing about people like Mary is that they just want to be in charge, they want to be at the top table. She will adjust.

She's difficult, even in love, and a cold mother?

She wants more control. I think that whole generation were fairly cold! We didn't have our children all over us until the sixties. When I was a child I saw my father once a week and lunch on Sundays, and we weren't grand or certainly rich. That was just the way it was done in England then.

What is the relationship between Mary and her mother, Cora?

Mary thinks her mother is sentimental, and she blames it on her being an American. Mary also has a modern impetus; she doesn't want to adopt the powerless role where all the decisions were being made by the husband.

And the relationship with her sister, Edith?

She can't stand Edith. The sister has two principal narrative roles. One is that some people are just unlucky and we have all known them. But the other is that the First World War didn't just open careers but also perfectly ordinary women were changed by the war because of the activities they got involved with. It means Edith publishes rather than selling the magazine and just letting it go.

Are the acting company like a family, and do they get on together?

They all get on very well and look forward to coming back to work each year. They are not together between August and February and they all do other things, and then they come back to go on with the series. It's a nice atmosphere on the set. I was there the other day.

Where is the set?

It's partly at Highclere, those are all the ground-floor rooms. The kitchens and the attics and at least one bedroom and Robert's bedroom are all at Ealing Studios. So they go between the two.

Are you friendly with them all? Your great friend is Maggie Smith?

I am pretty friendly with most of them and know some better than others and I have worked with Hugh and Maggie and Allen Leech before. They are a nice group.

They are very different from the characters they play?

Yes, some more different than others.

Would you like to change, or will Downton Abbey go on after the sixth season?

Our audiences have continued to rise. The largest audience we have ever had was for the last episode of the last series. *The Daily Mail* kept writing about how the audience was going down when in fact it was going up. We have something like one hundred sixty million in China and in America something like twenty-five million when you add them all up.

You are now writing the sixth season. Until when does it go? 1940?

I never answer those questions.

Are we going to get to the Second World War?

No, not yet.

Are you going to work in America?

Yes, I am working on *The Gilded Age*, which is a bit earlier than Downton, it's sort of 1870s Edith Wharton's New York.

Do you feel comfortable with that, even though you are not American?

I think it's a challenge. I have spent a lot of time in America and I am interested in American social history and the fast-moving social system. You come from nothing, within one generation you are a prince, but the mere fact that it was custom in America to divide your fortune between all your children meant that no fortune lasted for long.

Are you inventing a new family?

Yes. A student of the era will recognize many incidents, but they are mainly fictional characters. It'll be about American society, no doubt with some foreigners in it.

For me the key virtue is

SELF-KNOWLEDGE.

I think if we have a real understanding of who we are, then we are able to withstand life's buffeting.

What makes the success of your TV stories?

I don't know. I think you are trying to create a world in itself, a kind of universe. You want people to become involved with that world and they do it in their relationships with these fictional characters and sometimes their relationship can be surprisingly powerful, almost alarming. Quite what that is, it would take someone cleverer than I to define.

Do you have fun?

It's very involving and interesting and I am very lucky to have chosen a career that continues to interest me.

Will you use big stars in this American production?

Sometimes there's an advantage in an actor's baggage and you put that to use. You could say that we profited from Maggie's status and the aura around her to make our show instantly worthwhile, but on the other hand the advantage of the lesser known is that they become doubly real for you.

Will *The Gilded Age* be filmed in New York?

Most of nineteenth Century New York has gone, so we may find ourselves in another East Coast town that has been better preserved.

Are you writing in your house in Dorset?

Yes, but I write wherever I am. Writing as an actor means you don't get a fetish about a desk. I write on a computer, and not at a specific time of day.

Will you write another novel?

At the moment I haven't got the space to do another novel. I would like to.

Are you inviting people to come and live in your world?

People pray for my characters. They know it's all fiction, but they do worry about Cora!

London.
February 25, 2015

~

DANTE FERRETTI

PRODUCTION DESIGNER

Dante Ferretti is an Italian production designer, art director, and costume designer. Throughout his career he has worked with many great directors, both American and Italian, including Pier Paolo Pasolini, Federico Fellini, Terry Gilliam, Franco Zeffirelli, Martin Scorsese, Francis Ford Coppola, Anthony Minghella, and Tim Burton. He frequently collaborates with his wife, set decorator Francesca Lo Schiavo. Ferretti has won three Academy Awards for Best Art Direction; for *The Aviator* [2004], *Sweeney Todd: The Demon Barber of Fleet Street* [2007], and *Hugo* [2011]. He had seven previous nominations. In addition, he was nominated for Best Costume Design for *Kundun* [1997]. He has also won three BAFTA Awards.

On December 13th, you will be awarded an honorary degree in architecture at Rome's Università la Sapienza, in the Architecture Department's aula magna [great hall] in the Villa Borghese. How does it feel to receive this degree?

It is a great pleasure, because it is not easy to be awarded such an important degree. The fact that a set designer who works in the cinema, the theater, and the opera is given an honorary degree as an architect in appreciation for all the work he's done up to now is a great honor. Without a doubt architecture is an important part of my work, because every time I have to make a film that is set in a certain historical period I have to consider what I can do to avoid making a copy. Because when one copies, it looks like a film set, and I am a bit like the actors that study at the Actors Studio. I put myself into the role as if I myself were the architect from the historical period in which the film is set. If I make a mistake, it isn't important. Actually, it would seem more realistic. Moreover, the actual architecture would have been tweaked and reworked many times in the years since that period.

Unlike an architect, who builds bridges, buildings, and places of worship that then remain as symbols of their era, is your work a bit like the Buddhist mandala which is destroyed once it is finished?

Once a film is done shooting the set is taken down and space is made to shoot new films. This happens at Cinecittà as well as at Pinewood in London and in the film studios in Los Angeles, where everything is taken down and destroyed. Sometimes at Cinecittà they leave sets that can be reused for other films, even once the film is completed and shown in cinemas, but this happens rarely.

What are the most memorable sets that you have created during your career?

Federico Fellini and Pier Paolo Pasolini were my teachers. With Fellini I had to build the entire set. He had a very particular vision. You had to understand what he wanted, what he had in mind. We did six films together. I should mention that lies were very important with Fellini. He'd ask me, "Dantino, what did you dream last night?" I'd make dreams up. He knew I was inventing them, but he wanted to see how far my imagination went.

What was your experience when working with Pasolini?

I did eight films when I was an assistant, from *The Gospel According to St. Matthew* [*Il vangelo secondo Matteo*, 1964] to *The Hawks and the Sparrows* [*Uccellacci e uccellini*, 1966]. Until one day Pasolini called me to do *Medea* [1969], and from that time on we worked together, until his last film, *The 120 Days of Sodom* [*Salò o le 120 giornate di Sodoma*, 1975]. We always used the formal *lei* form when speaking to each other in Italian. He would give me the scarcest outline of something, and I would understand what he wanted and go and create it. Sometimes I did things all my own way, and he would look and say, "Good, good."

Was it after Franco Zeffirelli's film of "Hamlet" that you began working in the United States?

Yes, I met Martin Scorsese in America, and have done nine films with him. The most recent one, *Silence*, comes out in the U.S. on December 23 [2016], but the list includes: *The Age of Innocence* [1993]; *Kundun* [1997]; *The Gangs of New York* [2002]; *The Aviator* [2004]; and *Hugo*. . . .

You won two Academy Awards with *The Aviator* and *Hugo*. Then you won a third with Tim Burton's *Sweeney Todd*?

Yes. I have won three Oscars, and my wife, Francesca Lo Schiavo, has won three Oscars as a set designer. I have had ten nominations and Francesca has had eight.

Which of these films specially stands out in your own mind?

I think *Hugo* was the most thrilling. I had such a good time making that film. In any case, once I've chosen a film—and I always choose the films I work on—then I'm happy to have had the opportunity to work with great directors. I have to say that this is a huge privilege.

Can you tell us about some of the new projects you are now working on?

Yes. I'm doing *Diabolik* [broadcast 2012], which is based on a very famous Italian comic book of the same name. At Cinecittà I'm reconstructing the city in *Diabolik*, which is called Claireville. It's a TV series produced by Sky and Cattleya, and there are ten episodes. Once I'm done preparing everything, I'm doing a new Martin Scorsese film called *The Irish Man*, which will be shot in New York.

Do you think that television series, which are increasingly better and ever more sophisticated, will replace the cinema?

People are talking more and more about television series and are now used to the "serial" genre. The quality isn't always there, but it is usually quite good. Naturally this isn't only in Italy, but in the United States and England as well, where they shoot these series with important actors. Netflix produces really long stories. Yes, these series can be interesting, but it is unfortunate if people are going to the cinema less and less.

You have also worked for the opera and the theater, do you continue to do so?

Yes. Now I'm working on a musical called *Divo Nerone*, and then I'm doing the set design for Rossini's *Othello*, which is being put on at the Teatro di San Carlo in Naples and directed by Amos Gitai.

You also played a very important role in the new layout and reconstruction of the Egyptian Museum in Turin?

Yes, it's true. The first part was building out the statue gallery, which is still there today, and the second part was the new design with the Aimaro Isola architectural firm.

I have heard that you are increasingly focusing on painting in these last few years and months. Has painting become your new line of work?

No, but I have always loved to paint. I've always made sketches for my work, but if I have two hours of time I will paint. I can even finish a large painting in two hours. When I go on holiday I leave home with my canvases, and I often paint when I return from the beach or when everyone else is at the beach. It's something I really enjoy doing.

Do you think of yourself as a painter or as a set designer?

I consider myself to be a worker, and it is for others to classify what it is I do. I do my work to the best of my abilities.

Then I will ask you: What is your occupation?

I am a set designer. It is what I have wanted to do since I was thirteen years old. I like to create historical periods and change them. I like to tell stories by creating the scenes in a certain way.

You must really be very pleased to be going to receive an honorary degree as an architect in Rome, the city where you began your long career?

Yes. It is a great honor, one that goes along with other types of nominations like the Oscars, or the honorary degree that I received from the Accademia delle Belle Arti. I am also very grateful to President Napolitano, who nominated me as a Grand Officer of the State of the Italian Republic.

Rome

November 26, 2016

~

IN ANY CASE, ONCE I'VE CHOSEN A FILM – AND I ALWAYS CHOOSE THE FILMS I WORK ON – THEN I'M HAPPY TO HAVE HAD THE OPPORTUNITY TO WORK WITH GREAT DIRECTORS. I HAVE TO SAY THAT THIS IS A HUGE PRIVILEGE.

URS FISCHER

ARTIST

I have just finished a long interview with Urs Fischer in his huge studio in Brooklyn, not far from the bridge that I am now crossing. Today the sky is very blue, as it sometimes is in New York in winter. This amazing view of the city, its bridges and skyscrapers, must make a strong impression on the artist as he goes home from work. Urs lives in Manhattan with his family, and travels daily to and from his Brooklyn studio. He says, "I try to have a normal family life and not to work during the weekend."

The interview takes place sitting around his desk, in the midst of the noise that Urs' many assistants make. There are maybe ten or more, working at different tables in the very large industrial space we are in. Later we will move to a sort of mezzanine, where there are more desks, a few secretaries and an open kitchen with a long table where everyone eats together. Today, lunch is cooked by Mina Stone, who is producing *Cooking for Artists* with Urs' publishing house, Kiito-San, which also publishes all his catalogues and other books. Urs loves books and reading. The recipes and the photographs in the book are Mina's, and there are also some drawings by her artist friends. Her book is simple Greek cuisine, along with some other recipes; good food, easy to cook. Today's lunch is ceviche, spaghetti with tomato sauce and basil, and a green salad accompanied by San Pellegrino water, followed by espresso coffee. The atmosphere is happy and friendly.

After living in New York for eighteen years do you still consider yourself a Swiss artist?

When I am in Europe I don't see myself as a European artist. In America I am an immigrant artist.

It makes a difference?

I guess it makes a big difference. Recently I had the understanding that as a teenager I always liked the idea of America. That is the reason why I am here.

Is it because of the market?

It is the richness of the soil, the many layers. This is what is more attractive here, not the market. I tried to be in Berlin, in Amsterdam, and London, but it came back to the concept of being an immigrant. In the Netherlands, Germany, England, you will never become "one of them." Here it is a more open society and you don't feel like a foreigner.

Why did you leave Switzerland?

It is very beautiful and very small. I still have my family there, my old friends, my memories. I know all the laws and how a cowbell sounds. I don't know any other country where the cows are so close to the homes. I like the people and the culture, but I am not attracted to be there in terms of art. There were no schools for art, and I studied photography. Switzerland is not a country with a nobility, there was never a court, a system of academies, there is more a peasant humor or understanding. There is a smallness of view and no culture of big ideas; beauty in a grand way is not part of the system. Of course, Swiss artists like Hodler, Vallotton, and Tinguely have some beauty, but there are no cities with beautiful boulevards.

But there are many important private art collections?

Yes. Around Zürich people used to weave, then they started to build machines and they created industries and banks and insurance companies and food industries. I am thinking of Knorr and Maggi, and the chemical and pharmaceutical laboratories in Basel. All that generated a wealthy bourgeoisie, and these people have created their own castles and collections. I have a lot of collectors there, but I have not done a show there in seven years. Instead, for instance, I had five shows in New York in the last year.

How did you decide to become an artist?

By deciding I did not want to be many other things. I wanted to be free. Even if it is an illusion, at least to feel free. Of course I liked art, and mine was not a rebellion against my parents.

Since you left Switzerland eighteen years ago, has your work changed much?

Hopefully! You should stay open to new influences in your life. [He lights a cigarette, a Camel filter. Sometimes he smokes one of the new, fake cigarettes.]

Do you consider yourself an eclectic artist?

At the end of the day you accomplish what you can. I don't go in one direction. You just do what you do, and you are limited by yourself in making your oeuvre, it is the oeuvre of one person. So why limit it? Sometimes in the small there is more than in the big.

SOMETIMES IN THE SMALL

THERE IS MORE THAN IN THE BIG.

What is your scale?

Since the very beginning I wanted to be open to big and small scale. I don't think in terms of scale. If I make a mouse it is small; if I deal with a building, the building is big. If you think of an elephant, it is big in your apartment, but if you put it out of that space it is nothing. Unfortunately, today we have very large galleries.

And so, what?

For the private encounter size matters, because stuff gets lost. Large galleries, big works limit the use.

What about your sculptures, for instance the one big blue and two big yellow bears?

They are for outside, and outside is big. But in your own house how many sculptures can you have?

So are you now changing to small works?

I always made small too. Morandi is a great example. In the opposite of what I do he can show the whole world.

Does this mean that for an artist there are no rules?

There are many rules. Art is full of rules.

Like what?

If you decide to do this or that people react and they are very judgmental. For instance, a good example is an artist like Christo. Not much work, larger and larger, done for the public. He was pulled down, but I think that he is an excellent sculptor; it is just that he is very popular.

What about an artist like Jeff Koons? Is he to be taken seriously?

Jeff is very serious biographically. He is a very serious artist. A good example of what I wanted to say about rules is Dalí, who was not considered okay because of his going to parties or because he was too social. But why should you be like Carl Andre? It is not open-minded. If you work out of your field it can be seen as bad.

Would you like to be more free?

Sure, I am never free enough. I think that what counts for an artist is how you grow.

Where do you want to go?

I don't know. I am not sure.

Would you like to stop?

No, I love what I do. I am not complaining. If I was a writer of serious novels and then wrote children's books I would not be considered serious anymore. That is what I meant before about rules. As Kafka, you are not allowed to write *Harry Potter*.

Would you like to break boundaries?

No more than any other artist. Another good example of rules is Turner.

Why?

Because he was not accepted when he shifted to the inside and development as a human being.

But most of the time art is hardly recognized by contemporaries?

Yes, definitely. You can do better and better and what you try to share is a synchronization. Everyone else's artwork is how you feed your biographical energy. You don't make work out of nothing. Picasso, for instance, is a good case of biographical energy. He changed locations and women in order to find new energy.

Do you feel the same?

I try not to use other people and their lives for my work. For me to be a sensible human being is more important than anything else.

Do you take notes?

I have thousands of notes, but I don't look at them, ever. They are useful in the moment you make them.

How do you work?

I am more a sculptor, more than anything else. The life of a sculpture is different. It goes through many procedures and labor. A big part of sculpture is the metamorphosis of material. Somehow, as a material, working in clay is similar to oil painting. It is not stable in form, it is malleable and you can be very fast. [Dogs are walking around the studio. They are very quiet.]

As a sculptor do you like Giambologna?

I liked a particular sculpture of his, but Bernini is a better example of what I like. He is shocking; he did amazing, unbelievable things.

Who are the artists that you like?

In life it changes, you keep discovering. Two years ago I started to look at what I thought I did not like, to understand what I don't like.

What don't you like?

I did not know what to do with Chagall; I never connected. Another one is Kandinsky. I still don't like them.

Do you study a lot?

I love art. If an artist does not love art who does? There is so much great art. I go to galleries and museums to see old things and new things. The easiest way to understand is through books, they are great!

You don't talk about the Internet?

It is not good for art. It is very specific. If you look for instance at Medardo Rosso, on the Internet there are a lot of things you don't see! Of course I am not against technology, I love it, and in order to have some control of my work I made my own website.

What about your critics?

I don't read critics. I don't care. I think that criticism is a bit passé; there are so many other ways today. Criticism anyway, it is not written for me. I am personally interested in the positive of an artwork; an artwork is what it is. I believe that criticism has lost a lot. If you have an opinion it should be done with great effort and I don't see much effort anymore. Criticism is lazy compared to the effort. I am not interested in an opinion that is just good or bad.

What about curators?

I believe in synergy. Everything you do is based on synergy. The curator has an important role.

And the dealer?

Every dealer I worked with has different qualities. I am my own boss by now and I have many dealers. It depends on the work and who is better for that particular work. I used to have one dealer and a main gallery and everything else filtered through him. I advise all artists to be independent for the same reason that you move out of your parent's house.

Are you independent?

I don't sell myself. Never. I don't like it. I don't care; I don't want to deal with the business side. A lot of dealers and collectors are business people. I see the nicer side of the people that collect and I leave the business side to dealers. I don't follow the auctions, but I like the auction catalogues because you can see pictures that you would never see elsewhere.

Are you aware of your prices?

I don't particularly like it, but if you have a secondary market it changes your primary market. It forces you into another direction.

Do you work hard?

Not as hard as I should, you can always do more, better, rethink. Art is open, it can go on endlessly. I work hard, but sometimes you have to be a dad and help people, and it makes time smaller and smaller.

Do you have vices?

I don't drink anymore, or very little. No drugs, nothing. You lose a lot of time for a hangover.

What are your future shows?

This year I decided to do lots of smaller shows. One in April in Naples, one at the Modern Institute in Glasgow in May, one with Massimo De Carlo in Milano sometime in the summer, one small show maybe with Gagosian in L.A., one with Bice Curiger in Arles where she runs the Fondation Vincent van Gogh in January. . . .

What about money?

It is of great help, and I invest in my work and I buy art. I have a lot of different works from people I like and admire.

Do you think it is a lively period for art?

A great period, not dogmatic, and more difficult to read if you apply old models. As for the quality of art, there is a lot of great art, there is a lot that is new. No better art than in the past.

Are you afraid of losing your talent?

Whatever is, is. I was more afraid when I was young. Now you try your best. If it does not work, it does not.

New York
January 23, 2015

~

But the real question is what you do as a human being.

I AM **never** FREE ENOUGH.

I THINK THAT WHAT COUNTS FOR AN ARTIST IS HOW YOU **grow.**

NORMAN FOSTER

ARCHITECT

Lord Foster, nowadays you are one of the most famous architects in the world, but you had a very interesting and unusual start. Could you be so kind as to tell us, how did you become an architect?

Working in Manchester in my first job at the age of sixteen, I spent every spare minute wandering around buildings in the city. I wasn't consciously thinking, "One day I am going to be an architect, therefore I should be doing this." I was just drawn to buildings for the aesthetic experience. Some buildings and parts of that city were particularly inspirational—the cast iron tradition of Barton Arcade, the Victorian architecture of Manchester Town Hall, or the modernist *Daily Express* building, for example. When I returned after my National Service, I began looking for a job that appealed to my creative side—drawing had been a serious passion for me throughout my childhood. I had always been fascinated by design, and a short stint at the contracts department in a local architect's office spurred me on to build my own portfolio of drawings. It was this journey of self-discovery that led me to apply to the architecture program at Manchester University.

Who was your first mentor?

The people I was exposed to at Yale, in particular Paul Rudolph, Serge Chermayeff, and Vincent Scully, were hugely influential. Paul Rudolph created a studio atmosphere which was highly creative, competitive, and spurred on by a succession of visiting critics.

What was the first building you did?

The Retreat was an early project that we carried out as part of Team 4 in 1964. The clients were Marcus Brumwell and his wife, Rene, who had earlier commissioned us to build the Creek Vean House. The Brumwells and their family were fond of taking picnics just by the creek in the woods of Feock, where they had a small hut, and the commission was to replace it with a simple, all-weather gazebo, with built-in seating, electricity for a small stove, and piped water to a sink. The structure strips the notion of a house down to its very essence—a place of shelter. Fanning outward from a notional source within the earth, the gazebo breaks surface from the slope of the bank, and faces towards the sea, like the cockpit of a plane, maximizing the views of the waterfront. A simple glazing frame, the structure was inspired by the distinctive sliding canopy of the Hawker Hurricane, which was a remarkably agile wooden-framed fighter plane from the 1930s. These varied references were distilled into a minimalist glass bubble—a "cockpit" looking out to views of the Fal estuary—an "away place" in which to read, contemplate, or have picnics.

For some years you were associated with Richard Rogers, but you decided to work with your own company based in London. What have been your most important projects?

With Richard as Team 4, it lasted some four years until 1967. Since then there have been so many it is impossible to pick out from them—there have been different ones for different reasons.

Each architect has his own style. How would you define yours?

I have never subscribed to a particular style; each project is a unique response to the site, and its physical and cultural context. The values and philosophy are the constants. Design is always a collective effort, so perhaps you could say that the style is that of Norman Foster with his various teams. Some core beliefs: The quality of design affects the quality of our lives. A commitment to the principles of sustainability, performance, and "doing more with less." The pursuit of beauty. A continuous tradition of questioning, challenging, and innovating; a fascination with technology as a means to social ends.

You have built public buildings, homes, and skyscrapers. As you well know there is a large debate about skyscrapers. Are you keen on building skyscrapers or do you believe they are now obsolete?

I love tall buildings as much as low-rise structures. I do not believe that skyscrapers are now obsolete—I have often argued that denser cities are more successful and sustainable. Higher density does not mean we have to build tall. On the contrary however, skyscrapers can play an important role in the city when designed and planned for sensitively and considered in the wider context of transport.

I have always said that the true challenge of renewal is to continue the historic tradition of change, but with a sensitivity to the spirit of the past.

Nowadays all over the world, cities have exploded and are booming. What is your idea of the city today? Are you concerned by the ever-increasing transportation problems?

On the contrary, I am very excited by the prospects of new technologies that offer sustainable, quiet, and fast alternatives for transport that could transform cities for people. The issues of transportation we face in cities today are imminently solvable if we just take a bold approach towards infrastructure—just as our Victorian forbearers did in 19th century Britain.

Over the centuries there were architectural styles and fashions, from ancient Egypt, the Greeks, the city of Rome, the Renaissance, the baroque, the Gothic, Bauhaus, and Italian fascist. Is there a style of today? And what is it? Or is each architect simply doing whatever they want?

I think you need the perspective of time to be able to analyze the attributes of a particular time period. It provides a certain clarity that is not possible in the heat of the moment. For example, what we today call Gothic or baroque was not so clear-cut at the time. It is only after having the benefit of viewing the works of those time periods from a distance that historians have categorized them.

What do you think about the countries who have erased their own past? Beijing has destroyed its own past, unlike Rome. Is it a crime?

It is important to find a balance between new and old. I have always said that the true challenge of renewal is to continue the historic tradition of change, but with a sensitivity to the spirit of the past.

What do you think about the destruction of wars, from Dresden to the Twin Towers to Palmyra and Aleppo? Antiquity is menaced by such acts. How do you feel about it, and the rebuilding of these cities later?

Such losses are tragic and horrific. As an afterthought, perhaps our awareness of the vulnerability of true antiquities should lead us to record them properly for posterity.

How do the climate change debates and recent seismic catastrophes impact architecture?

Climate change is a very serious issue, and sustainability is not a matter of fashion, but of survival affecting architecture and infrastructure at every level, be it an airport or a small apartment. Sustainability requires us to think holistically and not about buildings in isolation. The location and function of a building; its flexibility and lifespan; its orientation, its form, and structure; its heating and ventilation systems; and the materials used, all impact upon the amount of energy required to build, run, and maintain it, and the movement of goods and people to and from it. Architects cannot solve all the world's ecological problems, but we can design buildings to run at a fraction of current energy levels and we can influence transport patterns through urban planning and infrastructure.

You recently built, at what they say is a cost of five billion dollars, the new HQ of Apple in California. How is it working in the Silicon Valley? You do a lot of work in the high-tech world—how is it to work with such conceptually advanced people?

As an architect I am grateful for enlightened individuals who commission buildings. The more passionate they are the more demanding they are likely to be—which is positive. Some are in Silicon Valley, some are in lots of other places. It is about the individual not the place.

The architecture of the past allows us to witness past worlds in the present. What will remain of our civilization in the future?
You will have to ask that question in say, a hundred years from now.

When you make a project, is your foremost concern aesthetic, or is it for example security, or usability?
Every project begins with research, and a return to first principles. You have to evaluate the site, its physical setting, climate, the culture of the place, the needs of the user—each of these aspects determines the final outcome, which is different every time. Let's just say that it is impossible to separate how it looks from how it works, from how it is made.

Since you began how much has changed in architecture. And are there new young architects that you praise today?
I praise all architects of talent, young or old, dead or alive. We all have to appreciate talent. The ends of architecture and core values have not changed. The means and technology have—and they will continue to do so.

Since a few years, even if you are based in London and spend much time in St. Moritz, can we say that your main house is your private plane? How much has your passion for flying changed your professional life?
For as long as I can remember I have been fascinated by flight. Relatively late, in my thirties, I started to fly. First sailplanes, then single engine light aircraft, then helicopters, then piston twins, then historic aircraft, then jets. So flying has been and still is a way of life. I realize that these words are written on the way to an airport!

The idea of how human beings inhabit space varies across the world. In Japan for example, the space for a human can be very small. How do you feel about that?
It is not about the amount of space—it is the quality of the space.

London
February 26, 2017

~

For as long as I can remember
I have been fascinated by flight.

Relatively late, in my thirties,
I started to fly.

ANTOINE GALLIMARD

PUBLISHER

Antoine Gallimard is a French publisher. He is the president of Éditions Gallimard and the Madrigall Group, which is the third-largest French publishing group.

Your grandfather Gaston Gallimard was one of the founders of *La Nouvelle Revue Française*, in order to please some of his friends, among them André Gide. You, Antoine, wanted to study philosophy, but your father, Claude Gallimard, encouraged you to study law. Did you become president of Gallimard by chance, or is it with regard to a sense of responsibility to your family?

My grandfather forged the family's destiny. I don't think I could have been a writer, but I would have liked to become a journalist. I think that I became a publisher because I was obsessed with series of books of a similar format, for example the *Bibliothèque de la Pléiade*. I was obsessed with these complete-edition series, and I loved the way books fill space, and I liked to arrange them in their proper order. I tried to have as many Le Livre de Poche paperbacks as I could. The presence of books is essential in my life, and I think that if there are no books in an apartment, it's like an apartment without windows. One book takes you to another, like in a chain. You know Gallimard has a formidable catalogue, and an heir is obliged to exist at the level of his heritage. I wanted to keep this building where we are now. I wanted to keep the garden. I wanted to keep the books.

Was it easy to take over control of the publishing house?

I became a publisher because I was faithful to my grandfather and to my father. I was helped by the fact that I had very good relationships with the people who worked in the publishing house and they were confident in me, and I also had good relationships with the writers. This is a writers' publishing house. Don't forget that André Gide, André Malraux, Albert Camus worked here. Writers feel at home here in Gallimard.

Your grandfather Gaston always said that he became a publisher by chance and that he much preferred vacations, playing tennis, or driving cars?

He always appeared to be very easygoing, but in reality he was very concerned about the future of the publishing house. He was very grateful to my father because my father decided to follow him. There are not many family publishers left nowadays in the world.

One of your daughters is following you and runs the publishing house Casterman, that is part of your group?

Yes, and I also have another daughter who is interested in publishing and they are both very motivated and attentive.

What kind of publisher is Gallimard?

What was specific to our publishing house's very good reputation was to give as much importance to the literary aspect as to commercial success. My grandfather Gaston defined a publisher as "A trader who has made a pact with the spirit," but what happens is that when we are very successful, like at the moment with some of the books that we publish, people say that Gallimard has lost its soul. But if we don't have success for a while people say that Gallimard doesn't work anymore! So this is what I have to face all the time.

Is Gallimard also so well-known because of the quality of its books?

Yes, we give enormous importance to the editing, to the typography, to the paper, to the jackets, and to the *mise en page* [layout]. We try to eliminate any errors as much as possible and certainly for us the quality is very important indeed.

You have had many Nobel Prize winners among your authors?

Yes, more or less fifteen. And also many other award winners.

Can we say that writers are at the heart of Gallimard?

It's very atypical, because we believe in literature. We believe that we can only exist if we support writers. Our objective is to consider literature above all.

And you publish writers of very different political and stylistic genres?

Yes, we published Louis-Ferdinand Céline and Paul Claudel, and we published J. M. G. Le Clézio and Philippe Sollers, people who are very different. We don't have any prejudices in our judgment.

Is reading doing well in France?

There are less strong readers. By strong readers I mean people who read three to four books per month. People nowadays tend to read bestsellers and children's books, and books for young people are also very successful.

Do people read more digital or printed paper books?

In France the digital book format doesn't do very well. It represents only two percent of the market.

What about paperbacks?

They always work very well and there is a large production.

Do you sell more novels or essays?

Many novels, biographies, and correspondences. For instance *Lettres à Anne*, the love letters of François Mitterrand to his mistress Anne Pingeot, sold more than sixty thousand copies.

Do you sell more in bookstores or on Amazon?

Amazon is of course a very important phenomenon, but bookstores do well if they are staffed by people who really love books.

How many Gallimard bookstores are there?

We have four in Paris, three in Strasbourg, and a very big one in Nancy. Altogether we have ten bookstores, including one in Montreal.

How is the state of health of the French language?

Of course French has lost its importance outside of France, especially in countries like Argentina, or in the Arab countries where the previous generations spoke French. Nowadays they only speak English. But of course in France people read in French. Very few read in English.

Is there a concern about the political situation? If Marine Le Pen wins the elections could it penalize the freedom of publishing?

Yes, if the Front National wins the election, we have seen it in the regional elections that when they get into power, they reduce the cultural budget. France is strong because there is a network of bookstores and there is no discounting, and in France the budget for culture is one percent. But, as I said, we are afraid that if the Front National comes to power they will damage our cultural tradition—and we are also afraid that they would close the borders.

Are there any new writers that you consider interesting?

Yes, we publish Jean-Baptiste Del Amo, his book is called *Règne animal*, and also Catherine Cusset.

Which are the classics that you sell the most?

Journey to the End of the Night [*Voyage au bout de la nuit*] by Louis-Ferdinand Céline sells around fifty thousand copies a year, *The Stranger* [*L'Étranger*] by Albert Camus sells a hundred thousand copies a year, and *The Little Prince* [*Le Petit Prince*] by Antoine de Saint-Exupéry is still another big bestseller.

And the classic foreign writers?

Ernest Hemingway always sells well, as do William Faulkner, Philip Roth, and Milan Kundera. We recently bought the rights and are republishing all the works of Italo Calvino, and it is going quite well.

Why did you buy the Flammarion publishing house?

Every enterprise has to think of its development. Gallimard is an authors' publishing house. Flammarion is a publishing house for readers, and Flammarion is very important in human sciences, in astronomy, in well-being, and also has a very popular collection of paperbacks called J'ai Lu. We also bought Casterman, who publishes *The Adventures of Tintin*.

Do you still publish some books with very small print runs?

Yes, for example we published the correspondence of Gide, and that of Jean Cocteau; we published the correspondence between Céline and Gaston Gallimard, and the correspondence between Marcel Proust and Gaston Gallimard.

What is your main job?

I take care of Gallimard and of the holding company, Madrigall.

What kind of publishing group is Madrigall?

It is small compared to Hachette, because Hachette is very important in other countries as well, like America and England. We are the third-largest group in France, after Hachette and Editis.

Are you the sole proprietor of Madrigall?

My family owns ninety percent of Madrigall, and ten percent is owned by Bernard Arnault. He was interested in the family aspect of the company and our catalogue, and he became a shareholder four years ago. This shows great confidence in our work.

Are there lots of risks in your business?

Yes, there are industry risks, and generational changes, and if people in France have less spending power they will not spend money in bookstores. We had a very bad month in January because it was too cold. A mild climate is best for book sales, with some rain but not too much. People don't buy many books when they are on vacation.

Are there fashions in book publishing?

Yes, for a while "autofiction" was very popular. Nowadays "docufiction," which fictionalizes real events, is fashionable. Mystery books still work very well, and we have also had immense success with the *Harry Potter* books. The last one sold more than a million copies.

How many people work in your group?

There are eighteen hundred people in the whole group, working in publishing, in bookstores and in distribution. We publish around nine hundred titles per year as Gallimard, and more or less the same as Flammarion.

Are you satisfied?

At the beginning I really wanted to be the publisher of a very small publishing house, but of course I am proud and happy that we bought Flammarion. Sometimes it is frustrating because they are too big. In Gallimard I can make some decisions. What I would say is that if a publisher is too much of an entrepreneur, then you are not a good publisher, but if you are too much of a publisher, this can become dangerous.

Do you have some leisure in your free time?

Not much. I see some writers, but it is not always very easy to be a friend with your authors. A publisher needs to practice the art of diplomacy.

Do you read many books?

Mostly I read readers' reports.

But you still have a passion for collected editions?

Yes, and I have my private library.

Is it hard to be an heir?

There are lots of jealousies around.

What did your father teach you?

He taught me that it is very important to be patient, and to have endurance, and to be close to the writers. He was very close to Kundera, to Jean Giono, and Le Clézio.

Which writer impressed you the most?

I would say Louis Aragon. I was impressed when he spoke. He could talk about everything, from politics—talking about Lenin and Stalin—to literature, talking about Malraux and Breton. He was very impressive.

What about foreign writers, who impressed you the most?

I would certainly say Borges for his delicacy, because he was funny and had a wonderful smile. I was also very impressed by Octavio Paz, and I should say that I am very close to Milan Kundera.

Were you very close to your grandfather?

Yes, I was. We had a typical relationship of a grandfather and a grandchild, which is a much easier relationship than with your parents. Gaston used to take me to good restaurants so I could learn about gastronomy, and he used to talk to me about his women.

Are you sometime frightened by the risks of your profession?

Yes, sometimes I worry about bankruptcy, but I am not afraid of the risks and I just have to be very careful.

Paris

March 2017

~

The presence of books is essential in my life,

AND I THINK THAT IF THERE ARE NO BOOKS IN AN APARTMENT, IT'S LIKE AN APARTMENT WITHOUT WINDOWS.

VALENTINO GARAVANI

FASHION DESIGNER

In Piazza Mignanelli—a stone's throw from the Spanish Steps—one sees an old palazzo and a large staircase where models are being photographed. Valentino is very busy. It is June 2004 and there's a buzz in the air. Valentino has given interviews to American television and Italian television. His models have been photographed for a Spanish magazine. He's smiling and elegant in a pinstriped suit, a blue shirt, a regimental tie, and brown suede shoes. He lets me into a large room. There are modern paintings on the walls and beautiful objects on two large tables with a desk in the middle. Valentino is always smiling.

How are things going?

Well. It's a happy moment for work. I'm quite pleased. But just like any sensitive human being, I am upset about what is going on in the world.

How so?

In the sense that the world is traumatized. Each of us is quivering, fearful of something. And this naturally influences our moods and our lives.

Are you talking about Iraq?

About everything. It's a really unpleasant time. I feel like we live with angst, and this makes us a bit less strong, to tell the truth.

One wouldn't say that looking at your creations.

Yes, yes. But there's worry in our minds that stops us from being serene.

What about work?

No. Work is certainly going forward. The show must go on.

THE WORLD IS TRAUMATIZED.

EACH OF US IS

qUiVeRiNg,

FEARFUL OF SOMETHING.

But does fashion seem too frivolous today considering the world we live in?

It is not a question of fashion or frivolity, but I have to be honest. These periods also have some influence on business. Fortunately, my boutiques keep selling, but people are scared and, in a certain sense, they have less desire to spend money.

Does that make you change the style of your clothing?

No. Absolutely not. On the contrary, those things that are dreams, like art, cinema, and fashion, have to do their best to keep distracting and distancing us from what is happening.

Do you have new ideas in mind right now?

Always women, glamorous women with great appeal. But to tell you the truth, I don't willingly talk about my future projects because they are perhaps still in the embryonic stage. Of course there will be many new details, and a Valentino with never-before-seen creations in the Paris fashion shows.

In your opinion, is that era of great models over?

No. They've changed. Actually, the greatest one of all may be a Brazilian model named Giselle [Bündchen]. And then there are stars from Russia. Gorgeous women. Dozens of top models come from the Eastern countries, and it's amazing because they are all girls who are between sixteen and twenty. Therefore, they are really young, but they are prepared, because they've studied younger than others have.

Why have you chosen to spend so much time in London over the years?

First and foremost because I have a house there. Then it's a city that has given me a lot of satisfaction, and it's a very masculine city. And if I have to be honest, I really appreciate the extraordinary traditions of London and the English.

You really like traditions, don't you?

Yes, I like them. Just as I've always liked those families from back in the old days with their rigor and severity. In Italy we lack this a bit. I have to say that we Italians are fantastic. We've always been fantastic, and I've always said that. But lately I see people around me who aren't happy. I believe they are a bit dissatisfied.

What is Valentino like?

Well, Valentino always tries to be happy. My upbringing and my way of seeing things require me to be this way. Naturally I have my ups and downs, but I've got a strong character, and I can change my attitude depending on the day or time of day.

Do you always work a lot?

Yes. I really like to design. I usually start late, around eleven thirty a.m., and then I go until eight p.m. or nine p.m. I have to create ten collections per year, and believe me, it's a big commitment.

Do you design every day?

Yes, yes. I design, I watch fittings, I look at fabrics, and I see people.

Do you really still do fittings?

No. Since the existence of prêt-à-porter, I no longer do fittings except in rare cases for some actors, actresses, friends, or even some young girls whom I love to dress as brides.

Do you need a lot of imagination to do this work?

Yes. You need imagination but, above all, you need a lot of time.

And do you have enough?

Well, I need to find the time.

Are you still able to see friends?

Yes. Absolutely. I have to leave room for my private life. I have had and still have many friends—extraordinary people. I need them to be able to continue and go forward.

Rome
June 6, 2004

~

AMOS GITAI

FILMMAKER

Amos Gitai's film *Rabin, The Last Day* marks the twentieth anniversary of the Israeli Prime Minister Yitzhak Rabin's savage killing in Tel Aviv on the evening of Saturday, November 4, 1995. The film sheds light on an ever-growing crisis of hate in Israeli society today. Rabin's killer, apprehended at the scene, turned out to be a twenty-five-year-old Jewish observant. Investigation into his brutal murder reveals the dark and frightening world that made this tragic deed possible.

Amos, your new film *Rabin, The Last Day* was shown in Venice and in Toronto, and will be officially launched in Tel Aviv on November 4th, the day Rabin was killed. Why did you feel the need to shoot this film?

First of all, as an Israeli citizen—because I am concerned by the way the country is going. I am not a politician, so my way of talking is cinema. I am concerned that, in the last twenty years since the killing of Rabin, Israel is going in a direction that is more and more isolating itself. They fight everybody without being selective, and it is more and more xenophobic. I think it is concerning for everybody who loves Israel.

How do you tell the story of his [Rabin's] last hours?

Twenty years ago Rabin put me on his plane to Washington and also to Cairo, and I interviewed him extensively in Jerusalem. Rabin was not a soft lefty, as people describe him. He understood that to stabilize Israeli existence in the Middle East he needed to make inroads to the Arab world. He also understood that the most important of all the regional conflicts is the Israel-Palestinian one. Israel has to find ways to reach a new form of co-existence with the Palestinians. This conflict is real, in the sense that there is occupation of the Palestinian areas for more than forty years, but it is also a pretext for the Arabs and Muslim countries to defer from the real problem in this conflict. Rabin understood that if Israel could succeed in dismantling this minefield this would help its security.

But wasn't he killed for his ideas by the Jewish extremists, by the right wing?

Yes, when he started to negotiate with the Palestinians there was a very well-organized campaign, supported essentially by three forces against him. The first one by hallucinating rabbis, who put on him all sorts of Talmudic witchcraft to kill him; by the lobby of the settlers who don't want to give any ground to Palestinians in the Holy Land; and by the parliamentary right wing, led by Likud and Netanyahu, who want to destabilize the Rabin government.

Did he know that they were trying to kill him?

No. He says, and this is in the film, that he does not think that they will kill him, and he has confidence in the security forces of Israel.

Do the facts that Syria has imploded, that there is a war against ISIS, that the whole region is in trouble, and that there is a new opening of the U.S. and the West vis-à-vis Iran, change something for Israel?

We are in a very dangerous neighborhood. But the question is if we should only believe in the *rapport de force*, and I think that being a Jewish state we should also believe in ideas.

But what does this mean?

Israel has first of all to keep its democratic structure, which is menaced by the extreme right that is now part of the Israeli government. They want to interfere, even in the judicial system. Judges will not advance in their career if they don't impose the most severe punishment possible on the Palestinians. The minister of culture wants to interfere with Israeli culture, and so on and so forth.

As an artist and a director, how do you feel in your country?

I feel continuous pressure on my colleagues and me, to be conformist and not to say anything that disturbs the current regime. This is a disaster and can destroy the Israeli project. Israel is strong because it has an open society and the young generation feel that they can be creative and free. If this project is menaced it will weaken society.

How do Israelis perceive the different relationship that there is today with the U.S., which has traditionally been the strongest ally to Israel?

I performed a play some years ago about the conflict between Judaea and the Roman Empire, in which the ultranationalists in Masada wanted to beat the Roman Empire. And we know how this episode ended. Exile for centuries.

You sound very pessimistic.

I cannot afford to be pessimistic, but we are not in a good period, and hopefully making this movie will make some people think.

. . . my way of

TALKING

is cinema.

Do you believe that the Israeli government is going to interfere and bother you about this particular film?

I am looking forward to the release of the film. It will be released in the auditorium of the Philharmonic Orchestra in Tel Aviv, just two hundred meters from where Rabin was shot.

Therefore you believe that cinema is still a way to express political ideas?

You and I are meeting today on a very special day, Yom Kippur. For all the Jewish world this is a day of memory and contemplation. For me it was also the day I was shot inside a burning helicopter, forty-two years ago in the Golan. We were flying to try to save an Israeli pilot who was shot down. On Yom Kippur the helicopter was shot by Syrian missiles. I was an architecture student, and I was supposed to continue the work of my father who was a Bauhaus architect, but when I came back from the hospital I decided to become a filmmaker and not an architect. I said to myself that I will tell what is on my mind. And since then I only made films that I thought were worth doing.

Why do you live in Paris?

I live between my hometown, Haifa, and Paris. I came to Paris in the eighties when I made documentaries which were not very much liked by my countrymen. I came for a few weeks and these became seven years. After Rabin was elected in nineteen ninety-two, I went back to Israel. During my Paris years I extended my knowledge, thanks to people like Jack Lang, the minister of culture, who facilitated my work.

What is your feeling about the relationship between the diaspora Jews and Israel?

There is a very strong feeling of solidarity, and anywhere I travel in the world I find people of the Jewish community with great compassion. I think this link is impressive.

Is this new film very important for you?

It's part of my body of work, which is telling the story of this big drama called Israel. In my mind it is a big story which deserves strong cinema.

Do you have any other new projects?

Some related to the film: They will publish my interviews with Rabin, and I will do a play on the same subject in Avignon next year. And then the actress Isabelle Huppert has proposed to me the idea of doing a film with her about a Jewish Marrano called Doña Grazia Nasi.

Paris
September 23, 2015

~

MARIA GRAZIA CHIURI

FASHION DESIGNER

You are the first female creative director of Dior, following in the footsteps of Christian Dior, Yves Saint Laurent, John Galliano, Gianfranco Ferré, and Raf Simons. How does it feel?

I have never thought about it like that, because then you have the weight of history on you. Having a healthy disregard for history helps me, because otherwise you are trapped by it and you can't move forward. This disregard is also part of being Italian, of being Roman.

Why is this a Roman trait?

If you live in Rome you get used to living surrounded by history, but this doesn't mean you shouldn't try to do something, even if you are aware that it's probably already been done better by someone else. When I started working for Dior I felt like a curator, tied into an untouchable heritage and brand. You have to live with that, and you have to know how to emphasize and promote it.

Were you nervous when you presented your first collection for Dior in the gardens of the Musée Rodin to the most important and influential people in the fashion world?

I was happy and in high spirits because it was a great opportunity. Obviously you have to be ready for people to like it or not like it, that is part of the game, but it is more important to put yourself out there. It was a great joy to have done something with my heart, with passion and enthusiasm.

Did you take inspiration from the book *We Should All Be Feminists* by the Nigerian writer Chimamanda Ngozi Adichie?

I asked myself the question of how to speak to women today. Literature is a reference point in my work and she is a woman who fascinates me. Dior is a brand for women and we can't use women from the fifties as a reference, we need to talk to the women of today.

Who is the Dior woman of today?

I don't think that there is a specific Dior woman. Today women aren't faithful to just one specific brand, so Dior must be a brand that approaches women in a different way. It has to offer its point of view, but at the same time it has to talk to all women, not to specific women.

Is it true that you look to how your daughter Rachele and her friends dress and think?

Yes, absolutely. It would be impossible to do this job without looking to that generation. Women in their twenties are the future. They live in a completely different way. They are completely connected, they have different inspirations, they are much more culturally aware. They are my reference point.

Why do you need to refer to them?

I am not a millennial, but today we live in a world where information comes from the web, where we are all connected. This change is momentous. It's incredible how Instagram, for instance, has come into everyone's lives. It doesn't just have a visual influence, it influences language. I wasn't born with a computer in my hand like they were!

You started out as an accessories designer. How did you first become involved with clothes and fashion?

My mother had a small dressmaker's shop in Rome. I grew up there. I saw *Vogue* even as a small child. The fashion world wasn't so complex back then, it was much simpler. I liked accessories, I've always liked shoes and bags, and I liked to draw. I would go to the vintage market in Porta Portese and buy vintage bags. Back then fashion was about designers who had their little fashion houses, simple family-run businesses. I've been in fashion for twenty-eight years, and when I was young it was almost like prehistoric times compared to how it is today. Prada was a store in Milan, not the Prada of today. It has been a monumental change. Even Dior has gone through an enormous change.

When working at Fendi with your long-time friend Pierpaolo Piccioli you two created the famous "Baguette" bag. . . .

No, we never claimed to have done this. We worked on the team that created the "Baguette" phenomenon.

After Fendi you again worked with Pierpaolo Piccioli at Valentino. Is it very different for you at Dior, being in charge by yourself?

No, because I worked with Ms. Fendi and all the founders of the company for nine years. Then I worked with Valentino Garavani and Giancarlo Giammetti for another ten years, again with the designer and founders. Pierpaolo and I were creative directors for eight years. Fashion is about the ability to work in a team—not just with one colleague, but with an entire company. At Dior I've found a great team. There is this romantic idea of the designer alone in a room, but fashion is no longer like that. A designer needs to have a vision, but the team needs to work day in and day out to execute that vision.

Valentino said that your feet are firmly planted on the ground. Is that true?

I don't intend to lose my sense of reality. I don't want to be too trusting. I want to keep my feet on the ground. This type of creative work also has a societal aspect to it, because so many people work in this industry. You need to have a good head on your shoulders about what you are doing and not just think about yourself. This is incredibly important from a societal point of view.

Does keeping your feet on the ground also help you combine the creative and business sides?

Having my feet on the ground helps me create a fit that works for all women. This work is also about professionalism. To make a jacket that fits well is important. There's also a very technical side to this job.

How does fashion work? What does your job as creative director of Dior entail?

First and foremost it entails having a global vision for the Dior brand, finding a way to interpret this brand while respecting the past. To promote the heritage, but also to use it in a contemporary way to speak to this new generation of customers who reflect our times.

Dior is a very big organization?

Enormous. It is a worldwide company. I've maybe seen one-tenth of it after eight months. There are about five thousand people worldwide and one hundred and ninety-seven stores. Dior himself had one thousand employees and five buildings in avenue Montaigne. I found this amazing book in the archives that showed a map of the world where he had opened his fashion houses. He was a worldwide brand, an amazing feat for the times. He had a branch in New York and immediately realized that American women had a sportier, more practical lifestyle than French women, so he decided to simplify his clothes.

What countries is Dior most successful in today?

This is a worldwide brand. We sell all over, to all women—French, European, American, Asian. Women follow fashion all over the world. You either follow fashion or you don't; it isn't linked to one country. I always say you either are fashionable or you are not.

What does it mean to be fashionable?

To be interested in fashion as a form of self-expression. To be interested in what designers do. There are many more people who are interested in the cultural phenomenon of fashion than you might think. Today it's easier to get the information, so there's more curiosity.

What future changes are you planning?

I'm creatively instinctive. I don't think you can plan all that much. Fashion is also absolutely instinctive, representing what you feel in the moment. It isn't a product that can be planned or it wouldn't be fashion.

Do you need a lot of money to follow fashion?

There is a big difference between following fashion and "consuming" it. You can easily follow it without "consuming" it. I am very interested in art. When I have time I go to see exhibitions, but that doesn't mean I have to be a collector. It is one thing to follow fashion or be interested in it, and it's another thing entirely to buy fashion.

Is fashion culture or art?

In my opinion, fashion is culture. In any case, it's a language. Therefore, as a language it might interest you, but you could just be interested in following it without having to buy it.

What have the biggest changes been since you began working in fashion?

Communications have completely changed fashion. There are more people interested and fashion companies have grown as a result. They definitely weren't this big before. Supply and demand have grown. Everything has gone from small organizations to really big ones.

What is the difference between working in fashion in Rome and in Paris?

In Paris the concept of fashion is linked to a tradition of haute couture, while in Italy, not just in Rome, there is more ready-to-wear. Ready-to-wear began in Italy with Armani, Versace, and Valentino. Haute couture started in France. This is the main difference between the two cultures. France emphasizes its tradition and its heritage in an incredible way, Italy is more ready for change because it is more tied to ready-to-wear and the seasonal nature of fashion. This difference changes your approach and how you work. Italian companies are incredibly fast in certain ways but sometimes they forget to promote their heritage because they are always pushing ahead, looking to innovation and what's new. France is very good at promoting its heritage, but at times it has a hard time with change and what's new.

Now that you work for Dior do you feel more French or more Italian? Will Dior become more Italian with you as creative director?

I am an Italian woman working in a French company. I have a daughter who lives in London, a husband in Rome—I feel European. Dior will always be French. I hope to bring the best from both cultures, to emphasize haute couture but make it work in a more updated dimension, perhaps more tied to the mentality of Italian ready-to-wear.

Fashion is also in the United States, Japan and other places . . . .

However, fashion started in France and Italy. There's no doubt that the United States and Japan and other countries have their own specific niches. Sportswear began in America.

What country do you think has the most talented people?

Talent can be everywhere. It isn't tied to one's nationality. Talent has no rules.

Many top brands were started in the twentieth century, but now there aren't so many new names. There isn't a new Gaultier or a new Alaïa or a new Armani. . . .

Today it is much more difficult because the world is totally different. Today, any talented young person who wants to create his own brand finds himself in a world that is so expensive and competitive, and this wasn't the case before. He needs to find someone to finance him. Today, if a young person, for example, wants to simply hold a fashion show, if he doesn't have a group financing him, how can he do it? It's impossible. Marco de Vincenzo, a talented young Italian designer with his own brand, was, thank goodness, picked up by the LVMH group. Otherwise how could he hold a fashion show in Milan, or create an advertising campaign, or buy the furnishings to open a shop, much less open a shop?

It seems that the trend today is for the old name brands to bring in new talented designers. Did you ever want to have your own fashion house and be like Elsa Schiaparelli or Coco Chanel?

For the love of God, no thank you! I have never thought of founding a fashion house, because it brings with it certain things that I have no desire to do. I prefer to work for a big brand rather than have my own brand. Also because, realistically speaking, it is very complicated to do something like this today. Even in other professions I don't see many people being that enterprising, because it's a more complex world where it isn't so easy to do these kinds of things.

Did you change the classic "D" of the Dior logo with J'ADIOR?

I haven't changed the logo of *"J'Adore"* by Dior. I have a playful side to me and fashion has a playful side. Women also want to have fun with fashion. I think J'ADIOR really represents women today because it really sums up the message. If I had to write a hashtag I'd write J'ADIOR. Today, everything is about speaking concisely, making up new words with this new way of talking.

Even in fashion there is the world before the Internet and the world after the Internet?

Yes, but even there clothes change accordingly because it's all a big change. What I am trying to say is that time passes in a different way. Even the past is going by faster. There isn't the normal sense of time that we used to have. Before something from ten years ago didn't seem so old, whereas today . . .

Is business better or the same in this new world?

I don't know how to answer that question because it is also much more complicated, but the fact is that we must pay attention to the business side of things.

How long in advance do you have to prepare your collections?

There are two ready-to-wear collections, two couture collections, and two pre-collections. It is a continuous thing, it never slows down and in this sense fashion is very fast. You need to really get out there, find inspiration, and understand what you are feeling at a particular moment so you can put it out there for discussion.

Why is black your favorite color?

I think we are the "black generation." Black comes from punk, it cancels out. It also allows you to think freely. It's like a shield, a uniform. It has an austere aspect. It is so full of meaning.

Do women still dream about long dresses, evening gowns, and bridal gowns?

Every woman dreams about fairy tale occasions. I often say that unfortunately fairy tales don't exist, but it is better to have a dream.

What colors would you make yours in?

If it's going to be a dream, it has to be a personal dream. I would ask a woman what color she wanted. As for wedding dresses, I don't think they need to be white. Today, a woman who decides to get married can choose whatever color she wants. What is important is that she is happy.

Do you ever run out of ideas?

Honestly, no. There are always things around you that inspire you, something that piques your intellect and curiosity. What's important is to know how to observe, and to be curious about everything. I am very curious. I am interested in everything. Reading, seeing films, and seeing exhibitions are all very intellectually stimulating. I love to learn and discover new things.

Then you go into your atelier and set right to work on these inspirations?

You start working on it, start doing research. You get an inspiration and it's like a wonderful treasure hunt where one thing leads to another. An image leads you to a book that leads you to a character that leads you to an artist. . . .

Do you like to work at a fast pace?

I am a woman that goes fast in life. I have the ability to be concise. Fashion is fast, the world is fast, and life is fast. I have a great desire to live, but there is not a lot of time.

After twenty-eight years what is your enduring impression of fashion?

For me it is a language, an expression. I have a great passion for this job, and I have a lot of fun. If the time comes that I am no longer having fun I think I will stop, but I think it's wonderful creatively to start anew with each collection, with new inspirations and new ideas. Even though twenty-eight years have passed I still have a lot of enthusiasm. As long as I have this attitude it's all okay, because it is a very challenging job.

What is your language?

My language is to create fashion where Dior pieces can become personal for each person. Each person can interpret them or wear them in her own way. My job is to create a Dior wardrobe where each woman can mix and match in a personal way. Nowadays there's a great desire to be part of a community, but at the same time there's a great desire to be unique. Each person, even if she recognizes the values of the Dior brand, still wants to be able to use those values in a strictly personal and unique way.

Paris
April 23, 2017

~

TO BE INTERESTED IN FASHION AS A FORM OF

self-expression.

MARK GROTJAHN

ARTIST

The interview with Mark Grotjahn takes place in a suite at Claridge's Hotel in London, where he has recently opened an exhibition of his masks at the Gagosian Gallery called *Pink Cosco*. The original masks are made from scraps of corrugated paper or cardboard salvaged from shipments of art supplies, beer boxes, or gifts sent by friends. The heads he makes are transformed cardboard boxes, transmuted into bronze heads. He paints the cardboard masks and the bronzes that follow them in a way that is freer than his usual studio work. The masks have allowed him to become an expressionistic painter again.

Mark Grotjahn is a tall man, dressed in blue jeans and a madras shirt. He has salt and pepper short cut hair and a pair of dark-framed Persol glasses. He is sitting on a couch. Sometimes during the conversation, he will lie on the same couch. He is wearing thick cotton socks and after we shake hands and start talking he says to me: "You are wearing New Balance shoes," and adds, "I have the same ones, and they are the most elegant, beautiful, and comfortable." Then he moves to another room and comes back with two pairs of New Balance shoes, one black, identical to the ones I am wearing, and the other red. He asks, "Isn't this red an extraordinary shade of red?" I smile, and then we start talking about art.

Do you think that in your work there are different periods, like for instance what happened to major artists like Picasso?

I do have periods, but in my mind I can go back and reinvestigate them. People know me for two different periods, my butterflies and my faces.

What about the masks?

I like painting them, it gives me a different freedom. It allows me licenses that I normally do not have in my paintings. I started making masks to wind down after a day of painting. Making the masks was like an athlete stretching before or after exercise. I was trying to let go of the intensity that was involved in the other kind of art making, but I did really like these. In my mind though, I thought of them as an exercise, as something very personal and not for public consumption.

Do you consider them to be like sculptures?

Yes, they are not masks. They are called masks, but they are not. What I like the most is that my head is getting away. Here in London, half of them are yellow and half pink.

For one night and two days you showed some new works in the house of Curzio Malaparte in Capri, the house that was built in 1937 by the rationalist architect Adalberto Libera and stands on a cliff thirty-two meters above the sea.

Yes, it is a red box with reverse pyramidal stairs leading to the roof patio. On the roof there is also a freestanding curving white wall. I have loved that house since a long time. It's my favorite house in the world, even if I never saw it or went to Capri before, but I so loved the pictures and images of it.

How did you know this house?

I knew it for the first time when I saw the Jean-Luc Godard film *Contempt* [*Le Mépris*], shot in 1963, that featured this house. Brigitte Bardot was the protagonist of the film.

But how did all this happen?

Larry Gagosian called me and asked if I wanted to do this very special show at Villa Malaparte. I answered that I needed two days to think about it, and then I said, "I will give you a minimum of seven drawings." But then, on second thought, thinking of this exceptional space, I suddenly wanted to show paintings, smaller-size paintings than I usually do. I must say that it takes a lot of submission to do a small painting when before I have always been thinking large.

So ultimately you said yes.

Yes, I found it cool enough. I wanted to see my paintings there. Sometimes I was doing a painting a day.

How many paintings did you do?

Around sixteen to eighteen paintings in two months.

Does the fact that you answered yes to Larry Gagosian mean that you like challenges?

I took this on, one of the few. I did the paintings, but I also have seven drawings.

That series of work is called *New Capri*?
Yes.

Does the *New Capri* series look like a smaller version of your series *Faces*?
Yes, in a way.

Is there a nuance between your work and the Malaparte house?
To me the house is very interesting because it's rigid, handmade, and severe. Just look at the location.

Could you stay there and work there?
Not by myself.

What kind of a painter are you?
An abstract painter. I want to be not representational. I would like to be more and more abstract. I want to feel meaningful, but I don't want any more to represent a face, a body.

Could you be a classical artist, painting landscapes or portraits?
I left this to my wife. I do not have the skill, nor the classical training for that.

How long have you lived in LA?
I have lived there since 1997, and I consider myself an American painter.

You started your career by opening a gallery in Hollywood with a friend?
Yes, I was already an artist at the time, but we opened a gallery with five solo shows. The work of the gallery in itself was a show. At that time very few galleries in LA used to show a young artist's solo exhibition, the main street was in New York.

In terms of art, do you think LA has changed since you started working?
Yes, there are now enough galleries with good artists.

Didn't you like New York?
Yes, I did, and I like the snow, but there is too much going on in New York. In LA I didn't have to work too much, and didn't have to do too much social life. What I loved in New York at that time was that there was a great mixture of artists: writers, musicians, architects . . . artists were living and gathering together.

How do you live when you are in LA?
I live in my studio.

Do you think there are many good artists nowadays?
There are lots of good artists, but I don't know who the young artists are any more. When I was young myself I knew who the good artists were.

Do you still have many friends among them?
Yes, I do.

Can we say that when you had your exhibition in Tokyo in 2010 and your work was entitled *Captain America* that you somehow referred to Jasper Johns's flags?
If you are good at languages, there are a lot of tools you want to use. Picasso had multi-eyes in multiple perspectives. When I make a work I see other artists come out, I recognize it, never hide it. They developed languages, and if I want them I try to use them.

Has the fact that you became so famous changed your work and your life?
It certainly has changed my life. Today I am a rich man and I must say that I prefer it, because I bought a house and a studio. But I must also say that my own criticality with my work has not changed. I am still very tough with myself.

Do you follow your work and the people buying it?
I do, and there was a time when it bothered me very much to see my work at auction. I took it very personally.

Do you prefer your work to be in private homes or museums?
It's nice to have work in museums, because in museums you are seen by many people.

Is there an artist you particularly admire?
I admire very much Mike Kelley's work.

Can we say that your work has been inspired by Kandinsky, Klee, and the Bauhaus?
Yes, somehow, yes.

London
June, 2016

~

ZAHA HADID

ARCHITECT

The following interview with Zaha Hadid DBE RA took place in the Royal Academicians' Room in the Keeper's House at the Royal Academy of Arts, in Mayfair, London. The invited audience has been generously welcomed by Charles Saumarez Smith, the Secretary and Chief Executive of the Royal Academy.

Zaha, you have said that architecture is not for people who want an easy life. Is this not the case for anyone who wants to excel in his or her job?

There are other professions that are very difficult, but architecture is particularly difficult because your career is reliant on the people you work with, and that's the first hurdle. The second hurdle is the people you work with as a client. You have no control over the developer or the economics.

Like when you worked in Cardiff?

Today is twenty years to the day for the Cardiff Opera House project, and people forget what happened. It was a very nasty experience, but it made us much stronger. It's a shame they didn't build the Cardiff Opera House, but I can't have everything.

You had it particularly tough because your projects are particularly ambitious?

My work is not within the accepted box. Maybe because I am a woman, also an Arab; there was a certain prejudice about these things.

You became a teacher in important universities all over the world: the Architectural Association, Harvard. Now you teach in Vienna?

I always thought teaching was very important. You learn from what you teach, and show people they can achieve beyond what they thought possible for them to do.

What do you teach?

I don't think you can teach architecture, you can only inspire people. In Vienna it is called a master class because you are a master and the students are with you for five or six years. At the end the students have learned your repertoire and your expertise.

Do they then come to work for you?

Some of the best people in my studio are from the Vienna program, and also the Architectural Association. I am investing in my studio. She laughs.

You studied mathematics in Lebanon. Can you say an architect is a mixture of many talents? Drawing, engineering, a diplomat?

Diplomacy! Not my best talent! I don't play up to people. I remember Rem Koolhaus when they asked me to join the Office for Metropolitan Architecture, cofounded by Koolhaas in 1975 and I said, "Only as a partner." I mean, honestly! I had just finished school. And they said, "As long as you are an obedient partner." I said, "No, I am not going to be an obedient partner." That was the end of my partnership!

For a long time you were a theoretician architect. Then something changed and you became a very productive architect, working all over the world?

I always wanted to build what I call the theoretical project. Work on paper was never intended just to be drawing, but to have a productive reality. At the Architectural Association in the early mid-seventies—when, post-'68, all faith in architecture had collapsed—they were still dominated by the dogma of modernism. Alternatives were historicism, postmodernism, and neorationalism. I thought there must be another alternative, and so I started to complete the modernist project, not knowing that in this endeavor I would discover other things.

At the end of the day your shapes are artistic shapes?

Architecture is semi-artistic, but you are inspired by nature, landscape, biology, all living things. You can be far more ambitious now, you can make great spatial experiences, but one thing which hasn't changed is that we have to deal with gravity, to land on the ground. I learned from a great engineer called Peter Rice to understand the logic of structure.

As an architect you have to know about practical things, for a stadium, about security and such things, not only the environment?

You have to know all these things, not completely, but the logic of all these aspects.

Compared to architects of the past like Michelangelo, Alberti, Brunelleschi, Boromini, whose buildings are still here today, do you conceive your work as built to last over centuries?

The idea of time has changed. The world is moving much faster, and they might change these things in midcentury. I can't predict if it will be necessarily here in twenty years or needed there in a hundred years' time.

Was the MAXXI contemporary art museum in Rome a very difficult project to achieve considering the layers of architecture in Rome—an eternal city where there is so much architecture of so many centuries?

I think Rome is paralyzed by its history, so it needs interventions. I like the MAXXI project in Rome and I remember every line. It was a project on the cusp between my semitectonic early work and semifluid later.

Are there some projects you like and some you regret?

I have not done too much, so I have not regretted them. We have been lucky in very varied experiences, from building a bridge in Abu Dhabi to the stadium here for the pool, or a school in Brixton, or a cancer facility in Scotland. Mostly they are big projects.

You also design furniture. Do you like that?

I think it's fun to do, it's like making a model. You design and within a few months make, unlike architecture which takes a very long time. A chair is the most significant thing, but we still have not done a chair.

Why is your office in London?

I am a very stubborn person. First, I like London. A great city that has become a greater city in the last twenty or thirty years. I always thought London has great potential in terms of architecture. It's proven to me, great potential, but not for myself!

London is your base. How much time do you spend here?

A lot, I am trying not to travel so much. I am very lucky to have lots of people in the office who can travel for me. I like to travel, but it's very exhausting.

You said Rome was difficult, but China, Japan, Azerbaijan, Beijing were easier?

Not easier, but it depends on the client. China, although they say they are difficult, they are not. I find China relatively comfortable to work in.

What is the process, how do you start working on a project?

It has changed. We used to start working with a sketch, a model, a painting, or a model cross section. With digital and visual technology, the skill base has changed. We still look at work in a three-dimensional way. It is not a linear process, it is a very back-and-forth process.

Are there many things you can do today with the new technologies?

There's more precision and it's seamless on many layers, not only on the design, but seamless on the process, from the design to engineering to manufacturing to construction. I think that's very exciting.

Often to win a job you have to win a competition?

Although competitions are very expensive and sometimes a waste of time, some of the best ideas came out of working against time, without client intervention, in a different kind of space mentally.

Is the cost of the building one of the most significant issues? Do you have to be good at economics, too?

I know what is going to become expensive and what is cheap. I think it very important that a project is affordable.

Is common sense an essential quality for your job?

To know where the limits are, but having said that I think it's also very important that cities have great work. Cities should invest in good spatial organization that has more impact than just making a terrible cheap building, which you see a lot of.

In Hong Kong you won a competition but you didn't build it. How did you feel?

When Margaret Thatcher went to Hong Kong, that was the end of that project. It was early in my career and the number of lessons I learned is far greater than if I had built it.

The project is still there. Would it change enormously if you did it now?

I still believe in the carved mountain idea that came into play in terms of landscape and typography in many other projects later. The idea of layering was the most important idea, that you can build almost simultaneously; as if the layering is compressed in one single moment of time instead of a thousand years.

Is there a *fil rouge*, a guiding light in your work?

The common thread was abstraction, now it is complexity. Thirty years ago it had to do with the modernist ideology, with mass production. To challenge that idea was much more complex, and also the idea of typology changed a lot. Typology was there as one type of library, of office building, of apartment, and I thought you could challenge these. From the twentieth century it came out that the public domain is very important.

What is the public domain?

Put a building on a particular site, part of a city, and you engage the site in the life of

Cities should invest in

good

spatial

organization

that has more impact than just making a

terrible cheap building,

which you see a lot of.

the city. Exactly as you do the squares in Rome. In London the squares are private. It is very important to create these public spaces.

You do monuments, public buildings, but what has influenced your taste, your fantasy?

I was influenced by the modernists, but also by constructivism, and the Russian experiment was never fully tested. I became interested in how the site influences the project. What emerged was to look at what I call a field, and the field becomes another topic.

When they invite you to do a hospital, a stadium, a church, do you first have an idea that very often becomes the project? Through intuition?

No, all these things come together. You are constantly thinking about what to do for the next space or tower. When you get site specific you might test some of these ideas on that particular site.

The swimming pool stadium in London was from a competition. How did it proceed in your mind?

Of course water, the pool, the idea of the wave was an obvious idea, and we were interested in the typology of the landscape and computation of the idea of the wave.

You said it was tough to be an Arab, a woman, also to be a Muslim?

I come from Iraq, and there were many Christians there and lots of Jews and Muslims. I am a Muslim who went to a nun's school and for six years of my life I crossed my heart. There was no difference between the Christians and the Muslims.

Sometimes wars are very troublesome for architecture. Have you seen many disasters?

I used to live in Beirut and that was completely destroyed.

What do you feel about Aleppo?

It's very disturbing. It's not just the architecture, it is about the people who are there. It doesn't matter if you are from the region or not. If I see people from Africa, I am not from Africa but I feel for them. At this day and age, there should be no fighting. It is very sad.

Do you think it's a good historical moment for architecture?

It's been a great moment for the past ten or fifteen years. I am always very wary, because I think the pragmatists, the conservatives, are always lurking around the scenes, happy to leap out any minute and scuttle anything interesting.

I was thinking about Rome in another way. What about fascist architecture?

It is now in London, it has migrated from Italy to the UK! Laughs. I don't think you can separate architecture from the situation. Some of these buildings are of course very monumental and very interesting, but if you look at that period in Germany, it's very austere and extremely oppressive.

Are you very comfortable in England?

No, I am not comfortable in England. I like London. I would just say, "I have no work in London!" It's not out of choice.

How about in the USA, a country that loves architecture?

We are doing a tower in Miami, a building in New York. My two earlier projects, one was in Cincinnati, we had another museum in Michigan.

What's the difference between England and America?

In America they mostly do metal steel frame, repetitive floors. Like London, most of the work is corporate, either residential or offices, not like Europe, where they have invested in cultural buildings. When it is booming in America, they like architecture; when it is not booming, they don't. That's why I say as an architect you are in the hands of fate.

What are your frustrations?

I don't have any frustrations. If you want an easy life don't be an architect. Ask anybody in my office. You have to work all the time. If you want a nine-to-five job and to go home and relax, just don't do it.

Is it not the same for any artist?

The artist is the same. Architects have to organize a plan: you enter here, walk through there, you understand the stairs, make a room. . . . Is it the right size, the wrong size? It is exactly like writing. This is the composition, and also you have to edit it, over and over again, so that it looks seamless and effortless.

What are the things you like the least and make you impatient?

People not understanding what I am saying to them! That is the most flustering thing. But if you have trained them, they understand you better. I'll be honest; it's very difficult to explain things to men. It's virtually impossible. The older generation in my office think they know everything better than anyone. The younger generation are much more flexible and adaptable. Sloppiness irritates me the most.

But the world today. . . ?

I am not hysterical about it. Laughs, but I would like them to be less sloppy!

You seem to have a very special feeling for Rome?

My parents took me to Rome when I was seven years old and it stayed with me. That flamboyancy of Italy was similar to Beirut. I love those cities, Baghdad or Cairo, which are very tense and dense and with rivers. I am not a romantic but there is something about waterways in that part of the world which has a certain resonance.

Are you inspired by Istanbul?

Istanbul is one of my favorite cities, I love it. It's a kind of composite. I like that Sinan [Mimar Sinan, the greatest Ottoman architect] wanted to do these cupolas as if it was a mountain. The Roman Istanbul alone is stunning.

And you like the Greek monuments, too?

I do. I like many things. This is what you learn from. When you do something you don't have to repeat it, but you can learn from it.

Do you dream of building something in particular?

A project on the level of urbanism and architecture. There are some enormous sites being developed and I would love to do something in London, but I am not keeping my fingers crossed.

Royal Academy of Arts, London
February 25, 2015

~

DENNIS HOPPER

ACTOR & DIRECTOR

Dennis Hopper, a director and, first and foremost, an actor, was in Salzburg in October 2000 to show some of his works of art.

Showing art is rather a different experience. Are you satisfied?

Yes. I sold two of my works for the first time, including a painting called *Fragmented Woman*, which is my *Mona Lisa*. It is inspired by a photo I took in 1964, and it has a woman with many mouths, each of which has different colored lips. I also sold a large sculpture and many photographs.

When did you get started with the plastic arts?

I have always painted, even before I became an actor. On February 16th, at the Stedelijk Museum in Amsterdam, I will show in a comprehensive retrospective with cinema, photography, paintings, and sculptures.

Will you continue to act?

This year I only worked on one film, with John Malkovich. It is called *Knockaround Guys*, and it is a mafia film in which I play the part of a mafia boss.

Tell me about some of the great moments of your life?

I was the president of the jury at the Venice Film Festival. I won the Leone d'Oro award in 1971 with *The Last Movie*, in which I directed and acted. I am very fond of that project. I shot it in Peru after the success of *Easy Rider* [1969], but I had it in mind even before.

Did you also write *Easy Rider*?

Yes. I wrote it with Peter Fonda and Terry Southern, who also worked on the screenplay for *Dr. Strangelove* [1964].

What significance does *Easy Rider* have for you?

It's the first film I directed, and thanks to that film, I won at the Cannes Film Festival for best first film. I was also nominated for an Oscar for that screenplay. It only cost

$350,000 and we made that money back in a week in New York in only one cinema. It represented the culture of young people at the end of the 1960s. Hollywood was still making films with Doris Day and Rock Hudson. Rock music didn't exist in films, and marijuana was completely ignored, as were the political changes that had taken place.

What did you do after *The Last Movie*?

Out of the Blue [1980], which wasn't distributed, though it did become a cult film. Then I didn't direct for ten years until I did *Colors* [1988] with Sean Penn and Robert Duvall. It was a great success and earned fifty million dollars in the United States alone.

You have had a career of highs and lows. You've also been an actor . . . .

Yes, because my films haven't been commercially successful. And to think that since 1969 up to now, I have only shot seven films. Even as an actor, I've had highs and lows.

Do you consider yourself a cinema intellectual?

No. More than anything, I am a compulsive creator. I work with the senses. I owe this to Lee Strasberg of the Actors Studio, who taught me to get in touch with my senses.

Has America changed a lot since *Easy Rider*?

Before, America was a country in which blacks and whites couldn't drink from the same water fountain. They couldn't use the same toilet. They couldn't sit in the same seats on the bus.

What kind of film would you make today?

I would make a film about the homeless and the people that live on the street, gravitating to the streets of Los Angeles. Or those that wander on the beaches of Venice or Santa Monica where there's a burgeoning homeless population. I made a small eight-minute digital film, and I would perhaps make a long digital film. I have trouble getting financing. I certainly do have a desire to make more films.

Do you feel frustrated?

I have the same frustration in sculpture as well, but I have always gone against those in power because I didn't have a choice. There's no other way.

What relationship do you have with Hollywood today?

I play golf with the head of Warner, the president of Columbia Pictures and the vice president of Paramount. But we never talk about work. They want to make money and they don't have time to waste. They only remember me for *Easy Rider*.

Have you tried working in Europe?

Yes. I lived in Paris for a year and a half, but I didn't find money there either. To make films, you need millions of dollars.

But don't you have a large art collection?

Yes. And I've let go of a lot of works. I am a compulsive collector. I live in a house full of pieces by Richard Serra, Jean-Michel Basquiat, Andy Warhol, and Julian Schnabel. Before I divorced my first wife, I also had paintings by Jasper Johns, Rauschenberg, Oldenburg, Lichtenstein, and Frank Stella. It was one of the first collections of pop art. And to think that then it was worth twenty-five thousand dollars, and today it would be worth almost a hundred million dollars. Many of my paintings are in German museums today.

How does America seem to you today?

I love it. It's a big country, and there is a lot to be critical about, but I love it all. I am very proud to be an American. I have always seen things through the eyes of a simple boy from Kansas. Sure, I have had a lot of problems, but that doesn't matter. I am happy, and I have no regrets for what I've done, because I know that a few of the films I've made will live on.

What do you think of Lucas, Spielberg, and Coppola?

They came after *Easy Rider*. They had a lot of money and they could make films. I don't think they are more talented than I am. But, and let's be clear, I am not jealous.

What do you think are the important films that came after *Easy Rider*?

Many European films that aren't distributed in America. But even in Rome, there's no more film industry like back during the Clint Eastwood and Charles Bronson period. Perhaps only in France, where there's Canal+, which sponsors more than fifty percent of films. In the United States, it seems like there's no more place for film history or foreign films. It seems like they prefer to make money off of the popcorn they sell at the cinema as opposed to on the films.

Are you saying that there is no longer any artistry in film?

I love many big films. And, all in all, I think there are good films today. Despite my age, I would like to continue to work.

Salzburg
October 8, 2000

~

I HAVE ALWAYS

s e e n

THINGS

T H R O U G H

THE EYES OF A

simple boy

FROM KANSAS.

HRH PRINCE EL HASSAN BIN TALAL OF JORDAN

HUMANITARIAN

How are you?

I am beginning to feel that voices from the region who call for justice, which basically is a call for enabling and empowering people for citizenship, are beginning to receive broad support. For the first time authentic ideas are coming from the region and being listened to. People are beginning to develop the content of the rule of law, and to recognize the difference between the mobility stakeholders and the development or national stakeholders. It sometimes seems that migration stakeholders are from one planet and development stakeholders from an altogether different one. With global warming raising the Mediterranean, forty-five million Egyptians are going to have to move from the delta region. I don't see anybody, but anybody, who is interested in building the infrastructure or who cares about crisis avoidance.

Nobody cares?

Shifting the emphasis from bombs and oil to citizens being the vector of stability or instability may be the way to propose a stabilization architecture for the region. You can't cherry-pick the community you want to protect because you want to protect minorities. You have to protect the minority and the majority. Iran has the same figure of forty-five million people potentially on the move by 2030, because the water they get is from the Zagros Mountains where the ice is shrinking. The water is deoxygenating and when you deoxygenate water you can't grow anything. So where will this ninety million people go before you can say, "Aleikum Salaam?"

What is your major concern now?

A major concern in the region is rampant corruption, alongside a lack of governance and of institutionalism. The problem we face is that all the slogans of the Arab Spring in 2011 were just that, they were slogans. "Democracy." "Freedom." What people are asking for is equal opportunity. In the Arab Thought Forum we have produced a charter proscribing discrimination at all levels; that means the handicapped, the elderly, all the things that are not written into constitutions.

What has changed since we met a year ago?

In my country, when we last met we were about seven to eight million people. Today we are eleven million. Since 2011, thirty-two thousand Syrian children have been born in Jordan. In several years' time these children will be the foot soldiers of the Da'esh.

What we call ISIS and you call Da'esh, is it a problem for you?

It is about the absence of identity. The Da'esh has three or four components, one of which is the former Ba'ath army which was disbanded. The second component is the Salafis, which is a sort of rejuvenation of the first Wahabi movement in British India. In northern Syria and northern Iraq it's basically a holding position. Staffan de Mistura's comments concerning making Aleppo an open city are so important, and also for Mosul, so that all the minorities have a chance to breathe as citizens.

Is Jordan the only stable state? Lebanon, Syria, Iraq—what is going to happen in this region?

Today is 1914 all over again. Margaret MacMillan at Oxford University has written a brilliant book, *The War That Ended Peace*, and Pope Francis has made a very important remark: We are not actually at World War III, but the world is at war, because every region is in conflict. The question is that between 1914 and 1918 and the Versailles Conference they had to go through a world war to get to a peace conference. Is there a possibility of seeing a regional conference, and this regional conference focusing on West Asia? Because of the five countries that have seen military intervention, four are in our region—Afghanistan, Iraq, Syria, Iran, and then we have Nigeria. What has foreign intervention achieved? According to the terrorism index it has not achieved anything.

You mean the bombing?

I mean the bombing on the one side and also the Special Forces and the Special Operations, this is the sad point. People cannot even think, they cannot focus anymore, because of continuously being hit on the head. These are the zombies that ISIS wants. As we say, the "dead-hearted."

Do you talk to the people of ISIS?

I believe in talking to everyone. The Arab Thought Forum invites anyone from the region who is willing to engage in conversation. When the vernacular of governance breaks down then these communities become ghettoized. There has to be an understanding of the fact that this West Asian region cannot be protected by armies and navies focused solely on gas and oil.

What about the regional conference that never comes?

At the regional conference in Switzerland we meet with the Israelis and the Iranians and we talk nuclear. We meet in Montreux at a technical level on water. When we come close to the point of a Helsinki Process, the Israelis say we have to go back to our government because now we have to negotiate. And I say, "Before you can negotiate you need a vision."

What is the issue that Iran has to solve?

The issue is that the Americans feel they shouldn't remove sanctions totally, and the Iranians want to get as many of the sanctions removed as possible. Desalination is one of the things that makes their request justified, as their country is going to be unmanageable if they can't get the possibility of desalination. It is not about beneficiation for military reasons. If there is a real nuclear confrontation and retaliation we are all finished.

This mask of religion, what is horrible is that there are lots of English and French who join. Do they love to kill?

Yes, that is exactly it. It is unbelievable.

It is depressing to see this horrible violence everywhere. . . . It hasn't been like this always. Where does it come from, this deep inhumanity that has suddenly arisen?

It is an accumulation of the horrors of every ten years. Every decade there has been a war in our region, 1967 and its aftermath, 1973, 1981, and the Iraqi war, thousands of people lost and killed and people seem to forget that. We talk about the remembrance of the First World War but what about our region? Central government wants to intervene in everything, then you have corruption. Boko Haram stands up and holds the holy book and says books are forbidden, women are chattel. What has this got to do with Islam? We Muslims believe in the Divine, for those of us who believe. They, by contrast, believe in war and their selective interpretation of the law.

The First and Second World Wars started and become terrible wars, and then they finished and there was a peace treaty. Now things start suddenly and then just as suddenly finish. Like Gaza, it's such a fluid thing, there is no beginning. . . .

I was with Shimon Peres and he said to me, "I have a problem. I am surrounded by enemies." I said, "You think you have a problem. I am surrounded by friends." The problem is that after the Second World War Churchill talked about the broader patriotism, but

we are not allowed to talk about energy and water for the hum
we need to get out of this mess is a regional policy. It's all very w
of the Gulf to the UK and the US, to so-called Islamic banking. W
for a social cohesion fund for the region, where you bring in the
who have masses of money to spend, and bring the Russians into a conversation over the threat of Islamists? I am focusing on human dignity not triumphalist architecture. I am talking about social cohesion. Seventy percect of the world's refugees are Muslims. So why don't you get the Muslims who can to do something about it?

And Jerusalem?

There should be a special status for holy places. There should be a return to the status quo pre-1947. The Israelis can't have it both ways. Inclusionist peace means everybody. It's not just peace between the Israelis and the Palestinians that matters if you want to stabilize the region.

What is the position of Jordan?

Unfortunately, in the days when we were negotiating the peace treaty, everything went wrong following the assassination of Yitzhak Rabin in 1995, and then there was the untimely death of my brother . . . . Our position is very much one of let's pick up some of the initiatives which have been disregarded. The country needs a regional peace because everything is interconnected.

When ISIS was marching close to Baghdad, taking everything, I said to myself, "My God, will they go to Amman?"

I was one of the very few people standing with my brother in 1970 when we were digging trenches a little north of Amman, expecting the Syrian army to advance. I have seen some pretty horrible situations and I take it as it comes. What we need today is a new regional architecture, to deploy the resources to addressing the needs of the human capital. We need to think about it as a region. People have to be given a feeling of equal opportunity and that they can participate in building their future. I am not asking for the west to resolve our problems, I am asking for the world to do so. The world today, let's face it, is not the Security Council.

What do the Muslim extremists want, to conquer the world?

Allegedly they want justice for all, however it remains clear that implicitly they want power. They have been excluded for so long and now they want to exercise domination. As long as the West doesn't really care about this concept of inclusion by 2018, and hold a conference equivalent to that of 1918, this is going to fall down.

In America your identity is American, not your tribal background, but in the Middle East that is completely contrary to everything?

In the Ottoman period there was richness in diversity. They were diverse and they were encouraged to be diverse. In the post-Ottoman period nations emerged. The breakdown of the basic commitment to my great-grandfather, self-determination, led to the search for alternative leadership and led to the Saudis and the Gulf, because they accepted that oil should be exploited. When my family were massacred in 1958 in Iraq, the Baghdad Pact disintegrated, and the first serious financial assistance to Israel only started in 1961 because the West felt they had—unthinkable today—Turkey, Pakistan, Iran, and Iraq in a western pact. Crossed wires, false promises, all of this came into play. It's not a question of us all being born genetically mad and that we can't stand each other. The Americans shoot each other as well!

Do you as Jordan have influence?

We are an oasis of calm, but obviously things can change very quickly.

In terms of influence is your family still revered?

Yes, ever since the days of the Prophet.

But does anyone have any influence on the false caliph you mentioned?

It depends on the realignment of forces in the region, Turkey and Iraq. How do you define influence? Is it funding? It is not about religion.

So religion is a screen for ISIS, a justification?

Yes, it is a mask, a brand name. Theirs is not a doctrinal wedding to caliphate, they see this as a better economic and empowering option.

Queen Rania of Jordan said you need to solve the economic problems of people and unemployment, the same problems some western countries have?

In 1994 at the MENA (Middle East North Africa) conference some of us proposed, including Shimon Peres and myself, that twenty-four countries from Morocco to Turkey be included in a strategy designed to sustain human dignity, clean water, solar power, electricity, and so forth. We went to Brussels and asked for thirty-five billion dollars over ten years as an international effort to make this good neighborhood policy a possibility by improving social-economic conditions. A regional bank? Nothing has happened. You can't solve a problem with promises, promises, promises. It is not unsurprising to most Arabs that the bombs and the airplanes are bought with Arab money and that the people who are dying are Arabs. So what is this vicious circle of stupidity?

We are witness to only a very small part of history in our lives, but Europe has had two world wars in the last century.

A Spaniard and an Arab were in conversation, and the Spaniard said to the Arab: "We have ojalá, what do you have?" "We have Insh'allah," said the Arab. "How is it different?" asked the Spaniard. The Arab said: "Insh'allah does not convey quite the same sense of urgency."

London

November 24, 2014

~

I AM FOCUSING ON

HUMAN DIGNITY

NOT

TRIUMPHALIST

ARCHITECTURE.

ISABELLE HUPPERT

ACTRESS

Isabelle Huppert is petite. She practically tiptoes into a salon of the Hotel de la Ville in Rome, wearing gray pants, a beige pullover, and a red scarf around her neck. Her hair hangs long and loose. It is a reddish brown, and her eyes are large and brown. She seems more like a student just starting out than an international star. We talk a bit about her day in the Italian capital spent with her companion and children. They had lunch with Mauro Bolognini, a friend who directed her in the film *Lady of the Camelias*, which she shot alongside Gian Maria Volontè. Isabelle Huppert truly enjoys spending time in Rome, but says she couldn't always live there.

Isabelle Huppert, have you just come back from shooting a film in Russia?

I was there for almost three months, and I enjoyed the privileged life of a tourist so I can't say I really know it well. But Russia is a fascinating country with a big soul. It has great strength.

And now you are in Italy to promote another film?

Yes, *Après l'Amour* [*Love after Love*, 1992] directed by Diane Kurys. I had already shot *Entre Nous* [*Between Us*, 1983] with her. It is like a sociological look at the life of couples in the mid-twentieth century in a large city. It could take place anywhere. Diane Kurys wanted to focus on what happens when love ends. When, after having lived for many years with a partner, a woman feels the need for different passions.

What role do you play in the film?

The role of a writer trying to live two lives. She has lived with a man for many years, but she is trying to be free and not deny herself anything. It's a film that doesn't set out to resolve anything. It has a bit of the truth of a documentary and shows reality as it is lived by many. Today's women don't want to deny themselves anything. They want to experience everything.

Do you often play the part of ambiguous women who are a bit negative?

I play characters in the midst of negative situations, but their cruelty is a reflection of the situation in which they find themselves. My characters face challenges and suffering. And they aren't ever people that have anything handed to them by life.

Are you like these characters?

No. I play the roles.

How do you choose which films to act in?

I choose a character when it suits my imagination. But the most important thing is the director.

Is Chabrol your favorite director?

I have a unique relationship with him. We have done three films together. I have had the opportunity to portray all the facets of certain kinds of sentiment and to bring characters to life that are often regular people. I am not attracted to big heroes.

Who has been your favorite acting partner?

I had a wonderful experience with Gian Maria Volontè in Mauro Bolognini's *Lady of the Camelias* [1981] and with Marcello Mastroianni in Marco Ferreri's *Story of Piera* [1983], but I've always worked with good actors like Depardieu or Trintignant. I love actors that don't cause conflict. To tell you the truth, I prefer actresses to actors. I think men have a negative way of relating to their profession. They want to dictate, to take control. Mastroianni and Volontè are great actors because they have not given in to the temptation to try to be in power, unlike many of their French colleagues who argue constantly with the director.

In your opinion, who are the great actresses?

Vanessa Redgrave in certain films and Meryl Streep. Perhaps there are some less famous actresses. . . .

Do you think French cinema is good?

It exists. It is better than nothing. But it is always a bit limited, small, bourgeois, and inward looking. Of course, at times it promotes amazing things, but that happens quite rarely.

Do you like the theater?

Yes, very much. I rediscovered it four years ago. I hadn't done theater for a long time, and it was greatly satisfying. I worked in a Shakespeare comedy [*Measure for Measure*] directed by Peter Zadek last year at the Odéon theater in Paris. Now I'm working on a show with Bob Wilson in Switzerland that will then move on to Paris.

Was it easy for you to find success?

Yes. I found success slowly, starting young and playing small roles. Success doesn't bother me in its outward manifestations. I have always lived a normal life. I can go entire days without thinking about being an actress.

How do you live your daily life?

Shooting my films. My life is very tied to my work and very dependent on my work. But I have a companion, two children, and a family life as well. Playing roles and having children are similar things. In both cases, there is always something taking place in your core. Actresses often have a strong relationship with maternity.

Are you a good mother?

I don't know. I am a mother. I am very present. I always bring my children with me.

Do you feel like a fulfilled woman?

Yes. I am becoming one, though there's always a bit of frustration in order to keep moving ahead. But the frustration is part of my self-realization. When you start out in life, you suffer a lot and then, little by little, you let yourself go and you suffer less.

Are you afraid of aging?

Yes. I am afraid. I doubt there are many actresses that aren't afraid, but I see some advantages because age is perhaps one way of getting more respect and perhaps finding certain types of affirmation. I am scared of aging, but I don't know if I fear being old. It's like when you dive into water. You are a bit scared because you think the water will be cold, but then you feel fine.

Do you feel beautiful?

It depends on the moment. I find beauty to be a funny thing. Yesterday, I was having some photographs taken and I felt gorgeous, but today I was looking in the mirror and I didn't feel beautiful. I found these differences strange, and I thought to myself that this is the power of illusion. I can be beautiful if I want, but a part of beauty must be fabricated.

What things in life do you find to be most difficult?

Dealing with breakups, all kinds of breakups. And then I find it difficult to get ahead. Becoming an adult and forgetting you were once a child.

What more would you like to do?

It is difficult to answer that question. Right now, I feel like my aspirations correspond to reality quite well. I don't have many dreams that are out of reach.

Can you paint me a portrait of Isabelle Huppert?
I never stop interpreting self-portraits. All one needs to do is see my films.

Rome
March 1, 1993
Originally published in *Amica* magazine

~

I CHOOSE
A CHARACTER WHEN IT SUITS MY
iMaGInATion.
BUT THE MOST IMPORTANT THING
IS THE DIRECTOR.

ERICA JONG

NOVELIST

Erica, what is your view of what is happening in the feminine world?

I think that more and more people are becoming aware that women's rights are human rights. The smartest men understand well that when women are educated the economy goes up.

Why?

Because when women participate freely in the economy, they improve it. Because they are less preoccupied with fighting meaningless wars and they are willing to improve the status of their children. Of course we need male allies to help us. We would be crazy to reject their participation as we did in the past. Men and women have to be partners in order to improve the world.

But doesn't this happen everywhere?

It is not like that in Afghanistan. In any case fundamentalism has to be defied because it hurts everywhere if one keeps women barefoot and pregnant. You stop progress. Nowadays women have very important roles in the world. I think of Angela Merkel, the new chairman of the Federal Reserve [Janet Yellen], and Hillary Clinton.

Do you think Hillary will make it as the next president?

I hope so. She is so gifted. It would be very important. It is possible, but it is going to be a struggle. She is obviously by far the most talented politician we have in the U.S.

What is happening in the U.S.?

As for the condition of women, for some time we went back to sleep. But younger women are awake. In our history we never go straight ahead. But now we are going through a new period. Hopefully Hillary will be president. I would like to see that. There is a prejudice against women, but she is the most qualified.

I think
that more and
more people are
becoming aware
that women's
rights are

human rights.

. . . YOUNGER WOMEN ARE AWAKE. IN OUR HISTORY WE NEVER GO STRAIGHT AHEAD. BUT NOW WE ARE GOING THROUGH A NEW PERIOD.

Can we say that women were always very influential in literature?

Sappho invented love poetry. Women were important from the very beginning. But there has been a transformation and women now have more of an equal place in society.

Erica, what are you writing?

I am finishing a novel about people getting older.

What is the title?

Fear of Dying. It is a funny book, all about the "crazy" of the aging. When you realize you are not immortal and you start to deal with not being around forever. The book is about facing mortality.

Do you consider yourself a Jewish writer? A feminist writer?

I consider myself an American writer, with all the craziness of American writers. We have these ideals of freedom and democracy, and we do not live up to our ideals. So the writer in America has to be constantly reminded of that. Obviously my Jewish identity and my beliefs in feminism are in my writings—but they don't define my books.

As a writer do you feel close to Philip Roth or to Saul Bellow?

They are many similarities between Philip Roth and me. Wild humor and a lot of views of one's own life.

Are your books mainly fiction?

A combination of autobiography and fiction. It is impossible to tell what happened and what did not.

Are you a good plotter?

I don't think my strong point is plot, but I like my characters to develop.

What is the position of a female writer today in American society?

We certainly have many good ones and we are freer to write about our life than we have ever been before. I think I broke through censorship and fear, and made it accessible for women to write honestly about their lives.

What about sex in your books?

There is always sex in my books because in part I associate sex with freedom. But it is not what I am writing about.

How did you start the New Year and what are your wishes?

I started by going to a great jazz concert in New York. My first wish is to finish my novel. I am very happy with my life. I would like to be healthy and finish all the books I am thinking about. I have a new idea for a book—but I don't want to talk about it; it is bad luck.

Is it a good time for America today?

It's difficult to speak about the entire country. I think we are changing. Nowadays there is a tremendous influence of Latino culture. I miss Italy, and from where I sit Italy seems to be in a terrible mess. It's hard to understand the politics. But at least you got rid of Berlusconi, and that's a good thing.

You always had a special relationship with Italy, didn't you?

Yes, it is a country that reminds you that life goes on. It is a country where I love the attitude towards life, much more fatalistic than in America. America believes in change—and sometimes the change is a disillusion.

Do you think people are still reading books nowadays?

Yes, I think so. I believe the form is changing, but people who read still read. It is never going to be a mass audience as it is for movies or TV. The audience is more intimate.

New York

January 1, 2014

~

PATRICK KINMONTH

OPERA DIRECTOR & DESIGNER

Patrick Kinmonth is an Anglo-Irish opera director and designer, filmmaker, writer, painter, interior designer, art editor, creative director, and exhibition curator. He is widely known for his many stage, costume, interior, and architectural designs and recognized internationally for the breadth and depth of his creative interests. His many collaborations have yielded landmark opera, ballet and dance productions, books, and exhibitions. Kinmonth's earlier role as arts editor at British *Vogue* included creative direction for fashion and portraiture shoots. He is working principally as an opera director, and has been described as "one of the most indefinable personalities of contemporary art."

Can we define Patrick Kinmonth? Is it true that you are a renaissance man?

No, because there is no Renaissance. The Renaissance is the period you live in, not the person you are, and I have been living in anything but a Renaissance. My diversity is the result of a kind of fear and a kind of guilt, the two things that are responsible for everything worth preserving in culture. I came from a medical family where the arts are not esteemed, in the face of ill-health the arts are quite irrelevant. You would give up all the Picassos in the world for air to breathe if you were dying of lung cancer.

Did your father encourage you in your talent?

Yes, but that was my decision. I decided not to go to art school and went to Oxford. My father went to Trinity Dublin and then trained at St Thomas's and the entire rest of my family went to Trinity College, Cambridge. The decision to read literature at Oxford was a total break from my family tradition.

Did you want to be a painter?

I was always drawn to the visual. It has been my most active and coercive sense. I just love the visual world. My eyes are my most precious organ.

You did so many things, but you don't like labels?

The problem is quite simple. I did have extraordinary talents: I was born very musical, very verbal, very physical. I was blessed.

Your first job was as art editor at *Vogue*?

Working with *Vogue* was a kind of atonement, a punishment for being talented. I put myself at the service of others in order not to be embarrassed at being good at things. I hope I have gotten over that. In any artistic field that I now work in, my vision is expressed upon my own terms for my own purposes. It took me a longer time than most people to give myself permission to be that kind of artist.

You graduated from Oxford at twenty, and so at *Vogue* you were a very young man in contact with the most important designers and artists of the time, photographers like Cecil Beaton, Tony Snowdon, Mario Testino. What did all of these people teach you?

They gave me above all a huge amount of pleasure, because they were all remarkably talented in their own right. I didn't have the courage to want to be like them. I was the youngest in my family of four children, and therefore represent no originality, as everything has been done by your siblings. My mother encouraged me to play the piano and enjoyed my character, but didn't promote it or allow it to bloom.

Yet you have done so much in all these fields?

Tens of exhibitions, many ballets, more than forty-five, operas from Dresden to India, Brazil to China to Paris. If I look at it on the page it surprises me, it doesn't look possible, yet I have really tried to do things well, including buildings. I made the Missoni flagship store on Rodeo Drive, and worked on the architecture and design of the lovely house South Wraxall Manor for John Taylor of Duran Duran and his wife Gela Nash, the founder of Juicy Couture, and subsequently have worked on other houses as well.

And you were called on to work on the redesign of the Costume Institute at the Metropolitan Museum of Art in New York?

It was a *Vogue* nexus of Anna Wintour, Hamish Bowles, and the Costume Institute itself, who were interested in the work I had done in Europe and asked me to do several exhibitions at the Costume Institute.

Is there a gestalt you have given to your life?

People say that in order to do one thing well you have to cut away all the weeds around it and concentrate on that one thing. My experience says there is another way to do things. If you respond to what the world offers you and say yes to projects, you discover it is the same skills in a different area. In her defense, Lila De Nobili, one of the greatest costume designers, is an example of someone who could have done many other kinds of creative work as a visual artist, but something in her character drew her to dedicate herself to costume. She learned her craft and dedicated herself to costume, but in my world, by doing many things, I reassured myself that the process, in visual terms, is the same.

Your artistic career is somehow comparable, for instance, to the combined talents of the Russian ballet?

Comprehension and intelligence, perception and articulation are the tools that everybody uses as an artist. If you don't have those things you are primitive. If you are intelligent you can apply your skills as an intelligent person to any kind of problem, and solve it.

Today do you consider yourself principally a director?

Not yet. The director is probably an overrated character, just because he is on the top of the pyramid. In the creative process of visualizing a production, the designer is of equivalent or greater importance than the director, whose job extends to the concept of the production. But that concept very often has to be comprehended by the designer before the director can apply themselves to the problem. The design for an opera is handed in a year before the production. The designer is the person who makes the shape of the production, which is why one would work with someone like Lila De Nobili, because she would bring an extraordinary articulation of the characters she was dressing.

So what is your job?

My job is to come up with the story that we are going to tell about a great work of art that may not have been seen in those terms before. I am working on Mozart's *La Clemenza di Tito* in Karlsruhe, and Wagner's *Tannhäuser* in Cologne. By working with great directors such as Robert Carsen many of my designs have survived. In Brno we made a revival of our *Káa Kabanová*, the first opera I ever did the sets and costumes for, more than a decade ago.

Soon you will revive it in the Teatro Regio in Turin?

Yes. I am going to show the revival of *Káa Kabanová* there, which has now been seen in La Scala, Brno, all over the place. Every time you return to a work it's different, because all the singers are different and I adjust the costumes as a result of their characters and how they color the role. The conversation I have with myself is between the libretto and the music. My work is to make these stories as compelling dramatically as possible.

Would you also like to be a cinema director?

Oh yes. I am obsessed by cinema and long to be a movie director.

Although born in Ireland, are you now very English?

At this point I am, I have become English. I am by birth Irish. My father and grandmother could not have been more Irish, I have thirty-two first cousins in Ireland. When I started as a painter I obsessively painted thirty or forty times a picture called "Wake," with obvious reference to the night spent with a corpse as you do in Ireland, traveling by boat between one country and the other and not belonging to either. As I've grown up I have become more and more grateful to England for what it's given me in my education and culture, and the more I travel the more I respect it and value its institutions.

Do you consider yourself a man of the present or of the past?

I am not remotely nostalgic. I am fascinated by the present. People say that I live in a seventeenth-century house in North Devon, but if you understand the passage of time you don't want to be constantly ripping everything down! I am more concerned about preserving atmospheres, a medievalist rather than medieval, as reconstructed in our character by the Victorians. My house is a statement of there is a way of being from the past as much as possible. It doesn't contradict modernity. It's now modern to think of the environment, but the Druids honored every source of water and how light moved, they made it a religion.

You have witnessed a very creative London of The Beatles, the Rolling Stones, the famous photographers. What's the difference between then and today?

We are grappling with the dissolving of national identity and the effects of globalization. Mutual dependence is optimistic, but also people are terrified of losing their identity. This connectivity tragically reduces variety. Technology means all sorts of accelerations in possibility. The physical fact of communication is redefined on a monthly basis. I embrace and adapt as quickly as I possibly can.

Are you at peace with yourself?

No. I am struggling to come to terms with the issues that surround us, which are extremely complicated. The "rage, rage against the dying of the light," of Dylan Thomas is attractive. I hope as a result of passion I will go on burning brightly until something cuts me down.

London
January 22, 2017

~

CALVIN KLEIN

FASHION DESIGNER

Calvin Klein gets out of a Mercedes and goes into an Italian restaurant downtown. He is dressed in dark gray and is wearing a crew-neck pullover without a shirt underneath. He is very thin and lanky. When he speaks, he moves his long, thin hands. His face is also thin, and his nose and eyes are very sharp and alert. He speaks quite slowly and his voice has no particular affectations. He orders a simple meal—salad, boiled fish, and sorbet. He drinks still, natural water.

Next week you are opening a shop in Paris on avenue Montaigne. In a few months, you will also launch a shop in the Red Square in Moscow. What is behind this expansion?

Three years ago we realized we had achieved the success needed to expand to the rest of the world. First we sold our fragrances, which saw great success. They were really popular just about everywhere, and this was a sign that the time had come to open clothing stores as well.

What is your impression of Moscow?

I wouldn't have believed this would have been possible seven or eight years ago. I have to confess that I hope to open a Calvin Klein shop or Calvin Klein Jeans shop in all of the most important cities in the world. The market has changed a lot, and now there is strong demand for our products. I would say that our style has become more of an international style than an American style.

Can you describe this style in a few words?

Minimalist, modern, pure, no-frills, sexy, and sensual. A luxurious casual elegance. I think people like and are interested in this today.

Well it's almost the year 2000. How do you think people will dress in the future?

I am not a prophet, but if I try to transport myself to the year 2000, I think women will want clothes in which they can work well and move well, and that can go from day to evening. Versatile clothing. Versatile because life is busier and women have less time to think about and try on clothing. I imagine a new kind of freedom for men that goes a bit beyond classic elegance. Lighter clothing, for example, T-shirts under jackets or sports jackets and turtleneck sweaters. The same goes for the home. People are working more and more from home with fax machines, telephones, and computers, and the aesthetic of the home needs to be cleaner, more modern, luxurious, and comfortable at the same time. Today I'm designing for homes. I see the future there.

Why is American style so popular from China to Brazil to Italy to Russia?

Well, I am an American born in New York, a city of eighteen million people from all over the world with many different influences. I am influenced by New York and this goes into my work. I think that people all over the world want the same things—to be beautiful, elegant, and sexy.

Could you describe your typical work day?

I get to the office early in the morning. I love to work and especially the work I do. In the evening I spend time with family or friends. I make time every day to do some exercise. I organize my time to be able to focus on diet and exercise. Being in shape is very important and my clothes reflect this. Many people want to be healthy and look good and they watch their diet and work out.

Do you follow a special diet?

I pay a lot of attention to what I eat. I eat fresh foods—a lot of fish and chicken. I don't drink, and I haven't smoked in years. I have to say that I'm very interested in health.

How do you choose your employees?

I look at their creativity, originality, and energy. Those who aren't conformists and that think and work like me. I work in a team and personal chemistry is really important. We have to work fast because there is a lot of competition.

Is it true that you wear bespoke suits from England?

Not any longer. I invented the men's line so I could wear me. I choose colors, fabrics, and things I'd like to have. Before, I went to London to get classic suits. Now I wear lighter, more elegant, and tighter-fitting fabrics.

Is it true that you don't like to have a lot of objects around and that you love homes with a lot of space?

Absolutely. Space in New York is an absolute luxury. Everything looks better in a larger space with fewer things. My Madison Avenue shop was created with an atmosphere of space, silence, and without distractions for customers. And beautiful light.

I

LOVE

TO WORK

AND ESPECIALLY

THE WORK

I DO.

How many houses do you have?

I have a new apartment in New York that I bought and that I'm renovating and a house in East Hampton on the ocean. I don't need any more than that. They would require work and stress that I don't want.

When you aren't working, what do you do?

I go to my house in East Hampton whenever I can, and when I'm in New York, I go to the theater, painting exhibitions, or I go out with my friends. I do the things New York has to offer.

What is the key to your long-lasting success?

I think I have a point of view I believe in, and this is the key factor in my success. From a business point of view, I have a strategy, I develop it very carefully, and then I maintain that strategy.

Are you a good father to your daughter?

I hope so. I try to be. Maybe I didn't spend enough time with her when she was little. But we are very close, and I am so proud of her. She has been very inspirational for me and for my work. She works in television and is very happy. She is not interested in fashion.

You are said to be a loyal friend. Who are some of your best friends?

Friendships are very important in the best and worst moments of life. I feel like our friendships and our families are the important things in life. More than love.

What are your values?

Honesty, sincerity, reliability, hard work, and a spirit of friendship.

What kind of advice would you give to a young person who wants to break into the world of fashion?

He needs to know what he wants to do. He needs to believe in himself. It is hard work. He needs to know how to see opportunity, be flexible, and be ready to adapt to change. And never fear believing in himself. To have faith.

New York
May 11, 1997

~

SOPHIA LOREN

ACTRESS

"You do not become a star, you are born a star. A star is born with that indefinable extra something. Actually, truth be told, I do not know if I really am a big star. And in fact that is not the most important thing for me. What counts in life is to bring about more of your own dreams. In such a way that your life becomes like a fairy tale. This is what has happened to me, it is just like that."

Sophia Loren is sitting on one of the velvet sofas in her house, located just a few steps from the old town of Geneva. Behind her is a big, black grand piano; there is modern art on the walls; there are tapestries. The furnishings are French. In one corner you can see the framed parchment of her official appointment as an Officer of the Legion of Honor, an Oscar nomination, some book covers. She is smiling, tanned, lean.

She is wearing a beige skirt and an olive-colored Armani blouse. The contents of this library room tell of other chapters in the life of a star: in pride of place are the Oscar she won, her six David di Donatello Awards (the Italian equivalent to the Oscars), her Golden Bear from the Berlin International Film Festival, her Telegatto (comparable to the American People's Choice Award). And there are more: German awards, Japanese, her Golden Globe.

Sophia, what makes the most impression on you, now that you are reaching the sixty year milestone?

There is so much importance given to this birthday. But I do not feel at all in my sixties. I did not even realize it was happening; until the other day I just did not remember.

How have you stayed so beautiful and young looking?

It's my nature, it's my makeup. It's necessary to have an energy that carries you forward. You need the will to live, to have a great curiosity. To look for the best in life, to find new interests.

When did you realize that your life would become an extraordinary life?

Well, I believe that rewards in life are deserved. Every reward is the fruit of discipline, of dedication and of sacrifices. And of stubbornness.

For example?

An Italian doctor told me that I could not have children: I always disagreed and in the end he finally was proved wrong. I always disagreed.

What quality has most assisted your good fortune?

Perseverance.

And in your work?

Luck, you need to catch the moment. Otherwise the opportunity fades.

Have you lost many opportunities? What are the most important milestones in your career?

Well, meeting with my husband Carlo Ponti. And then also meeting De Sica. Carlo and De Sica have made some really fantastic projects for me. And then Joe Levine, the American producer, played an important role; he distributed the films in America with great fanfare. This had never happened before for Italian films in the U.S. Besides all this, I was able to get the Oscar for *Two Women* [*La ciociara*, 1960], and this was the first Italian-language film to get the award. Then the following year I was nominated for *Marriage Italian Style* [*Matrimonio all'italiana*, directed by De Sica, 1964], and then two years ago I won an Oscar for my career.

What does winning an Oscar mean to you?

It is the most important event in the career of an actor, an extraordinary moment, beautiful. Some people live their whole life just to win an Oscar.

And what is the most important thing in your life?

Well it is being with my mother, my sister, my sister's children. In other words, my family is the most important thing for me.

And who are the most important actors you have worked with?

Mastroianni, he is a completely unforgettable colleague. Even in the last movie, *Pret-à-Porter* [1994], which we just shot with Robert Altman in Paris, it was completely extraordinary meeting up with him again. The two of us, we're so good together we can do anything. Ours is always a magical encounter.

YOU DO NOT BECOME A STAR. YOU ARE BORN A STAR. A STAR IS BORN WITH THAT INDEFINABLE EXTRA SOMETHING.

But who else have you loved to work with? Who would you say? And what do you remember about Marlon Brando?

I was expecting a catastrophe when they told me that I was cast with him. Everyone told me it would be a disaster. But it did not turn out that way. Even though he was grumpy and very shy.

And what about Charlie Chaplin?

Working for him made little impression on me. Strangely, for the first ten days he only ever looked at me through the camera. It was as if he was intimidated by making a movie with me. Imagine how I felt, as I was intimidated by him. I remember him as a very kind man, always full of smiles, with nice hands. His wife was always on the set, he loved her in a crazy way.

And Cary Grant, what do you recollect about him?

He was fascinating, and then he fell in love with me.

And you were also in love with him?

I confess that I had a big "penchant" for him. Yes, there was something special between us.

Did you often fall in love on set?

Maybe little infatuations, but falling in love is quite another thing. Perhaps in life you fall in love only once.

And which of your directors do you remember in particular?

Ettore Scola, Lina Wertmüller, who I adore. My favorite, however, and for the record the one I most remember, was Alessandro Blasetti, who discovered the pair Loren-Mastroianni in *Too Bad She's Bad* [*Peccato che sia una canaglia*,1954].

But Sophia, you have lived abroad for years, do you still feel yourself to be a Neapolitan?

I exist only because inside of me, and above all else, I am only a Neapolitan. Naples exists inside of me, and always will. Fortunately for me there is this treasure that I have inside of me and, when I need it, then I pull it out. When we want to say important things among ourselves and the rest of the family, we still speak Neapolitan.

Another Neapolitan with a rising career is your niece, Alessandra Mussolini. What do think about her?

Alessandra is the daughter of my sister, Elizabeth. Everyone can take their own road in life as they want, I do not make judgements. But I do see that Alessandra carries herself well, and with dignity, because she is an intelligent woman, a witty woman with a sense of humor. And may God bless her and protect her!

Do you like fashion?

Yes, I like it. But only if it corresponds to and suits today's way of life, and in this respect Armani has realized that fashion needs to be fast and convenient and he has chosen wonderful colors, colors that really did not exist before.

How do you get on with your children?

They are talented young people who respect their parents and have good moral principles. I have to say that they have turned out very well.

Have you changed over the years?

I have gained experience and matured, but my principles, my way of seeing things is still the same.

What are the commanding principles for you?

Honesty. Be honest about what you can get. To make a sacrifice and to get what you want you need to be very certain. In other words: always think about your objective, have a clear goal, and commit to it from the heart. You will get nowhere with words. Believe me, it is actions that count.

Do you have film projects on the go?

Yes, in America and one in Europe. But, for now, nothing concrete.

Is the cinema your number-one priority?

It is something that is very important to me. I would like to act for one hundred and fifty years. However, the children are my first priority. I want to be near them, to try to help them. For sure, I do not want to be too much of an imposition, and I help them if they ask me. Then there are many things I would still like to do, because maturity has improved me and there are many things in life that I had not understood before: many small nuances of life that make me understand I have a lot more to give.

Are you a jealous woman?

Fortunately I have not needed to be. I find that jealousy is a miserable feeling. It means you aspire to something that you cannot have. Even in love, it is better to leave, better not to waste time.

What do you think of divorce?

I think that it is better to divorce than to argue in front of the children.

And your view on abortion?

Having had several miscarriages it is not easy for me to talk about. I do see however, that, in certain dramatic or very special situations, abortion is indispensable.

So you do not agree with the Pope?

I find this Pope to be extraordinary: he is a pilgrim, he goes everywhere, he is interested in everyone.

Are you religious?

Yes, but not practicing.

How do you see Italy to be?

There is a great future, Italians are very creative. They are unique in the world. Italy, I'm sure, will find its resources and will be back on form at the appropriate time. I say this with anger. Things do not go so well. Let's promote Italy and be optimistic. Italy deserves it and is worth it.

What will you do now?

I will celebrate my birthday with my sister. Then I will go to Paris.

What is your favorite place?

This is now my city. I live in Geneva because my children were born here. It is where our family home is; it is the place where we find ourselves.

Geneva

September 3, 1994

~

PETER MARINO

ARCHITECT

Architect Peter Marino has one golden rule: never work with lawyers. Understandable when you've collaborated instead with the likes of Andy Warhol. One should never mention personal friendships in writing an interview, but Peter Marino is a special case as, with Andy Warhol, I was one of his first clients in New York in 1975. Peter was twenty-five years old, just out of Cornell University and had short hair, a proper suit, a white shirt with a bow tie—not how most people know him today. He had a little office, and he went around town with a huge bag full of drawings, pictures, and samples of materials, tiles, carpets.

I chose him to help not only because he was considered good, but also because he was asking very little money, and as I was also twenty-five, I had almost none. Peter was very precise in his taste, very patient, and listened carefully to what we really wanted. Then—because I really had no money—I went to the Salvation Army to buy a couch and an armchair. We did one apartment in the Upper East Side together and then a little Victorian house in the country in Alpine, New Jersey.

Thirty-eight years have passed since and Peter is still working in the Architects & Designers building at 150 East 58th Street in New York, but he now has three floors that look like a museum. Everywhere there are paintings by Kiefer, Richter, Warhol, and Clemente, mixed with antique Asian sculpture and bronzes (Peter is one of the most important bronze sculpture collectors). This is not even the largest part of his collection: that is in his apartment on 57th Street. He is proud of his new look: a sort of antique Roman leather chest fitting, large leather bracelets, leather trousers, motorcycle boots, silver rings and a silver chain with little knives hanging, from it. He has a very well-trimmed beard, and his hair is shaven into a Mohawk. I ask Peter about art, style, France, mediocrity—and motorcycles.

The salon in Peter's apartment has very high ceilings because he took two floors, so it looks like a classical temple, although with Empire or *retour d'Égypte* furniture

mixed with German pieces. On the walls hang Warhols of Vesuvius and Pompeian wall paintings. Everywhere there are bronze sculptures from Giambologna onwards, and around the dining table paintings by de Kooning. Below are some choice excerpts from our interview. Peter took to rebelling early, he tells me.

REBEL REBEL

I saw my first show of de Kooning when I was still in school; my teacher was against it, but I liked it. At first I followed my teacher's point of view, but in the back of my mind I thought that my teacher was wrong. In 1990 I bought some de Kooning at a very reasonable price and I think I was right. [De Kooning's record is $137.5 million in a private sale.]

In the sixites and seventies there was so much distraction around, but it was a very important cultural moment, and students felt it all over the world, and it was time to change. Before we were not very much into rebellion. I always hated to be banal. What is important is to be honest with yourself. I need to see things clearly. I love everything to be clear. Lies do not work. I don't have the energy and I need it all for my creation.

ON COLLECTING

Andy Warhol made me understand that good art defines the entire society in which it was created. If you look at a Vermeer you know everything about Dutch society of that time. If you look at an Elvis Presley by Warhol on a silver screen, you know everything about American celebrity mass production.

The reason why I look at artists when I do a new building is because they are outside of society and they are futurists. Contemporary architects are not as fast as artists and fashion people.

I have more than ten Kiefers. They are perfect for my house in Aspen. From the large windows I see the landscape of the Rocky Mountains, and inside, against the walls, the Kiefer paintings match perfectly with the landscape. I have so many because of the design of the home, and they are tough enough to challenge the mountains!

I still draw: on white paper, eight-and-a-half inches by twelve inches, with a black pen—always the same for thirty-two years. I like the lines.

ON HIS STYLE

You would recognize a Peter Marino building because of its modern architecture, with the use of very elegant and beautiful materials. I use a lot of natural light and space. I stay away from orange, which I find vulgar—and violet. I like all the rest.

I like to look at the Italian architects of the early Renaissance, like Alberti and Brunelleschi, who were also artists. Or Carlo Scarpa, who was a medical student. But I should say that my work comes from the fact that I was a painter.

ON BEING GLOBAL

Many of my clients are from foreign countries and I learned a lot traveling, visiting them, and especially working in so many different places, and with so many different types of people. I spend fifty percent of my time between Asia, California, the Middle East, and Europe, but I only travel for work. I work in so many different countries, but my base is New York.

ON MEDIOCRITY

I only like very high and very low. I hate the middle and often I reject clients for mediocre projects. I like visual people, and that is why we have one rule: We never, ever work for lawyers. They are only interested in words; they cannot see things.

ON FRANCE

I like the way the French discuss things: Every person has an opinion on everything. Americans in general are horrified and they think that French people are mean. I find it refreshing that French people tell you things to your face.

ON MOTORBIKES

I have seven, one for everyday—a KTM—and in the country I have Harleys. For me, riding my motorcycle is a way of meditation, a way of feeling free from my work and daily stress. I especially like to ride in the summer with some friends.

ON CLOTHES

My daughter suggested to me that for next Halloween I should wear a suit—because nobody will recognize me!

New York

2013

Originally published in *Spear's Magazine*, issue 34

~

WHAT IS IMPORTANT IS TO BE HONEST WITH YOURSELF.

I need to see things clearly.

• I LOVE EVERYTHING TO BE CLEAR.

Lies do not work.

I DON'T HAVE THE ENERGY AND I NEED IT ALL FOR MY CREATION.

MARCELLO MASTROIANNI

ACTOR

I can say that Marcello Mastroianni was a friend. We used to see each other in Dr. Severini's apartment in Rome. He was our doctor and the doctor of Alberto Moravia and Gian Maria Volontè, among others. We met for Sunday night dinner and were all very relaxed and friendly.

I remember once being in Cinecittà, at the press conference for Federico Fellini's new film *Ginger and Fred* [1986]. Marcello and Giulietta Masina were the two protagonists. I was going to write a profile of Fellini for American *Vogue*. At a certain point one of Fellini's assistants said to me, "Mr. Fellini would like you to ask Mastroianni a question." I asked him, "On Friday you finished a film in Naples with Jack Lemmon [*Machheroni* (*Macaroni*), 1985]. The director was Ettore Scola. How can you start being Fred in this new film by Fellini on Monday, without a pause?" He answered, "That's how it is for a bank clerk. He closes on Friday and opens again on Monday." That was Marcello.

In Paris I once asked him if he wanted to be interviewed for *La Stampa*. He said, "Not now please, we have time." One morning a few months later, it was around eight o'clock, the phone rings. "It's Marcello. Do you want to join me for coffee in a café in boulevard Saint-Germain?" Mastroianni is in Paris to make a film, written and directed by Agnès Varda, about one hundred years of cinema, *Les cent et une nuits de Simon Cinéma* [*One Hundred and One Nights*, 1995].

It is June 15, 1994. Mastroianni is reading the Italian newspapers in the café when I arrive. He is dressed in a creased raincoat and a dark-blue shirt. Of course he is smoking one of his endless cigarettes, only nowadays they are filter slims: he was obliged to give up his much-loved Esportazioni. After a while he asked me, "Do you still want to do an interview? Let's do it." I had nothing. I asked the waiter if he could find me some paper. He gave me his little notebook for writing his orders, and he gave me his biro pen. Then we started the interview. I did not think that it would be the last one.

I was working in a movie with Robert Altman and now I have started a film with Agnès Varda: it's a tribute to cinema on its centenary. I am acting with Depardieu, Piccoli . . . .

Marcello, were you acting with Sophia Loren in Altman's film?

Yes, and it's so much fun working with Sophia. We are really good friends. We have made thirteen films together. In this film she eats all of the other actresses; she plays a very powerful character.

Will you spend the summer in Paris?

That depends on the movie business and what's going on.

Have you been following Italian politics?

A bit, but not with any great seriousness.

Does Silvio Berlusconi's victory surprise you?

The left surprises me, he surprises me, they all surprise me, but I am really not that interested. In France they have been talking negatively about Italy and neofascistic ministers. Maybe the fact is that I am getting old. Perhaps it's old age that makes me so skeptical.

Do you believe that there is a danger of fascism in Italy?

There are a few signs, but no need to give them too much importance. Of course, if that did turn out to be the case I would be very concerned.

You find it boring?

I am much more interested in my work. More than ever before. At my age one has less distractions. Work is what makes me feel on the ball.

How old are you?

I will be seventy this September.

How does that make you feel?

I don't think I'll live to be a hundred and twenty. Of course everyone would like to live that long, but it isn't possible.

Were you in shock when Giulietta Masina and Federico Fellini died?

Of course, it's a shock when the people you love so much, especially when they are so hugely talented, disappear out of sight.

Do you find death unsettling?

I love being alive. I enjoy seeing how things turn out in the end. I want to be around to see things, as a spectator. I am not very streetwise, perhaps that's my limitation. I have my own view on things and I've never wanted to upset other people or be upset by them. My character is Mediterranean, I take life one day at a time; I know that's sometimes not so good.

Are you a cheerful person?

I am extremely grateful for a life that has dealt so generously with me. I have had good luck, loves, success, money. . . .

What will you do with your money?

Let me think about that.

Will you leave it to your heirs? So that they can live in luxury?

I am generous and I was never shrewd enough to be really well paid.

But how much do you make for a film?

I could make more, but I'm not complaining. It's my good luck that the Lumière brothers invented the cinema.

Making movies is actually great fun?

That's the irony of it.

Do you worry about being out of work?

I make good use of my time when I am not working. But if I was not working at all, then I really would have a very big hole in my life. My profession is a hugely privileged one. At the end of the day, a movie is about fifty people meeting up to share a meal and a joke. It's a lot better than going to work in an office.

Do actors really kiss each other on the set? Do they fall in love?

Of course it can happen that a love affair starts between colleagues who think highly of each other, but it's a rarity. I have made one hundred and fifty movies; I'd be in prison if I fell in love every time. We pretend to be in love, but that's not unpleasant. It's better to kiss a beautiful woman than dig the soil. Oh yes!

What do you remember most about Fellini?

For us actors, it was his brilliant imagination. Making a movie with Fellini was a nonstop party and as a director he was really easy: Great fun, you said it yourself.

Every time you make a movie, however, it's always a treat, it is just so much fun. Sometimes I read interviews with American actors who talk about their "suffering." What are they talking about? On account of what does one suffer? People love you, they ask you for your autograph, they pay you to travel on wonderful journeys. Where's the torment in that? Let's leave torment to the poets, to the musicians. An actor is a fool, a pet, but has his own distinct characteristics, is not forgettable; you can't be a half-wit and be any good.

Which actors did you take as your models?

In my youth I loved to watch Gary Cooper and Clark Gable. I don't really have such strong attractions any longer. After the war Marlon Brando made a big impression on me: good looking, magnetic, a gigantic personality, great class. And also Montgomery Clift. I never really much liked James Dean. In Italy I have great admiration for Gassman, he always gives so much and is endearing; but then he is a very unusual actor, well educated and funny. He is also lionhearted. How many times have I said: make Gassman president of the Republic! I was also a fan of Tognazzi, and Volontè. I saw the pre-war actors as my heroes.

But then you became a hero?

So the Americans used to say.

Are you always traveling...?

I enjoy being out and about. The film industry allows you to travel first-class, to be one of the beautiful people, to be greeted with a warm welcome all over the world. Given the choice between Rome and Viterbo, I would rather go to Viterbo.

But you really like your freedom?

As much as my commitments allow. One postpones everything and says, "Soon I'm going to shoot a film, then we will see."

Are you a good father? Are you very much involved with your daughters?

I am a big pain in the ass! A disciplinarian, blinkered.

Your daughter Chiara has become an actress. Are you happy about that?

Yes, but with misgivings if she doesn't succeed in carving out a career. If you had to choose between being an actor who can't make a career and being a normal worker, I would prefer to be a worker. If you're not in demand, you're condemned to stay at home and wait for the phone to ring and sometimes it just does not happen; that's demeaning. Better to have a serious job.

Are you skeptical about Italians?

They are skilled, enterprising, courageous; it's a pity that the political class does not know how to respect the many people who have worked for their money and who pay their taxes. I don't have much love for politicians, nor can I stand fashion. Why do the newspapers give so much importance to fashion, when everyone has already made up their minds to wear blue jeans?

And what about the movie industry?

I would say this: It's such a shame that we have never had our own Armani, Benetton, Ferrè, Versace. Italian producers can't see beyond their own noses; they make it up as they go along. Our rulers are even worse. After the war, they were complaining to De Sica and Rossellini: We do not approve of your films being shown abroad. "Dirty clothes are washed at home," that's what they said. Nobody really understood the fact that the movie industry could be the most important ambassador for Italy.

And what about television?

I only like factual documentaries or programs about historical events. What a lot of nonsense: and what a bore! The presenters really annoy me, all dressed up in their jewelry and their fashionable clothes. But who pays for all these clothes they wear? It would be better to wear a less over-the-top, pretty dress.

So, in conclusion, do you mind being nearly seventy years old?

I am happy to be reaching seventy, but in truth I could not care less. So there you are: that's how it is.

Paris
June 15, 1994

~

I LOVE BEING **alive**.

I ENJOY SEEING HOW THINGS **turn out** IN THE END.

I WANT TO BE AROUND TO **see** THINGS.

AS A SPECTATOR.

SUZY MENKES

JOURNALIST

Suzy Menkes is a leading British journalist and fashion critic. Formerly the fashion editor for the *International Herald Tribune*, she is now International Fashion Editor for nineteen editions of *Vogue* online.

Why did you become a fashion editor? Is fashion your lifelong passion?

There's a difference between having a lifelong passion for fashion and being a fashion editor. I was always interested in fashion, according to my mother I started my passion for fashion at the age of five when I did little drawings which of course she kept until the end of her days. I was also always interested in writing. When I went to Newnham College Cambridge to read English literature and history I joined *Varsity*, the Cambridge university newspaper, on my first morning. In my third year I became Editor of *Varsity*. I was the first female editor, making history. Nowadays it's not something a smart woman from a university would want to do particularly, to edit and write a woman's page in a newspaper, but when I graduated I joined the *Times of London* specifically to be a contributor to the woman's page. This was something incredibly new, because we're talking about 1967.

Do you consider yourself a journalist, or a critic, or a writer?

A journalist first. I consider that part of all journalism is a kind of curiosity, to find out the why and the how and the where. I put my criticism in the context of what I think is around, whether I see a reflection of what's happening in society, whether I see in the designer a change in her or his aesthetic or whether it seems a bit stuck in the rut.

You were the fashion voice for the *International Herald Tribune* for twenty years. Why did you move to *Vogue*?

I changed before they threw me out when the *Herald Tribune* became *The New York Times*. Luckily Jonathan Newhouse offered me a fabulous job at *Vogue*.

Do you really think that they would have thrown you out?

Yes, I do more or less. I think they never really understood the *Herald Tribune* or what it stood for in a lot of people's minds. Right from the beginning I always loved the paper, because I felt it did give a kind of pan-European view of the world; and not just Europe, the world in general. *The New York Times* is a fantastically strong paper and it has wonderful stories in it, but it has now become about America. I don't think it has much of an international perspective.

Has journalism changed in the last ten years?

Yes, the world changed. The point about writing is that words are words. They were scratched on Greek marble or in stone, and then they were written with a quill pen in ink on beautiful paper, and then they were turned out in rough printing. Now they're online in your telephone, but words are still words and I still care about what I read. And I hope that other people care about what I write.

Is impartiality your trademark?

I try to be impartial, and I've always tried to tell my assistants that it's not good because you like it. You like it because it's good. None of Coco Chanel's work has ever worked for me personally, but that doesn't mean I think less of what Coco Chanel invented and what Karl Lagerfeld has continued with. With me it's not personal. I don't have to want to wear the clothes personally to give somebody a good review, but the opposite really.

Did you meet Coco Chanel?

I have a shameful story about myself and Coco Chanel. When I was fairly junior I saw what was one of her last collections. There we were in the rue Cambon, and she sat on the stairway, and she was a very wrinkled up old lady and I thought the clothes were unbelievably boring and total grandmother stuff.

Did she impress you as a person?

What she actually achieved is extraordinary. She foresaw so much of women's lives, how they wanted to be, and to be more like men and dress more like men.

What do you expect from designers?

I think that what designers do, or are supposed to be doing, is making clothes. It's very interesting this thing that Maria Grazia Chiuri did for Dior, taking the message about "we all should be feminists" and putting it on a T-shirt selling at five hundred Euros or whatever. I admire her, I think she's a very energetic woman, a modern woman. She's married, she has children, she had a great success at Valentino, and she's building her way at Dior. But I don't want to go out wearing a T-shirt saying "we're all feminists." You won't see me wearing it.

How do you feel about the famous brands that have an endless succession of new designers?

Your question gets to the heart of what is happening in fashion now, and in the world. I think this idea of next . . . next . . . next . . . is very confusing in terms of established brands. There seems to be an idea that nobody can keep an established brand alive for much longer than three or four years. I'm not so sure that it's going to work in the long term.

Why did Gucci suddenly become such a huge success?

When they started, Gucci was making handbags, they weren't making clothes. Tom Ford made Gucci into this sex pot, extraordinary, kind of look, a sort of anti-Armani look. You've got Alessandro Michele there now, who was in the company all those years before he was allowed to break out. He went to François-Henri Pinault and said, "Give me a chance. I believe I can do something. I've worked here a long time." And he was given a chance.

What will happen next in fashion?

I don't know. If I knew I wouldn't be a simple journalist, I would be making my fortune by setting up a new fashion world. The huge groups, like Kering which owns Gucci—and Bernard Arnault's many companies—have decided to have a fashion system. I don't know whether it is the best thing for fashion.

What is this fashion system?

Finding a new designer—Dior's getting a bit boring, let's get John Galliano—or John Galliano is out let's get Raf Simons—and then he's out—so let's get Maria Grazia. I'm not meaning to be dismissive, because these people are very good designers, but the idea of continuity that you have had with Chanel, having one person in Karl Lagerfeld, is clearly not in these brands.

Is there anything new in fashion?

For the first time since the Victorian era bustles are back. You know what I mean by a bustle, things that go under skirts to shape them? Suddenly the back of the woman has become tremendously exciting—the Dernier Cri as they used to say—with Kim Kardashian going around. I'm somebody who from the age of about fourteen thought that I had much too large a behind and spent my whole life trying to hide it. And now you go out in the street and you see that Kim Kardashian look is everywhere. Women all get stretch trousers and they're hoping that they will have a large bottom in order to show it off to the world. It's a genuine change of fashion.

What does it mean?

This isn't some fashion designer who invented it. This is something that's actually happened and I think it goes with quite a big change. It's really the whole sense of vulgarity, that of course is not just about looking vulgar and waving behind your derriere in fashion, it all goes much deeper than that. You got the Kim Kardashian look first and all that, a general sense of vulgarity—and then you get Donald Trump. In this case, as is so often with fashion, the fashion comes first, except nobody realizes. People in the fashion world are very snooty, they look down and say: "Kim Kardashian has to be the worst dressed person you ever had going down the red carpet." But there is a whole mass of women now who for their own reasons want to copy that.

Is this vulgarity something that didn't exist before?

I'm not saying it didn't exist before, but people didn't want to display it before.

Has the concept of beauty and elegance changed?

One of the things that I do for Conde Nast are international conferences on luxury, which I also did for *The New York Times*, the *International Herald Tribune*. I have been doing conferences on luxury for seventeen years. I wanted to do a conference on mindful luxury and last month we went to Oman. I discovered somebody on Instagram, Huda she's called, and Huda Beauty is the absolute person on Instagram. I believe she now has eighteen million followers, probably since yesterday it's nineteen. She does beauty, and for as long as I can remember beauty has always been considered fairly unobtainable. If you are a beauty you are blessed. All that the houses selling makeup can do is to help you try and achieve a glimpse of this perfection which you see in the pictures. Huda and Huda Beauty take exactly the opposite view, that if you want to make your eyes look bigger, here's how to do it. If you want to make your nose look smaller, here's how to do it. Showing you how to do it. That's an example to me of how things change and I'm sure if you are the head of whichever company it is you never saw it coming.

Is it Paris that delivers international fame?

To make their presence felt almost everybody comes to Paris to show. You have to make it in Paris. This was the case, and I think it still is to a large extent. If people like Rei Kawakubo of Comme Des Garcons and Raf Simmons had not come to Paris to show they would have been local heroes. But there again, now it's different, because using social media you can make yourself known by pushing yourself on the Internet.

Is there still a place for eccentric artisan designers like Gaultier or Lacroix or Alaïa or Westwood?

I hope there is always going to be space for the poets and artists of fashion. I mean God help us if there's not space because it's only going to be H&M that produces fashion. You've got to have somebody who starts something. It's so easy to criticize people who do super cheap clothes, but Uniqlo, for example, make a lot of good basic clothes that are very well styled and very well thought of. I certainly remember having an experience with Alber Elbaz, who I am a great admirer of, and he, like so many other designers, worked with H&M to do a collection. And I remember my disappointment when I picked up one of the dresses that they had done—in obviously not pure silk or what Alber would have used for Lanvin, but you know it had nothing of the Lanvin, it was not the same thing. But it's too easy in fashion to say everything cheap is rubbish and everything expensive is good. I believe more than anything else that you find a lot of really sharply dressed people are mixing the two.

Who still makes artisan craft?

Italians for a start, and I find it interesting in India, where they turn out clothes very cheaply for the mass market but also the Indian Government has decided that craft is one of their strengths. They're very much encouraging people to take up craft, embroidery for example. Go and ask Alessandro e from Gucci. He will tell you, he will be so enthusiastic about the embroideries that he has done in India. When I made my last trip to India I went and saw a studio where they're making things by hand. Very beautiful, and they make for a lot of the big houses.

Is it a good thing that Italy invented pret-à-porter and industrialized fashion?

I think it's good, the question is how is it then used. The problem for Italy, as for any country, is that if you're only industrializing it then you can always find somebody cheaper somewhere else.

What is chic today?

I am not sure the word still exists, does it? It would be a good test to go out in the streets of London and find out if anybody under the age of twenty-four knows what the word chic means. Fashion is very fluid now, it really is about choice. There are people who put themselves together in a very elegant way, just not with the obvious signs and symbols that were used even twenty years ago. I think so many people wear jeans because however wealthy you are, you put on a pair of jeans and then you put on a fabulous jacket and then you are considered to be stylish and you'll also feel comfortable. So I think that's the change for women. Of course it's men as well, because sportswear hardly existed when I started writing about fashion, sportswear was for the tennis court and for whoever played football.

What about your clothes?

I wear a lot of Issey Miyake because it doesn't require urgent attention all the time.

I really feel strongly my clothes have to work as hard as I do. I do not w complicated. I don't want anything that's going to crease and look a m I have even got off the plane. I don't want anything that's going to require ar tion in the hotel because they're not as fast as me, and if I ask them to press some ing I'll have gone by the time it's done. That's the way the world has changed, the speed of everything.

What is an example of a landmark in your professional life?

Often those moments are about two people facing off each other. For example, Rei Kawakubo with the torn things with holes in, we called it the Gruyère Cheese sweater; and Azzedine Alaïa at the same time. Rei Kawakubo with these very much plain flat clothes; and Azzedine Alaïa with these amazing curves. Two absolute opposites.

Who gave you emotions?

Giorgio Armani with the real way that he got tailored clothes, mannish clothes that made them look feminine. Very powerful. Tom Ford at Gucci, when he did all those super-sexy things. Christian Lacroix when he did his amazingly imaginative froufrou decorated kind of clothes in such exquisite taste. Almost anybody who has made it, there's been a moment when there's been a fantastic show.

Are you still expecting emotion when you go to a show?

I am. I shall always be. You are looking for talent, but it's the emotion and the feeling that this is something new. I don't know that new is the right word. It's the exceptional, the something rare, the extraordinary. On a wall in my office in my home is a picture of people who cry at fashion shows. Hamish Bowles is one of them, and I am one of them.

When did you last feel that?

The last time I felt that was with a French designer who goes under the name of Jacquemus. There's something so fresh and so different about his work. You feel: "Yes! This is somebody interesting."

Is yours an endless passion?

Yes, it's an endless passion.

London

May 17, 2017

~

JOHN MICKLETHWAIT

EDITOR

The editor in chief of Bloomberg News has an extraordinary platform of observation to what's happening in the world.

What do you at Bloomberg think about the new President Trump's aggressive attitude towards journalists and the press? Do you think the freedom of the press is in danger?

I think the freedom of the press is enshrined in American life and we should measure the new president in the same way as we did the last one: by what he says and does. If he produces "alternative facts" that are not actually facts, then we should point that out. If his actions threaten the liberty of the press, then we should point that out, too, and fight back, but he has not done so yet; being rude to journalists does not count. Donald Trump has caused problems for what might be called the upmarket press right from the beginning: in the primaries he kept on saying outrageous things that we had to report and thus hoovered up the airtime from his opponents. The interesting thing is that these gaffes and insults, and the accompanying negative coverage, did not destroy him in the same way that they might have done other candidates. Indeed, as a candidate, Trump was like a fish that can survive at greater depths than other creatures. (If, say, Jeb Bush had been rude about the Pope, we would now be saying, "If only Jeb had not called the Pope 'disgraceful,' he might be president." For Trump, it was a two day storm, before he was rude about someone else—and the caravan moved on). Voters judged him by different standards to the mainstream media: to borrow that much used phrase, newspapers took him literally but not seriously, while many voters took him seriously but not literally. Despite his locker-room talk, a majority of white women voted for him. So Trump the candidate has rewritten some of the rules, but now he is president—and I think voters will increasingly hold him accountable for what he says and does. From the press's point of view, we should not treat him as different, or set special standards for dealing with him. He is the duly elected leader of the world's most important democracy. We should just get on with reporting what he does, and point out when he says things that are untrue and when he does things well.

You recently had the opportunity to interview Vladimir Putin. What is your impression of the man?

Putin is a poor economic manager but a cunning politician. His stewardship of Russia's economy has been weak, cronyism has been rampant, and he has failed to move away from oil. The resulting economic weakness will always put a limit on his other ambitions. Abroad, though, he has combined nationalist prejudice with opportunism. It is hard to detect a strategy, just a consistent desire to make Russia great again and a willingness to seize opportunities to achieve that, whether it be Barack Obama's retreats in Syria or Donald Trump's hero-worship. He has the advantage of having few scruples—whether it be in Syria, the Ukraine, or just telling the truth. On television, Putin is courteously combative; in private, he is more aggressive and a relentless observer of people's strengths and weaknesses. The level of fear he generates around him—the anxious members of his retinue—is both impressive and troubling: who tells him the truth? In the long term, he faces the problem of a peaceful exit: too many people around him have stolen too much, so he has to hang onto power.

Do you think that there will be a strong alliance between Donald Trump and Vladimir Putin, and do you think that this is going to destabilize the world and ultimately destroy the European Union?

I worry about the future of NATO in the light of some of the things Trump has said. But I also suspect that the Putin-Trump bromance has reached its peak. For Putin, to have reached a position where he is a force in U.S. politics and where the Russian bear holds the fate of parts of the Middle East in its paw is a remarkable achievement, but probably an unsustainable one. Now he has a problem: to keep his nationalist supporters at home sweet, he has to keep on jabbing at America; but in so doing he risks alienating his new friend, Donald Trump. As a candidate, Trump liked pointing to Putin's successes against America as a way of illustrating Obama's weaknesses. But now he is president—and he will not like to be seen to be weak. If an airliner is shot down, it will be Trump whom the world looks to; if Putin foments rebellion in Estonia, it will be harming a NATO member on Donald Trump's watch, which would enrage Republicans. Margaret Thatcher never cared much about the Falklands until Argentina invaded them.

Do you think that the news about Russian hacking and interference in the presidential elections could result in an impeachment if proven to be true?

I am not sure how it could result in impeachment unless there was some direct link to the Trump White House.

As a candidate, Trump liked pointing to Putin's successes against America as a way of illustrating Obama's weaknesses. But now he is president—and he will not like to be seen to be weak.

Under Barack Obama's presidency we perceived a recrudescence of the Cold War. Is this going to change with President Trump?

My instinct is that there will be an immediate thaw, followed by a gradual refreezing. Trump-Putin obviously starts from a warmer position than Putin-Obama, and there may be one or two deals to be done. But, as outlined above, I sense that the expansionary, anti-Western Russia that Putin believes in is always going to be in some conflict with the West.

Theresa May has chosen the so-called hard Brexit. Is England going to be a new middle man between Russia and the U.S. in its new adventure outside Europe?

I think Britain is never going to be a middleman between Russia and the U.S. London may be most oligarchs' second (or first) home; but diplomatic relations have been cold—and indeed bloodstained. France, perhaps under President Fillon, will look on the Kremlin more kindly. On Brexit, having been a "remainer," I would prefer a soft Brexit that keeps as many links with Europe as possible. I am deeply skeptical about Theresa May's new strategy to make Britain into a Singapore on the Thames; too many of her instincts are to intervene and Britain's forte is services, which are much easier to export to your neighbors than to, say, Australia. But I have to admit that Trump's willingness to do a trade deal with Britain gives a little more life to the idea of Britain being a free-trading entrepôt. But it is not just to do with tariffs and import quotas. In the long term I worry about Britain's soft power. People may mock the Eurotrash, but London is a far more cosmopolitan city than it once was—and it has been a talent magnet for the whole of Europe. For the past fifteen years, if you went for dinner in Milan, Madrid, or Malmö, the one thing most people have had in common is that their children have wanted to come to London; now that is in doubt. Vienna used to be Europe's entrepôt once; now it is a much narrower place.

Do you think that President Trump is going to create dangerous tensions in the U.S.-China relationship?

Yes, this, to me at least, is the most dangerous part of Donald Trump's presidency. There are plenty of people (including in China) who insist he is a pragmatist who believes in nothing—and that we should discount his talk on China. Normally these optimists point out that he is just a real estate guy who begins every negotiation by asking for an outrageous price and then settles for something reasonable. And the optimists argue that the Chinese are pragmatists, too; they will make a few compromises and trade will continue. I hope that is the case—and I think the probabilities point in that direction. The Chinese showed restraint when Trump spoke to Taiwan. But I have two nagging worries. First, to the extent that the new president does believe in anything, it has been America First: He has been skeptical of free trade for a long time (he opposed NAFTA) and the people he has appointed to trade posts are of a similar mind. Second, I am not sure that [Chinese President] Xi Jinping has as much room to compromise as the optimists or Trump assumes. This is a crucial year for Xi—we may well discover whether he wants to stay in power beyond the traditional ten years. From a domestic political viewpoint, he will not want to be seen kowtowing to foreign powers. My worry is that things unintentionally get out of hand: Trump makes an unreasonable demand (for instance over the currency), and Xi feels obliged to fire back. Again, I think the probability is that a deal will be struck: The two superpowers need each other. But history is littered with examples of nationalism trumping economic logic, especially when a new superpower is on the rise.

How do you think that the new U.S. Administration will handle the Middle East regional crisis? Is President Trump going to change attitudes vis-à-vis Syria, Turkey, Iran, Israel, Libya?

Trump has somewhat contradictory approaches to the Middle East: He wants to stay out of it while also obliterating ISIS. My guess is that, like Obama, he will end up being a form of grumpy policeman, albeit one with greater anger-management issues. He may be a little tougher on Iran and less tough on Israel, and he will look for some kind of deal with Russia over Syria. But I would expect his presidency to be reactive in the Middle East.

Donald Trump's election has created a deep fracture in America. Do you think that America will become a very different country?

Trump did not create the biggest fracture. America has been a fifty-fifty nation for some time, albeit one that has looked pretty conservative by the standards of other Western countries. So for the most part, he is a symptom of the problem, not its cause. What Trump has done is to recast the fracture—his coalition of voters included lots of working-class whites who voted for Obama as well as people who had not voted before.

Do you think that other powers, like Congress, the Senate, the Federal Reserve, will be able to limit the actual effects of Trump's Twitter mania and impulsive statements?

The genius of the American constitution is its balance of powers which restrains the ability of any one person or party to control everything. But it is hard to see how that would limit his ability to tweet—which is just another form of communication. There were previous debates about whether presidents should use TV and the radio. If it is useful, they use it. My guess is that Trump will keep tweeting. He had a chance to stop tweeting at the end of the campaign—and did not take it. But I also think his tweets will become gradually rarer and more boring—a little like other politicians. One reason is that his audience is now inured to their shock value. People already see them as examples of him mouthing off. Another reason is that he is now part of the legislative process: He may discover the virtue of silence.

Do you think as a consequence of all this there will be major changes in the world's economies?

There are some economies that look especially exposed to Donald Trump: Mexico would suffer enormously if goods can no longer cross the Rio Grande so freely. On the plus side, America's economy could be buoyed by deregulation, tax reform, and infrastructure spending. That explains why the stock markets have soared. The biggest worry is trade; see the China discussion above. The other worry is the budget deficit: America's biggest entitlement programs will begin to kick in, while the abolition of Obamacare could yet lead to an even more expensive situation.

Are we going to see new wars?

I hope not.

London
January 29, 2017

~

STAFFAN DE MISTURA

DIPLOMAT

Staffan de Mistura is the United Nations Special Envoy tasked with seeking a peaceful resolution to the conflict in Syria.

What is your job about?

My job is first to reduce the violence of the conflict in Syria that has produced two hundred and twenty thousand dead people and three point two million refugees. Second therefore is to try to increase assistance to these people. We are trying to find a basically political process, because everybody agrees at this stage that there is no military solution. Everybody agrees that there has to be a political solution, involving all Syrians and the regional and international countries which have had an interest and an involvement in the conflict. Officially my job is to reduce violence.

Is this idea not like a dream of utopia?

No. Maybe there is a different way to look at ending the conflict, because everything that has been tried has not worked.

But what is the situation?

Terribly tragic, because there are new factors that have come into the issue. One is ISIS, which has made the situation of the Syrian people even worse. And meanwhile the people of Syria, wherever I meet them, are exhausted. Eleven million are displaced. The economy went back by thirty years.

Is the Assad regime still in place?

Not one of the players in Syria at the moment, including Assad, can consider themselves stable, because the situation should currently worry everyone. However, since half of the population is still under his control, we cannot ignore that fact.

Are both sides against ISIS?

Everybody is concerned, in view of its violence, but they are also worried by the conflict between the opposition and the regime.

Officially
my job
is to
reduce
violence.

What are you doing in Aleppo and what does it mean?

First of all, I want to pay tribute to the first ones who raised concern about Aleppo. That was the Community of Sant'Egidio. It led to the very effective report by the international crisis group, indicating that if Aleppo falls it will be a tragedy for at least four hundred thousand people. We have to start somewhere in order to send a signal of hope. And to show that there can be some reduction of violence, which could facilitate a political process. We have to start somewhere in order to send a signal of hope. And to show that there can be some reduction of violence which could facilitate a political process.

What are you going to do for the people of Aleppo?

First thing is to find a way in which we can "freeze" the situation. These people have been under siege for two years. The city is very close to collapsing. If we do not do anything and the city collapses it could fall into the hands of ISIS, which is only twenty kilometers away, and that would be an even bigger tragedy.

And what is going on now?

Intense discussions with the Assad government, the opposition and the concerned countries. There is a lot of distrust between all parties, but the people of Syria have no time. As I said, they are exhausted.

What happens if it works?

If it does work in Aleppo, in a hurry, then we could replicate it in other places and meanwhile use that example in order to promote a national political process which should lead to the end of the conflict and a Syria which will hopefully be a country which can start reconstruction in line with what has been indicated in the Geneva conferences.

But that will not stop ISIS?

You are right, but ISIS cannot only be stopped by air campaigns. It needs to be stopped by the fact that ISIS takes advantage of the weakness and internal conflict of countries. It is like a political Ebola.

And what about Iraq?

Yes, if the country is in turmoil. If any community is excluded or marginalized, in particular the Sunni community, you will find a fertile ground for ISIS to enter and take over as it has done in some parts of Syria and Iraq. Therefore they need to stabilize these countries in order to be able to isolate and fight ISIS.

Is ISIS getting weaker?

That is a difficult question. They do find it more difficult to progress in their campaign. The example has been Kobane. They insisted, but they did not take over.

Is this experience of yours similar to the ones you had in Iraq or in Bosnia, Afghanistan and Somalia?

The answer is yes, but it is very different because this is probably the largest humanitarian crisis of this current century. Because there are so many players and so many countries involved and because this conflict has been going on for three and a half years and it is getting worse. Two highly dignified and respected mediators, Kofi Annan and Lakhdar Brahimi, have tried very hard to get a solution, but they could not find sufficient support in order to achieve that because the countries involved and the Security Council were divided.

Won't the oil crisis change things in the region?

The Syrian crisis is more complicated than simply to link it to the oil crisis.

What motivates you?

When I was seventeen I saw in Cyprus a child killed in front of me by a sniper, and that produced in me a level of healthy outrage that pushed me to choose a profession which could contribute to counter such horrors. Then there is the incredible dignity and courage of the many civilian victims which I have met in the nineteen conflicts where I have served as a UN envoy.

Do you have a real hope of peace for Syria?

Two answers. I am affected by a chronic disease called optimism, and therefore I have hope. Second, I can see in the eyes of the Syrian people that they are all asking for the end of this terrible conflict. No one has a strategy to win it militarily, and the risk is that the entity who could take advantage of this conflict could be ISIS. Therefore I believe that it would help all concerned countries and governments to realize that there is an urgent need to end this conflict through a political process and not through fighting.

Syria

December 18, 2014

~

ALBERTO MORAVIA

NOVELIST

Whenever I read Alberto Moravia's interviews, suddenly he comes back into my life as if he were still alive: Alberto's brief answers, his judgements about people, artists, ideas. He really was very unusual, special in his way of thinking. In his answers he was always unexpected and somehow naïve—somewhere between a child and a wizard. He adored cinema, and I know he was quite impressed by the fact that De Sica, Godard, Maselli, and Bertolucci had all made very important films out of his novels. He and Fellini had a mutual respect for each other's genius. They were not close friends, but Fellini took great account of what Alberto Moravia wrote about his films in the magazine *L' Espresso*, where he was the film critic. You can decide for yourself how original Moravia was from the acuity of his discernment in this short interview. I really wish he could still be with us!

How did it come about that nearly all your novels were made into movies?

Because in a way they come from the cinema, because actually they are theatrical, and then they return to their origin. My novels are almost all dramas dressed up as novels.

Of the films that have been made based on your books, which do you particularly remember?

A film directed by Vittorio De Sica with Sophia Loren, *Two Women* [La Ciociara, 1960]. Some movies made with important actresses, such as Gina Lollobrigida in *The Woman of Rome* [La Romana, 1954]; Catherine Spaak in *The Empty Canvas* [La Noia, 1963]; Brigitte Bardot in *Contempt* [Le Mépris, 1963]; Dominique Sanda and Stefania Sandrelli in *The Conformist* [Il Conformista, 1970], etc. And then I also had the best directors: Bertolucci for *The Conformist*; Godard for *Contempt*; De Sica for *Two Women*; Citto Maselli and Mauro Bolognini for *A Time of Indifference* [*Gli Indifferenti*, 1964], etc. Good directors make good movies, therefore I really cannot complain too much.

And do you know all these directors personally?

I know them, yes, some more than others. Bertolucci is the one who I know best, because he is also a friend. I only barely know De Sica, Godard a bit better.

But when they released *Contempt*, were you not also involved?

Of course, although my introduction to Brigitte Bardot and Godard was not very encouraging. I asked Brigitte Bardot, after witnessing all the hoo-ha that took place during the press conference for the film, if she was interested in doing an interview for *Candide*. She said, "Let's do it," but the interview never actually happened.

How was Brigitte Bardot?

Quite a bit different from how she looks in her photographs. Her body, yes, very pretty and graceful, her walk is most elegant. In real life though her face is like a Pekingese, more pug-like than you see on the screen. The movies sweeten such features. In her case that was quite difficult. I can't altogether believe that I ever had quite such a crush on Brigitte Bardot.

How was Claudia Cardinale?

I was asked to do an interview with Claudia Cardinale for *Esquire*. I agreed because I needed the money, but I was a bit uncomfortable about it: Doing an interview with a diva can be very annoying, especially if they turn on their star status, playing all those film star games with the journalist. I had the idea that I would turn this into a philosophical interview. To give consideration to what can be said about La Cardinale as a manifestation in space. I said to her, "I do not care who you are, nor what it is that you do in your life, nor that you are an actress, nor what you think of the movies. All I am interested in is your body." And so she told me what she thought of her legs, her breasts, her eyes, her hair, etc. The interview was a great success, and it went really well. I believe it was imitated all over the place. Anyway, then I wanted to do an interview with Bardot about her Marxism, given that she was a middle-class person, or so I thought. So okay, I am going to do this interview with her based on her ideas about capitalism. But she dodged the issue. I remember she said: "Je n'ai pas fait son premier film, je ferai son dernier." ["I did not make his first film, I will make his last."]

About who?

About Godard.

Do you think Godard is a genius?

Godard is a genius, yes, but when I say "genius" I do not mean a great artist. I do not even mean a great creator, I simply mean he is a genius and nothing else. In fact, what I just said is wrong, he is a creative man.

Fellini?

Fellini is a great artist.

While Godard is not?

Actually, he is a great artist as well, but he is more creative as a revolutionary than as an artist.

Bertolucci?

Bertolucci, he's another case again. You can sum it up like this, Godard revolutionized the cinema, at least he started a revolution that has gone on for quite some time. If you compare a Godard film with any other film, you see immediately that this is something quite different. There is a certain way of contextualizing, of framing the images . . .

Is Godard the Joyce of cinematography?

No, not really Joyce, no, I would not say Joyce.

His is a new kind of cinematographic storytelling?

There you have it, if anything, yes, more like Robbe-Grillet or a surrealist like Breton. Joyce is the super naturalist, naturalism inflated to the nth degree so as to break through naturalism. Joyce went beyond naturalism by sticking with naturalism.

But when it comes to surrealism, then it is Fellini, right?

No, Fellini is actually a bit of everything. Fellini is like Buñuel. There are two points of contact between Fellini and Buñuel. Fellini makes use of avant-garde experiences, Buñuel does, too. Buñuel has a strong Spanish foundation, into which he has integrated his own surrealistic experiences. But Buñuel's personality is bigger than what he does, he is not of any one school. It's the same for Fellini. Fellini is a man who has made use of a bit of everything. But he has his own personal style. . . . On the other hand, Godard is a real revolutionary in the way he uses his lens, how he looks at the human form; and I must say, to tell the truth, for me it is Godard, then Fellini, and next comes Buñuel, he is the third director that I love.

Bertolucci?

He has many points of similarity with Visconti. He is a cultured director, with a cultural sensibility. But then he's also a sensationalist, as the English say. He makes you feel a punch in the stomach, just like Visconti. *Bam!* He gives you a punch in the stomach, he makes you look at a boy as if he was a pear with a fork in his veins. Then he has a social conscience, this is also very important. And, like Visconti, he has a fantastic feeling for the past. That is the characteristic that I admire in him the most. Because even though he was just a child during the fascist era, even so films like *The Spider's Stratagem* [*Strategia del ragno*, 1972] or *The Conformist* are miraculous as reconstructions of an atmosphere, of a way of life that has completely disappeared.

Where does he dig this up from? He will have seen documentaries . . .
You know, it's not the same thing, in his films he creates precisely the right atmosphere. I must say this, both Visconti and Bertolucci are special directors. . . . Bertolucci is almost a more operatic version of Visconti. In short, they are scene setters as much as they are directors.

Is being a director different from being a writer?
No. A real director like a Godard or a Malle has his own style, in fact he writes. He writes with pictures. To sum it up, cinematic writing is no different from that of literature.

Rome
September 13, 2008
Originally published in *La Stampa*

~

HELMUT NEWTON

PHOTOGRAPHER

Helmut Newton is sitting in a light green chair in his studio on the thirty-third floor of a high-rise in Monte Carlo with a view of the sea, the Tennis Club, and the peninsula where designer Karl Lagerfeld has his house up on high. The great photographer is dressed completely in white with a cashmere pullover, blue-jeans-style pants, and tennis shoes. He is wearing round glasses with mother-of-pearl frames. His studio is full of paintings—a Vesuvius by Andy Warhol, a blow-up doll, and a painting by Roy Lichtenstein showing an interior setting.

How many years have you lived in Monte Carlo?

Since the end of 1981.

Why did you come here to live?

I was in Paris for twenty-six years, and I felt like I was getting old. I realized that my accountant only spent five months of the year in Paris. He spent the rest of his time in the south of France or in California. I was paying seventy-five percent of what I earned in taxes, and so I decided to come here. I felt the need to make a change. At first I thought about Los Angeles, and then I chose Monte Carlo, and I don't regret it at all. I have to say that now I do ninety percent of my photographs here and a part of the printing and archives.

And what is life like in Monte Carlo?

It is fantastic because the climate is great, and the light is extraordinary even when the sky is gray. I have binoculars to look out at the sea. I like to watch the sea, and I like to look into the windows of my neighbors. I did that for a long time until I discovered that they are too boring, so I stopped.

What is your life like?

When I am in Monte Carlo, I go to bed at nine forty-five p.m., then I read and watch television until at least ten thirty p.m. Then I go to sleep. I wake up at seven thirty a.m., and I am in the office by nine a.m. My apartment is near my office and my studio. In the summer, I go to the beach at midday. I have lunch and then I work under a beach tent. In the summer, the beach is my office.

When do you take photographs?

Preparations are long and detailed, for advertisements as well as for more artistic photographs.

How often do you take photographs?

It depends. Sometimes I don't work for three weeks. Lately, I haven't stopped working at all.

How do you choose your models?

I like very professional models. I know them all very well, and we've worked together for a long time.

Do you have favorites?

They come and they go. Today top models like Cindy Crawford or Claudia Schiffer are a bit a thing of the past. I always look for new models. I need to change. I don't remember their names, because I change so often. I have to say that recently I did a big job for designer Thierry Mugler, and I'm very proud of it. I like my work not just for the preparation it requires, but because of the personal issues you need to resolve, especially in advertising. I have to say that now I have enough money, and I only take on the jobs that interest me. The ones I like.

How many years have you been married?

I've known my wife for fifty years, and next year we will have been married for fifty years. She helps me a lot in my work.

How did you become a photographer?

I bought a camera for myself at age twelve in Germany. It was as small as a box and was an Agfa. I started to take photographs.

And it became your passion?

Yes, and the older I get, the more of a passion it is.

More than anything, you are curious, aren't you?

Certainly. I am a voyeur.

I LIKE VERY PROFESSIONAL MODELS. I KNOW THEM ALL VERY WELL, AND WE'VE WORKED TOGETHER FOR A LONG TIME.

How would you define your photographs?

They are photographs. Each one speaks for itself. Some people hate them and hate what I do. Others think they are beautiful.

Who are some of your favorite photographers?

I was good friends with Brassaï, and he influenced my work a lot. When I go to New York, I see Irving Penn.

What actors or famous people do you most remember?

Sigourney Weaver is a friend of mine in Los Angeles. She is a very intelligent woman. I am friends with Billy Wilder. He is a great friend, and is over ninety.

Other friends?

Andy Warhol and I were friends. Then I did a portrait of Margaret Thatcher I am very proud of. Today it is hanging in the National Portrait Gallery in London, and I want to point out that when one enters the gallery, they see the Queen as painted by Andy Warhol on one side and then my photograph of Margaret Thatcher. Chancellor Kohl also made an impression on me, and he's so charming. I did some gorgeous photographs of him.

Other people?

I remember Elizabeth Taylor very well and then David Hockney and Yves Saint Laurent. I photographed him for many years and many people that work with him. Many models.

Is Yves Saint Laurent the king of fashion?

He is most definitely a master.

Are there other masters?

Yves is a great master, and Thierry Mugler and John Galliano are also good because they break with tradition.

What about Versace?

I knew him and his family well. I went to his house in Miami, and I photographed him in Como. He was a very kind and generous man. It was a terrible shock to hear about his death. Gianni had a wonderful personality. I photographed him nude, and I promised him to never publish his photographs. Only perhaps as part of an exhibition.

What about Lady Diana?

I didn't know her. I would be really interested in photographing Camilla Parker Bowles. She seems like a fascinating woman, but it would probably be difficult to be able to do that. It wasn't easy for Margaret Thatcher either. I took years to get the authorization.

Would you like to photograph the Pope?

I would like that very much. To tell you the truth, I like photographing people I love, that I admire, and even people that I hate. I photographed Giovanni Agnelli in Turin. He's a fascinating and very charming person. I photographed the Aga Khan and Baron Evelyn Rothschild. All fascinating, different people.

How do you feel when you shoot a portrait?

Portraits are an extraordinary seduction. As I said, I can photograph people that I don't love. That I hate. I hated Le Pen considering I am Jewish. But I photographed him anyway.

What about Salvador Dalí?

I remember a fantastic photograph. He was very ill, and it was at the end of his life, but he put me through my paces. He was dying, and he was still perverse. He said, "Come photograph me because I'm dying. . . ."

Who is the wildest woman you have photographed?
Veruschka was interesting but not wild. Perhaps we were all wilder when we were young. Maybe the wildest women were strangers I met in Los Angeles.

Have there been big changes in photography?
Computers now produce photographs that are boring and ugly.

Are you a happy man?
Yes. I would say so.

Do you like food?
I am not interested in restaurants. I like pasta very much. In Milan, I go to the restaurant Torre di Pisa with my friend Ettore Sottsass. I have to say that you eat very well there.

Do you drink?
My doctor doesn't want me to drink more than one glass of champagne with two ice cubes before dinner and one glass of red wine with meals.

Tell me about a dream of yours?
I have always loved cars since I was a boy. I have had beautiful cars. I would like to have a Humvee, the enormous American military vehicle. I have to say I love trucks. I drove trucks when I was in the army.

Monte Carlo
November 30, 1997

~

TO TELL YOU THE TRUTH,

I LIKE

PHOTOGRAPHING

PEOPLE

I LOVE,

AND EVEN

PEOPLE THAT

I HATE.

ANTHONY D'OFFAY

ART DEALER

This interview with the distinguished art dealer and philanthropist Anthony d'Offay takes place in his elegant first floor office on London's Dering Street, a historic wood-paneled room where he works with his young assistant. Downstairs is Postcard Teas, a shop selling exquisite rare varieties of teas, which is run by Anthony's son, Timothy, and his Japanese wife, Asako. At Anthony's request a pot of delicious caffeine-free Chinese tea is bought up for us to drink during the interview.

How did you become a legend in the world of art?

I was very lucky. I opened a small gallery in 1965 and moved here to Dering Street in 1968. For two to three years at the end of the seventies we began to plan a very large new international gallery. Anne Seymour and I got married in 1977. Anne was one of the curators of the modern collection at the Tate, and she made it her ambition to change me into a modern person. So there were three of us—myself, my wife Anne, and Marie-Louise Laband, who joined in 1976 and ran the operation faultlessly for the next four decades. Our first exhibition when we opened in 1980 was Joseph Beuys. The new gallery had eight rooms; some of them really large.

Because you wanted to show big works of art?

We had the idea that if we could have a big gallery, like the New York SoHo galleries of the time, we could invite the world's greatest living artists to show here, and that this new program would help to make London a destination for the international art world. We imagined that people would come to London to see those shows and it would have a great impact, and I think that really worked. Beuys's *Stripes from the House of the Shaman* was the opening exhibition and this was Anne's idea.

What happened to that sculpture?

We sold it to James Mollison, the brilliant director of the National Gallery in Canberra, Australia. I really admired James, and when I rang him and said we had a Beuys sculpture which I thought would be perfect for Canberra, he said to me, "If you really,

really, really think it's true I shall buy it sight unseen. If it's not true, I shall murder you next time I see you!" James had previously bought one of the most famous works of art of the twentieth century (which is in London at the moment), and that is the great painting called *Blue Poles*, by Jackson Pollock. He had also bought two sculptures of *Bird in Space* by Brâncuşi. That's ambition for you!

In 1970 you began to represent Lucian Freud?

A wonderful experience. Such an extraordinary person, a great artist, and friend. He was the best man at our wedding.

And later he was represented elsewhere?

Yes, which was great for his career. It happened in an interesting way. In 1988 we showed an Australian performance artist called Leigh Bowery. Freud saw him, became fascinated by him, and started to make unusually large nude paintings of him. This became a great international breakthrough for Lucian and changed his career. The New York dealer, Bill Acquavella, started to show Lucian's pictures, and this led to an important retrospective at the Metropolitan Museum of Art.

Was Freud a fascinating presence?

Absolutely. A young lady, a client of ours, said that one of the greatest experiences of her life was walking past Lucian in Kensington Church Street. After thirty yards, she stopped and looked back and it was so thrilling, because he had also stopped and was looking back at her. She said this was the number-one romantic moment in her life. There's a marvellous film which was shown on the BBC after his death, a documentary called *Lucian Freud: A Painted Life* [2012], which includes footage of him as a child with his grandfather Sigmund, and ends with him painting in his studio at the end of his life. In the film there's a meeting between Lucian and Bill Acquavella. They shake hands on working together, and then Lucian says, "Would you be kind enough to look after the money I owe my bookmaker?" And Bill says, "Oh yes."

How much did he owe?

Two point seven million pounds. And Acquavella paid! Acquavella made an entirely new market for Lucian and achieved prices in millions of dollars. A decade before, we had a problem selling Lucian's pictures for over fifty thousand pounds. Bill Acquavella was able to say, "This is the greatest living painter," and charge accordingly.

Your artists were British and international?

Yes. They included from Europe: Joseph Beuys, Gerhard Richter, Anselm Kiefer, Sigmar Polke, Georg Baselitz, and Jannis Kounellis. From America: Willem de Kooning,

Cy Twombly, Jasper Johns, Ellsworth Kelly, Andy Warhol, Roy Lichtenstein, Vija Celmins, Carl Andre, Lawrence Weiner, Bill Viola, and Jeff Koons. From the UK: Richard Hamilton, Howard Hodgkin, Richard Long, Gilbert & George, and Ron Mueck. We tried to think of who were the world's most interesting artists.

Did you enjoy working with Willem de Kooning?

One of the most wonderful experiences of my life was representing Willem de Kooning. His dealer was Xavier Fourcade, who became a great friend, and we had two fantastic exhibitions, the first one of paintings and sculpture from the seventies and eighties and the second of paintings from the early eighties. de Kooning, coming like Erasmus from Rotterdam, was a poor immigrant to America, becoming a great painter in the late forties. As a young man in the early fifties he made these magnificent abstract expressionist paintings. Then came the extraordinary women paintings in the mid-fifties, against a background of other artists telling him that he was a traitor to do figurative painting.

And you worked with Andy Warhol?

Yes, I worked very closely with Andy Warhol and I commissioned the *Self-Portrait* (*Fright Wig*) paintings of 1986. We bought the whole show in advance. At that time people didn't have very good things to say about Warhol's work, and the accepted view was that much of the work of the seventies and early eighties was disappointing. "Mao was the last great image," people liked to say at the time. In 1986 our self-portrait exhibition was a colossal success, and we sold important paintings immediately to great international museums. The auction houses today call these works "Warhol's last masterpiece."

It was soon after this that he died?

I was working with him on a portrait of Samuel Beckett when he died. He called me before going to hospital and said he'd be out on Tuesday and would then go to Paris to see Beckett. He told me, "Beckett is very keen on this project, and I'm going to make you an exhibition in really pretty colors." Sadly Andy died in hospital. I remain proud that we achieved one big project with Warhol in London and that it had such an extraordinary success.

You have also shown Jeff Koons?

I said to Anselm Kiefer we were going to show Jeff Koons. He said, "Well, I hate his work, but I think it's a very good idea for the gallery." We had several Koons shows, all of them a success.

Looking at art is not about being schooled in art history. It is about asking questions, and getting young people to think in a new, creative way. And this is crucial for the future.

Damien Hirst?

Damien Hirst worked for us as a technician in the gallery before becoming a famous artist. He painted the walls for exhibitions, and was thrilled to meet great artists, such as Gerhard Richter.

Did he show with you later?

No, but we bought very beautiful works of his for the Artist Rooms collection.

Who is another very significant artist for you?

Richard Long, the great British sculptor, was always a very important artist for us, achieving international fame in the late sixties when he was barely out of art school. Also, Ron Mueck, who was included in Charles Saatchi's iconic exhibition *Sensation* at the Royal Academy in London in 1997. His sculpture *Dead Dad* became the star of the exhibition. Here was an unknown artist who made a sculpture that became famous immediately the world over.

What about your relationship with Francis Bacon?

He became a good friend. As a child in Leicester my mother used to take me to the museum while she went shopping. She left me, a boy of eight, in the care of the doorman at the museum, and I had the fantastic experience of being alone with wonderful works of art. When I was a teenager the museum was given a painting by Francis Bacon by the Contemporary Art Society. It was a totally astonishing thing for me to see this mysterious and powerful work of art and to be able to spend a considerable time looking at the picture. I remember thinking, the colors are wrong, the drawing is clumsy, I don't know if it represents a man or a woman. . . . But I felt incredibly excited and moved by the painting. When I left Edinburgh University, where I studied art, and came to London in 1963, my first thought was how thrilling it was to be in the city where Francis Bacon and Henry Moore showed their work. When I was in my thirties and we represented Lucian Freud, I saw a lot of Francis, because Lucian and he were dear friends.

Who else stands out for you?

We showed Maurizio Cattelan. An extraordinary artist, an art world trickster—think about *Him*, the sculpture showing Hitler kneeling—it's impossible to forget that image.

Then you suddenly closed your gallery, with the last show by Bill Viola?

Yes, we had extraordinary reviews for the Viola show and almost a hundred thousand visitors. Then we closed.

Why?

We had run the gallery for twenty-one years and felt we had completed what we had set out to do. I did not want the gallery to become tired or repetitive and the only way to close was to do so suddenly at the beginning of the new season, in September 2001.

How do you close a gallery?

Normally galleries go into decline well before they actually close and we wanted to avoid that. We also felt there was an opportunity to have another adventure, to make a collection which would travel to cities all over the UK.

How long did it take you to make the collection?

Seven years. We gave about one hundred works by Andy Warhol, a great collection of drawings by Joseph Beuys and have loaned *Blitzschlag mit Lichtschein auf Hirsch* [*Lightning with Stag in its Glare*, 1958–85, an installation by Joseph Beuys], the only sculptural installation at Tate Modern which has been there since the museum opened in 2000. We also gave significant works by Gerhard Richter, Diane Arbus, Robert Mapplethorpe, Jenny Holzer, Agnes Martin, Bruce Nauman, Ed Ruscha, Vija Celmins, Jannis Kounellis, Robert Therrien, Jeff Koons, and Damien Hirst, works by artists who we thought it would be really important that young people saw. If you are aged eight to twelve, a teenager or a student, what might change your life?

You call the collection Artist Rooms. Who does the collection belong to now?

The collection belongs to two museums, Tate and the National Galleries of Scotland on behalf of the nation.

Are you the curator?

Ceri Lewis is the managing curator, and there is a team of seven or eight people working full time. The Artist Rooms collection is for the UK, and allows regional museums to have exhibitions by artists they would never normally be able to show.

What is your role?

Having worked with the artists closely, I like to help curate the exhibitions. It is important that the artists are shown in the way they had taught me to install their work.

Is the collection still growing?

Yes. Since the donation of 2008, we have added the great international artist Louise Bourgeois, whose work is currently on display in the new Artist Rooms Gallery at Tate Modern. We have also added works by Dan Flavin, Roy Lichtenstein, Alex Katz, Don McCullin, Martin Creed, and Douglas Gordon.

Do you still work as a dealer?

I work with Hauser & Wirth to look after Ron Mueck. Hauser & Wirth are on Savile Row in London and Durslade Farm in Somerset. They also have large galleries in Zürich, New York, and Los Angeles.

What is the current status of London in the world of contemporary art?

I would say that London is the second city in the world for contemporary art, but the range of galleries in London now rivals even New York. Look at the colossal attendance in the first five or six months at Tate Modern with its new wing.

Was New York important for you?

In the eighties it was very important to be in New York once or twice a month to teach myself to think like an American, to make great friends with the museums, to try to do everything to the highest possible standards.

Are the most important collectors in America?

Not any more. We dealt with museums and the world's greatest collectors. I felt our job was to put on iconic exhibitions for the public in London and then to sell as much as possible to the most important international museums.

Do you think Brexit will ruin this?

I think we have to wait and see, but I have no impression of that. Everybody loves London. You have to ask yourself, which cities would you want to live in? For me, these would include London, New York, San Francisco, Kyoto, and Sydney.

Who are the new artists of today?

For us to have shown Jeff Koons was exciting, and we were proud to have put *Puppy* outside Guggenheim Bilbao. We included a few of the younger artists in Artist Rooms, like Damien Hirst, Douglas Gordon, Martin Creed, and Ellen Gallagher, and we have really beautiful works of theirs.

How do you spend your time these days?

Working with sixty Artist Rooms takes all my time! For me, getting young people to think creatively is what Artist Rooms is all about. Looking at art is not about being schooled in art history. It is about asking questions, and getting young people to think in a new, creative way. And this is crucial for the future.

London
January 8, 2017

~

Having worked with the artists closely, I like to help curate the exhibitions. It is important that the artists are shown in the way they had taught me to install their work.

AMOS OZ

WRITER

In his book *A Tale of Love and Darkness* [2002], which has been translated from the original Hebrew into many different languages, Israeli writer Amos Oz tells of his youth and his relationship with Jerusalem, where he was born.

What has changed since the 1940s and 1950s–the period you describe in your book?

Jerusalem has changed completely. It was a small town with many neighborhoods, and each neighborhood had its personality and its life cycle. Today it is a metropolis, a city of more than seven hundred and fifty thousand inhabitants, and it is much more lively, though it is still full of tensions, like when I was a child.

What kind of relationship do Israelis have with Jerusalem?

It is impossible to answer that, because every Israeli has his own Jerusalem. There's the Jerusalem of the religious and of the secular, the Jerusalem of the new settlers, and of those who have been there for many generations. The Jerusalem of the Jews and the Arabs . . .

So why did you go to live elsewhere?

At age fourteen, I rebelled against my father's world. He was an academic, and I became a tractor driver. He was on the right, and I became a socialist. He was an intellectual, and I wanted to be a farmer. So, at age fourteen, I moved to a kibbutz, and I later moved to another kibbutz in the desert. Since then I've been back to Jerusalem many times, but I've never been a resident. It is the city where I was born and where many of my books take place.

Do you set them there because a writer needs to know the places he describes?

I need some distance, however. I can't paint with my nose pressed to the canvas. I also kept my distance because the city is full of all kinds of extremists—Muslims, religious Jews, and nationalists. The whole city is like a big question mark.

You saw the birth of the state of Israel, which is now sixty years old. What has changed? Is the country stronger or weaker since then?

Israel was born out of dreams, not because of geography or demography. There were many different dreams: the dreams of the fathers and mothers of Israel. Some dreamed of recreating the days of the Bible. Others dreamed of creating a replica of the Jewish cities of Eastern Europe. Others dreamed of copying Austria-Hungary in the Middle East. Others wanted a social-democratic Scandinavia. Still others aimed to create a Marxist country. Those dreams canceled each other out and couldn't be achieved. After sixty years, Israel has a sense of disappointment precisely because it was born of a dream. But it isn't disappointment about the nature of Israel as much as the nature of dreams. The only way to maintain the sense of a wonderful, perfect dream is to never try to fulfill it. The moment in which you fulfill it, the disappointment starts. Israel is a dream fulfilled, and thus there's disappointment.

Does that mean it is a failure?

No. It isn't a failure.

Could there be other dreams?

Yes, always. But then if they are fulfilled, there's disappointment.

What about the reality of it?

The reality is that it is a very Mediterranean country much like Greece, Italy, and Spain. It is a loud, passionate, materialistic, and generous country with a warm heart, and it creates a lot of noise about it. I can say that Israel belongs more in a Fellini film than in a Bergman film.

What about the war aspect, the conflict with Palestinians?

War is the greatest tragedy of Arabs and Israelis. Peace is the greatest dream of Israelis, and I think it will come. I don't know how soon. I can't give you a date. It is difficult to be a prophet in the land of prophets, but I know that one day there will be a Palestinian embassy in Israel and an Israeli embassy in Palestine. These two embassies will be just a few kilometers away because there will be a Jerusalem West and a Jerusalem East.

Are you saying Jerusalem will be divided in two?

I think Jerusalem West will be the capital of Israel and Jerusalem East will be the capital of the Palestinian state.

Who will get the Wailing Wall?

I don't know what the exact borders will be, but I think the holy places need to remain outside the territories and open to all believers.

Do you think Israel will exist in one hundred years or do you agree with others that think it won't survive?

I believe it will still exist. I see no reason why it won't be that way. I think that one day, as has happened in Europe, there will be peace. But it won't take one thousand years, and much less blood will be spilled.

What about Iran, enemies from outside, and the threat of the atomic bomb?

I fear that within about fifteen years, all countries will have the atomic bomb, and there will be the same precarious balance that existed between the United States and the Soviet Union, or that exists now between India and Pakistan.

Do you think there could be new world wars?

It is difficult to predict.

What about literature?

It is blossoming on the slopes of an active volcano. Even when the world is dangerous and uncertain, people go on with their daily lives. They dream, plant gardens, work the land, and read and produce literature. In Israel, it's a golden age for literature today. Israelis read and write many books. And, most of all, they discuss many books. Occasionally a taxi driver will recognize me when I get in and will start talking. Not with me or about me but about the characters in my books.

Haven't you chosen the wrong line of work? Aren't you actually a failed farmer?

I wanted to be a farmer, but, in the end, the rebellion against my father took an almost three-hundred-and-sixty-degree turn, and now I am talking to you sitting in a room full of books, and I'm writing even more books. It is exactly what my father wanted me to do, and I didn't last many years as a tractor driver.

Was your father able to see your success?

He saw my first three books published.

And what did he think about them?

He was happy about my writings, but he was against my political ideas. He died forty years ago, and I still have political discussions with him. I have the habit of inviting the dead into my home every once in a while. I ask them to sit down and have a coffee and talk about the things we never talked about when they were still alive. After coffee, I send them away because I don't want the dead living in my house. But occasionally I invite them in for a coffee or a conversation. I think this is the right way to live with the dead, and with our dreams, we invite the dead to return.

Israel
August 21, 2009

~

I THINK THAT

one

DAY,

AS HAS HAPPENED IN EUROPE,
THERE WILL BE

PEACE.

ANITA PALLENBERG

MODEL

Anita Pallenberg is an actress, model, and fashion designer. Born in Italy in 1944, she was the partner of the Rolling Stones' guitarist Brian Jones and then the partner of Keith Richards.

Anita, you have worked in the worlds of cinema, music, and fashion. Would you define yourself as an eclectic person?

I would say that my life has been based on charm, living life on charm. Just in order to show my father, I spoke five languages, and my father said, "With that you will be a secretary." Now that I have got older I very much appreciate that they forced me to be at least bilingual, Italian and German.

Were you educated in Italy?

I went to school in Germany and I did not go to school in Italy. I think I learned more in museums in Italy.

What did you think you would do in life?

I wanted to be an archaeologist or an anthropologist. I never did it.

How was your life in Rome when you were young?

Mario Schifano was my first boyfriend, and in Rome I was seeing other artists, intellectuals and friends from the cinema world. We used to meet at Caffè Rosati: people like Furio Colombo, Giorgio Franchetti, Cy Twombly, Giulio Turcato.

You met Brian Jones when you were twenty-two years old?

Yes, I met him in Germany where I was doing a modeling job, and the photographer said there is a band playing and you should come, so I went to see them in Munich. I met Brian, who was speaking German and was very erudite. He said come with me, and we became friends. There were also the others like Keith and Mick there. At the time we were smoking hash and I used to travel with hash.

I asked them, "Do you want some?" and Brian said, "Yes," but his friends didn't. Later I went on a tour in Germany with Brian. I was working as a model in Germany because they paid on the day, that's why I liked to work there. In France or Italy, they paid several days later.

Were the Rolling Stones already famous at the time?

No. They had not written "Satisfaction" yet.

How did you change from being with Brian Jones to Keith Richards?

We were friends, and we were together. We were taking loads of acid, but Brian had horrors and bad trips, he did not take acid well. When we got busted in London we all decided to go to Morocco and Brian started to get very violent. We went by car, a Bentley with a driver, and Brian got sick and ended up in hospital. He had asthma. He was very sickly, fragile. So Keith and I drove on and left him there, and that was when we had a physical relationship.

That lasted fifteen years?

He was the biological right man to be the father of my children. It was more respect and friendship than mad love. Keith is very generous. In those days we did not plan families. I certainly did not want to get married, but I got pregnant. And then because I had to do a film, *Performance* [1970], I had to have a termination to do the film. I resented it very much, and so when I finished the film I got pregnant again. If you were not Sophia Loren with Carlo Ponti behind you it was difficult to be treated properly.

Which was your first film?

The first film I did when I was with Brian, he did the music with Jimmy Page. It was a Volker Schlöndorff movie, *A Degree of Murder* [Mord und Totschlag, 1966]. Then I played in *Barbarella* [1968] with Jane Fonda. Roger Vadim was the director.

How was Vadim?

We were doing one take a day at around six thirty in the evening. All day waiting. Probably I got into drugs because of that, it was so boring to wait. Vadim was funny. He thought he was a little boy and he behaved like a little boy. I spent a lot of time waiting on the set together with Jane Fonda. She had a very tragic life, and she was very professional. Keith was coming to see me, and Jane fell in love with him. After the film she came to our house in Cheyne Walk in London where I had Marlon my baby, and Keith did not let her in. She reminded him of his aunt.

What kind of person is Keith?

He is a musician. My father was a musician as well.

You saw a lot of Mick Jagger?

Me and Marianne Faithfull were always left alone, as Keith and Mick were recording and we were friends. We hung out together, taking drugs together, and we went to John Paul Getty's house, the Rossetti House, because he was the last resort, and he always had some drugs.

How was London in those days?

I always lived in Chelsea since we had a house; before that we were living in hotels. I was shocked in Chelsea by hippy girls who were walking barefoot in the Kings Road. I am Italian, and in Italy shoes are a sign of wealth. Only very poor people walk without shoes.

Was Chelsea different at that time?

No, just that now there are more bars and coffee shops.

Fashion was different?

It was hippy time, but I never was a hippy. At that time I worked in *Dillinger is Dead* [*Dillinger è morto,* 1966], a film by Marco Ferreri with Michel Piccoli and Annie Girardot. London was a little cliquey group of people who worked in galleries . . . artists, musicians . . . some aristocrats. There were some parties and some events, like Ravi Shankar playing or something like that.

How was it to raise two children in such a lifestyle?

We were on the road a lot, traveling on tour, and I took my son everywhere. I did not send Marlon to school until he was eight years old. I taught him how to read and write while Keith's mother looked after my daughter. My daughter (Angela, also known as Dandelion) was born in Switzerland. I took her on the road, but with a girl it is different, sometimes it was an unsafe environment. The difficulty with Keith is that he sleeps all day, and ideally I had to be up with the children all day. I couldn't have made the tours without the protection of drugs.

Did you meet many interesting people?

I don't think so. People are people. I was not a fan. I was not excited to meet John Lennon. It is not my personality. Of course I met John Lennon, and for me he was like an art student. I had a lot of respect for Jimmy Page, that's about it. Sometimes we would go out to a club called Ad Lib, but I also used to go out by myself to see the Pink

Floyd or Jimi Hendrix. I was not allowed to do it, because all the rock stars are male chauvinists in their own camps. If you were in the Beatles camp, or The Who, you could not be in the Rolling Stones camp.

Why did you break up with Keith?

Because of the growing of the children. My son also used to say to his father, "Dad, you are never there."

What happened when you finished with Keith?

I was happy that I could score my own drugs. That's the reality. I lived in Long Island and Westchester for about nine years. I was there alone with Marlon and Keith's father, who lived with us in America as well. I had some boyfriends, but nothing serious. Then I came back to England to clean up from drugs and went to rehab. I was a very bad alcoholic and it took me twenty years to come out of it.

How did you manage to stop?

I went to rehab. I did a baccalaureate in textiles at Central Saint Martins. I studied.

You became a designer?

I was more interested in fabrics. Then I worked with Vivienne Westwood. I did a lot of things, all sorts of things to save my life.

Do you still think of drugs?

It is like the love of my life. It is a love affair I had to give up. I was on my own, my family did not want to see me. I was disgusting, aggressive, a very hard drinker. I was morose, not a happy drunk. I wanted to live. I took care of myself. I went to AA meetings and all that. People were dying, there was AIDS. It was a dark period.

You managed to stop all by yourself?

How can you stop if not by yourself? That's the most important thing.

And you did it?

It has been fourteen years now with no drugs, no alcohol. I should be able to say that I am thirty years clean. Then I had a relapse with magic mushrooms and I started the cycle again for another ten years. It is a big battle. Now it is finished, unless I get very sick and they prescribe me morphine, which they won't! Today I can sit at a table in front of people who take cocaine or drink, without problems. I just get bored. People who drink get very boring. They repeat themselves and say the same thing over and over.

Where do you live when you are not in London?

Since four years I have spent the winter in Jamaica. Rome is too cold in the winter and so I look after Keith's house and garden in Jamaica where the climate is perfect, and I paint. I also went to Cuba and South America.

What about your children?

I see them, but they don't come to Jamaica.

Do you feel Italian and still speak Italian?

Yes. *Romana di Roma, romanaccia.* When I was young I was a so-called 'Pariolina' and then when I lived in New York in the seventies, I realized that there are many Italian dialects in New York that they don't speak in Italy any more. So I started to cultivate my Roman accent. Also I had a very great friend, the singer Gabriella Ferri, who was singing Roman songs. My children are English. My son speaks a little Spanish, but like all English people they don't speak other languages.

How would you describe yourself?

A vagabond. An adventurer. I am not a person with one specific talent. I wish I was.

Was it difficult to find your identity?

I don't want to get stuck in the sixties, like platform shoes. Fashion is probably my closest thing, but I don't like it. It is the thing I spend the most time on.

Who do you like in fashion?

Vivienne Westwood. Then I became a fashion style queen myself. They all want to take pictures of me and write articles about me and my style.

What is your style?

Boots, belts, cashmere, hats, sunglasses, furs as well. I am not politically correct. This is ruining the world. I like lamé fabrics, I worked in India for six months. I like jewelry, all jewelry. I used to wear a lot. Now I get more sensitive—I can barely wear anything. I am not afraid of change at all. I think change is the best thing one can do, quite honestly. I do a lot of gardening. I love that. I have an allotment garden in London and I grow Italian things. I do it with a German friend who grows German things like potatoes. I have a garden in Italy. I look after Marlon's garden and Keith's Jamaican garden. This year we had two crops of bananas for the first time. I paint and design. I do botanical paintings, an ancient art. I like everything that has been there for a long time. I love the

Chelsea Physic Garden in London where I go for lunch from time to time. I stopped going out at night since the smoking ban.

How much do you smoke?

About twenty a day, but I am not a cancer person. I do yoga, and also bicycle.

Do you live by yourself?

I have lived alone for twenty years. If I want to see someone I call them, but I don't like to be called. I have a couple of good friends from the sixties. I don't go out, now there are only paparazzi. I don't like it, I am tired of it.

Are you still friends with Marianne Faithfull?

We are very close. Now she lives in Paris, but we have seen each other a lot recently. She is incredibly strong, talented.

Any regrets?

I do not regret. I liked it better before, when political correctness did not exist and things were less tedious according to me.

Are you afraid to get older?

I am ready to die. I have done so much here. My mum died at ninety-four. I don't want to lose my independence. Now I am over seventy, and to be honest I did not think I would live over forty.

Chelsea, London
September 4, 2016

~

LUCIANO PAVAROTTI

OPERA SINGER

Pavarotti was a man of very clear ideas. Like all Italians, he was an Italian that followed *calcio* (soccer) and politics. But in these very few lines you will find that he was a man of great common sense, and maybe that helped his great talent to become recognized, and for him to become such a star.

I remember well when I went to visit him in 1994 in his house in Pesaro, where he was living with his second wife. He was eating with old school friends who came from his home town of Modena. They all had white hair, but Luciano had instead very black hair and eyebrows. They drank happily many bottles of Lambrusco, the red wine from their region, and Luciano by then was ready for a long siesta. Nevertheless, he talked to me about his forthcoming trip to America.

I also remember Luciano from years before, in his house in Modena. He was on a diet, and every few minutes he was screaming with his special voice, "*Adua*!"—the name of his first wife—because he wanted another glass of water and lemon. Then I saw in the dining room an enormous amount of raw vegetables and asked him, "Why?" He answered that they had no calories and he could eat as many as he wanted!

Then I asked him what his relationship with money was and he told me that when Mirella Freni and he were still very young and poor they had asked Herbert von Karajan, the very famous conductor, about money. von Karajan answered, "Sing well and money will come." That very simple sentence was for Pavarotti, and for me, a great lesson.

Was he a very special person? Yes, he was a star and a showman and he wanted to be like that, but he had in his way of speaking something very human, almost feminine. I am sure that he still has lots of fans all over the world. This short interview is an homage to the maestro.

I meet Luciano Pavarotti in Pesaro. Soon he will be staying at the Peninsula Beverly Hills Hotel in Los Angeles; already he is preparing and getting ready for the ultimate challenge, a concert he is going to give with Placido Domingo and José Carreras.

Do you like to sing with the other tenors?

Yes, it's good to be competitive. And then again we are friends and we respect each other.

What do you think of the Italian soccer team?

This is the real game changer. Now the game is beautiful, now you will see who are the hard men. Now we need to win.

But will Italy succeed?

That's what I predict.

What do you think of Baggio?

I think he is a great player.

Have you watched the matches?

At five in the morning!

And Sacchi, how does he seem to you?

Everybody criticized him at the beginning. Now he is either good or he is lucky. We criticize these people continuously, for example we have attacked Bearzot endlessly, we have criticized Vicini. Today we are fifty million technical experts, everyone has their own idea, an ideal team in mind. Despite all this the World Cup has been able to keep the team together. Do not forget that our boys are real champions, great professionals. I think we can very well do it, we are a super team.

After the concert will you go on holiday?

Yes, I will let the breezes blow across me.

Will you be at the Rossini Festival?

I will still be out and about then. I will resume work on September 13th, when I am going to sing in a concert in Modena. The actual program is still uncertain. Then I will go to the Metropolitan and will open the season with *Pagliacci*. Domingo will also be there.

Pavarotti, what's your opinion of Maestro Muti?

He's a very great conductor, he has a great family and he and his wife make a beautiful couple.

And Maestro Abbado?

He's a great conductor and a great man.

But is there competition even among conductors?

One wants there to be competition. We are talking about incredible levels of talent, technique, musical experience. People ask which one I prefer, but I will not name him.

And what is your favorite orchestra?

I am not going to say, I do not wish to offend anyone; but truly there is one orchestra that is really quite extraordinary.

Are you not going to sing in Italy?

Yes, I am doing the San Carlo in Naples on December 1, when I appear in *Un Ballo in Maschera.*

What do you think of what is happening in the world?

My ideal is that there would be no more states. I have a circle in Modena, Europe 92, founded in 1980, but a Europe such as this has not come about in the way I would have hoped.

What do you think of the Italian government?

I see the birth of the Second Republic. I have seen Andreotti found the First Republic with De Gasperi. I remember the elections at that time and the monarchists saying that for at least ten years it would be better not to change things. These days things have changed.

For better or for worse?

In a domestic house there is a head to that house and everybody works together, but in Italy there is not only no collaboration, there is not even a real democracy. To govern takes just two, not four hundred and fifty thousand people.

And Berlusconi, what do you think of him?

I think he's good. Now he's been elected, okay, so let's move on; let's stop putting a spoke in every wheel.

Can it be said that at the end of the day you are an optimist?

I am optimistic and it upsets me that people always see the glass half empty instead of the glass half full. Unfortunately, when one is an optimist, one is very often considered a simpleton. It is true that there are many problems in life and in the world, but I believe that there are also a great many solutions.

Pesaro
July 16, 1994

~

ONE WANTS THERE TO BE COMPETITION.
WE ARE TALKING ABOUT INCREDIBLE
LEVELS
OF
TALENT,
TECHNIQUE,
MUSICAL
EXPERIENCE.

SHIMON PERES

FORMER PRESIDENT OF ISRAEL

The year is 1999. On the ninth floor of a modern building in the center of Tel Aviv, there's a little door with a small nameplate. One rings the bell and a plain-clothes guard opens the door and asks a few discreet questions, a bit like in the airport. Shimon Peres is waiting with a smile on his tanned face. He is wearing dark-brown pants and an electric-blue shirt without a tie. In Peres's library, there are biographies of statesmen and photographs of him with American presidents, and especially with his mentor and former boss David Ben-Gurion.

Shimon Peres, you are the minister for regional cooperation in the new Barak government. How do you see the first steps taken by the new government?

After a three-year "glacial period," there's a new feeling of things opening up toward peace, which is a big change in and of itself.

Do you believe Barak is doing a good job as prime minister?

He is doing things his way and moving in the right direction. Everyone is entitled to his new successes and new failures.

What does that mean?

It means that Barak thinks the Americans should have a different role—not as a police force but as intermediaries for peace.

And what do you think?

I don't think the United States is trying to act alone or as a police force. And I don't see problems with the U.S. as long as the peace process goes ahead. The United States has an enormous role in the negotiations among Israel, the Palestinians, and other countries in the Middle East. It certainly can't be replaced.

Which United States presidents, in your opinion, have been most important in the journey toward peace?

I'm not here to give out marks. I can say that President Clinton is a president who is very well informed and whose heart is in the right place for Israel and for the Palestinians. In a certain sense, he's the best president out of them all for the peace process.

What about the Netanyahu era?

It was a waste. Unfortunately, we can't turn back time. We most definitely lost three years.

You didn't meet with Assad, the Syrian president. Barak will probably meet with him. What do you think of him?

Assad doesn't want to meet with us before there is peace, and this is a mistake because he is necessary for peace. When I was prime minister, it seemed like Assad wanted to reach a peace agreement as well. He said we could meet but said he couldn't give me an appointment yet!

They say that Assad in Syria—as well as Algeria—wants peace with Israel so they can have peace with the United States. Do you think this is true?

In a certain sense, yes. As there is no longer a Russian superpower, they no longer have a choice. They no longer have money or weapons. It's normal that countries like Syria, Algeria, and others want to enter into a new era and are therefore looking for the road to Washington. Syria sees that Jordan and Egypt have new weapons. They don't have old Russian weapons like they do, and they aren't as poor as they are.

What do you think about Iraq?

I think they have a psychopath, a crazy man for a leader. There are other countries with leaders like this as well—like North Korea and Yugoslavia, for example. But I don't think Saddam will last long. His people are living in such a terrible state, and you can't continue to govern a country with the secret police.

What do you think about what is happening in Iran?

The ayatollahs don't have the answers for the real needs of Iran. Reason ends where holiness begins. Saying you are holy doesn't lead to anything changing. Young people can't take the oppression that you have in these countries. I don't know how long change will take, but I know that the ayatollahs' prayers don't bring answers.

Is it true that Islamic fundamentalism is getting weaker?

Yes, because it's self-destructive. It is definitely decreasing in Algeria and in Sudan because people want two things more than anything else—food and freedom.

What about Israeli fundamentalists?

Yes, they exist, but they don't have weapons and they aren't in power.

But they killed Rabin.

It was one person and not an organization that killed Rabin.

Has society changed a lot from the times of Ben-Gurion's Israel?

Ben-Gurion was a strong character. Perhaps without him, Israel wouldn't exist today. But when Ben-Gurion became prime minister, there were six hundred thousand of us. Now there are six million. He went to war before having an army. Today Israel is a big democracy with a big army and an important economy. Thus Israel beat communism, and this is why Russian Jews come to Israel, and it's not the Israelis going to Russia.

Are there still remnants of the pioneer era?

The democratic spirit of the pioneers is still here. The big effort to bring together Palestinians and Jews and have them live in a democratic country was, in and of itself, a huge success.

And why do you think Israel is so important today? Why is it constantly talked about in all of the newspapers, especially in the United States?

Because it is an exception, a vision. In past centuries and in previous years, everyone said this was impossible, and yet it happened. I think that in Israel, it's a bit like a Shakespearean play. It's something that is unreal. After two thousand years of exile, Jews returned to their land, to their language, and created a democracy. It's more of a play, a drama, than a country. Perhaps it is the most dramatic country of all. A good drama doesn't depend on the number of actors as much as on the quality of the actors.

What about the Palestinians?

We need to help them to construct a prosperous, democratic country. The Israelis need to think about how the better off the Palestinians are, the better of they are. They also need to have their freedom and prosperity.

Is that a utopia?
Israel is a utopia as well, but it's a utopia that can become a reality.

Is Arafat a great leader?
Yes, even though he's made mistakes.

Do you have a lot of respect for him?
Absolutely. A lot.

Do you trust Arafat?
He certainly hasn't become a Zionist! But Palestinians need to believe in him.

Do you think there is a successor to Arafat?
Even if we don't like to [think] about it, everyone has a successor. This is how life goes.

What about the new king of Jordan?
He describes himself as an Internet man. I hope he represents an old tradition in the new world. His father was certainly a great king.

What about the new generation? The new king of Morocco, for example.
The new generation is more professional and more globally oriented. Young people don't want borders and walls. Today's economy is the result of science and technologies that definitely don't have borders.

Do you think the future is peace?
Yes. Peace and competition. And I believe that the new generation wants a world that is most definitely democratic. Take T-shirts and blue jeans. They are a declaration of equality just as that terrible McDonald's, and computers are as well. Young people don't love borders. They don't understand why they need to kill or be killed.

But there's still a big army here in Israel. And in Jordan there's a big army.
Listen, the future doesn't mean that the past is over. The future is always lesser and the past is always greater.

Why is it then that Moshe Dayan, General Rabin, you, and today Barak—all men of war—are the ones seeking peace more than any of the others?
Because the time for peace has come. Wars have clearly failed. We were attacked five times, and we won five times. We've had enough.

How are young people today taking this? Will they continue to want to do military service or are they reluctant in Israel?

As long as there is a difficult situation. As long as Iran and Iraq exist as political and military problems, it will be necessary to do military service. They have no choice.

What do you think about what is happening in Kosovo?

There's a lack of a political solution. You can't bomb Yugoslavia just to bomb it. If you don't want to Balkanize Europe, you need to "Europeanize" the Balkans. I think it was a really unique war. The Americans fought for a matter of principal, but it was a war without military victims for those on the attack, without ground troops. I don't think it created any solutions.

What do you think about the pope visiting Israel? Do you think it will be possible?

I think this pope is a great pope that uses his influence and not the power of the church. He has fought hard against anti-Semitism. He was the first pope to enter a synagogue and the first pope to say that the Jews didn't kill Jesus. He changed the character of the church. There's no doubt about it. I was Foreign Minister when we established diplomatic relations with the Vatican, and today that relationship is excellent. A visit from the pope to Israel would be very important. What I want to say is this: I would like a world of tourists and pilgrims instead of a world of military soldiers. But there are still great difficulties. Nothing can be great without great difficulties.

What is your secret, Shimon Peres?

Life is too short to be a pessimist, which doesn't save you from danger. If you are an optimist, you pick up on important things as you go. Things never end well for hateful people.

Many leaders have fought for peace and then were killed. Why is that?

It's true but others are still alive.

What do you really think of the new government? Are you supportive of it?

I am in favor of the new government because it is fighting for peace, and I have always been more passionate about politics than government.

So it's not true that there is friction and jealousy between you and Barak?

I am working for peace. If this government works for peace, I will work with this government.

Tel Aviv

August 3, 1999

I AM WORKING FOR

peace.

IF THIS
GOVERNMENT
WORKS FOR

peace,

I WILL WORK
WITH THIS
GOVERNMENT.

GAETANO PESCE

ARCHITECT & DESIGNER

Gaetano Pesce has just arrived in his office in downtown Manhattan, at 543 Broadway.

I have lived in New York since 1980, for thirty-four years. I love the city, but this summer we have heavy rain all the time, and it is quite inconvenient after the very cold winter we just had. I normally love to eat outside in the summer like one is used to doing in Rome or other Italian cities, and also in New York we are taking the same habit. But this summer, no way.

Why did you decide to move to New York and to become a New Yorker?

Because New York in one way or another represents at its best the modern concept of a mix of diversity, in its population, in its values, in its languages. My home is uptown, my office downtown. Every day, when I come down to SoHo it is like changing country. This city became the capital of the world in the second part of the twentieth century. Before it was Paris, then London in the sixties. London is still very intense and lively, but Paris has lost the cultural leadership that it had for the first part of the twentieth century. This is my opinion. You know, as humans we get old, animals, trees get old, and so do countries and cities.

So in your opinion, which will be the next capital?

They say Shanghai, but I don't believe it. Maybe Hong Kong will be a very strong place, but not for the next thirty years. New York will keep its leadership. The quality of life is created by the energy and the presence of young people, and young people come to New York from all over the world because they think that here you can dream and realize your dreams.

But do you still consider yourself Italian?

Yes, because even if I have been here since 1980, I have not been obliged to change my habits. My mother was from Venice, my father from Florence, and I did not have to change my habits. I don't believe that I am American, but I stay here because it is everybody's city, Jewish, Korean, Latin American, European. It is a cataloge of human beings.

Speaking about your work, you have a retrospective show of your work on at the MAXXI museum in Rome, the museum of contemporary art designed by Zaha Hadid. What can you say about it?

First of all I will say it shows many disciplines. There are architectural models, drawings, sculptures, a record that I made in the seventies, a movie that I made for the Museum of Modern Art in New York. The title of the show is "The Time of Diversity," because from the time of the French revolution, where one of the three main words was *égalité*. Today *égalité* is no longer a symbol of our society. When two things are equal they have nothing to say, but things were never equal. Never. And when some political movements like communism tried to transform society into an equal one, they failed. Today we live in a time of diversities and my show in Rome is about it. I also want to add that in the show, in the little square just outside the museum, there is a big armchair seven meters high. That is an enlargement of an armchair that I created thirty-five years ago in the shape of a woman's body, with a sphere attached to the foot—like the image of the prisoner.

What are your new projects about?

I am drawing on resin and I call the drawings "skins." They allow me to work in three dimensions, and it is an imaginative way of drawing on a material that I have known for a long time, and I work it. It is a material of our times and not like paper. Paper is an old material.

Is the art world particularly alive today?

Yes, absolutely, more so than others. In New York all the time there are so many interesting exhibitions. I myself have an exhibition of drawings in New York.

Don't you think that prices are going too high?

Maybe, but I don't find it so relevant. Prices go up and down and artists go on working all the time. Art in general moves where there are good economic conditions; Venice and Florence were rich cities during the Renaissance and art was flourishing, like it was afterwards in Paris and in New York. . . . There are of course always surprises, but it is part of the game.

And what about you?

I absolutely keep on working.

New York
July 2014

~

RENZO PIANO

ARCHITECT

The architect Renzo Piano meets me shortly before the ninth Biennale dell'Architettura opens in Venice on the theme of metamorphosis in 2004.

Renzo Piano, in 2000 you won the Leone d'Oro for career achievement. What does this show mean for you?

I think it's a good thing because it is continuing—albeit in a different way—to keep the general public's attention on architecture. Architecture has come out of its limited arena. It's less of a lofty niche art, and it's finally art for everyone, and people are getting passionate about it because it is imposed on them. Imposed in the sense that if someone makes an ugly building or an ugly city, this is imposed on people. It is wonderful that architecture has come out of its narrow space, and I would invite people to go visit the Biennale. What I think is important about the Biennale is the fact that the architecture is able to breathe in the light, in the wind, with transparency and depth. For thirty years now I personally, since the time of the de Menil Collection in Houston, have had buildings designed by light. Today all the immaterial elements, like sound, color, and transparency, come into play to create a feeling. This is why the title of the Biennale, *Metamorfosi*, is just right. For example my Kanaki building in New Caledonia is a building that breathes and makes sound. The building I'm working on now for the headquarters of *The New York Times* is a three-hundred-meter tower that gets its color from the surrounding environment and the reflections of light.

Do you have works on display at the Biennale this year?

Yes. There is the new project for the Paul Klee Museum in Bern, which will open to the public on June 21, 2005. It will be an anthology of Klee's works, where all of the collections, including those of his grandson, will come together. Then they chose the auditorium project in Rome. I think it is right that the Biennale's curator, Kurt Forster, chose these projects, because they are both metamorphoses. Klee's is like a transformation of the land, and the auditorium is a metamorphosis as well because we are talking about large buildings . . . using different themes, the Biennale is going ahead, seeing ever greater participation in architecture as a social issue. And this seems like moral and civic growth to me. Forster is right. Architecture is a metamorphosis.

However this is also true of great examples of architecture like those by Alberti or Brunelleschi?

Yes. For example, if one looks at the cupola of Santa Maria del Fiore in Florence, not only is it a great work of architecture from a classic, scientific, and constructive point of view, but it's a creative masterpiece in terms of space—that enormous space that "floats." In churches, for example some churches by Bernini, often there is an element of extraordinary expressiveness, such as that ray of light that suddenly cuts through the semidarkness. We should never forget that architecture isn't just expressive, or a way of communicating. There is always invention in terms of the collective consciousness and scientific invention because there's research, the challenge of man. We are always anxious to make discoveries. And then we can add in the big theme of "sustainability of the city." The theme of waste, renewable energy, rebuilding the suburbs, and new uses for abandoned industrial zones.

Is the Biennale's function to show the avant-garde and new trends?

It bears witness to the desire to make discoveries. Research is a very wonderful, important word. The avant-garde often seems like a parody of research, and so it's less interesting to me and whoever is interested in research. I think that saying that the Biennale shows the avant-garde is dangerous because it isn't just about surprising, but about doing real research. Often *avant-garde* is spoken in the same breath as a big word that I think is overblown—the word *freedom*. Freedom is a wonderful idea. But there's, for example, something Stravinsky wrote that says that it is very important for an artist to be limited to focusing on a specific idea. Self-discipline brings additional strength, a greater ability to go in-depth. It is better if one has the ability to stay focused on an objective. The artist's extreme stubbornness is often being self-disciplined in a specific area. The avant-garde often creates an interesting, multicolored world, but then at a certain point one needs to understand what really comes out of that; it can get caught up in the headiness of apparently meaningful research and become a purely theoretical exercise. Naturally there's a bit of everything when you hold a big show. Architecture is a serious thing, because it is a craft that people rely on. Architecture represents man, and it is, first and foremost, a refuge for man himself.

What about the problem of security in today's world?

It continues to be the same problem. There is no technical urbanistic solution to terrorism. The response is human and political, and not technological. The only technical response to terror could be to live in caves, and that wouldn't be a response then. The security I'm talking about, however, is that the work needs to be, first and foremost, a solid refuge.

Can the proof of this solidity in your work be seen definitively in the Georges Pompidou Center in Paris?

Yes. It is a building that has had almost two hundred million visitors in twenty-five years.

What is important to you?

The most important thing at my age is to know what I'm looking for artistically and professionally. It's about finding it.

Haven't you found it yet?

The philosopher Norberto Bobbio once said something wonderful to me: "In my lifetime I've reached the threshold of the temple various times, but I've never been able to go inside." In a certain sense, the day I was satisfied, I would stop. It is true that I've found myself at the threshold of the temple, but I've never gone inside.

What are you looking for?

In every project that I carry out—for example if I'm working on the Whitney project, on New York's Madison Avenue, Columbia University, or other projects—I try to apply the sacred principle of freedom, but I do so carefully. Another thing that I like to do is to try to pass on what I've learned to young people, and I do this via my small Workshop Foundation, which is based in my Genoa and Paris studios. The only way to pass things on to others is through example. The *bottega*, which is an idea as old as the world. Young people learn by standing alongside you as you work.

Do you like teaching?

It's what would be called the "senior artisan" in a workshop. At a certain age, you need to know what you want. At this point, my compass is taking me in a certain direction, but I'd like to slow this thing down, because the nature of being human limits us.

What kind of mark would you like to leave on the world?

Instead of making a mark on young people, I'd like to plant seeds in them. When they work with me, students understand that many things they learn at university aren't true. We mix poetic moments with pragmatic ones in architecture. It is the most materialistic and idealistic art one can imagine.

A final question. Can contemporary architecture be built and placed in the historic centers of ancient art cities?

The Georges Pompidou Center in Paris was a classic case of evolution and layering, so it was logical to continue to build there. The Beaubourg area is not, however, historic in terms of art. I would have a hard time doing something similar in a historic/artistic context.

Venice
September 8, 2004

~

THE MOST IMPORTANT THING AT MY AGE
IS TO KNOW WHAT I'M LOOKING FOR

artistically and professionally.

IT'S ABOUT FINDING IT.

FRANÇOIS PINAULT

BUSINESSMAN

François Pinault is a humble country boy who now bestrides the world of luxury goods like a colossus. The first time I met François Pinault was when we briefly crossed paths on the terrace of the Hotel Monaco in Venice, where he was having lunch with Jean-Jacques Aillagon, the French minister of culture under President Jacques Chirac. Pinault was relaxed and smiling and I introduced him and his guest to, appropriately, the Italian minister of culture, Lorenzo Ornaghi, who was there for the Venice Biennale of Architecture and the Mostra del Cinema, the Venice Film Festival.

It was quite the impromptu eminent cultural gathering. I liked Pinault's smile and his attitude, which was measured and open at the same time—sure of himself but not pretentious. We made an appointment to meet in Paris, at the headquarters of Artemis, his holding company, which owns a controlling share of both PPR—the luxury goods company that owns Gucci and Stella McCartney, Saint Laurent Paris and Bottega Veneta [renamed Kering in 2013]—and his many other activities and properties, which include Christie's auction house.

His office is in a very grand *hôtel particulier* in the rue François Premier, close to the avenue Montaigne and the Grand Palais, a few minutes' walk from the Elysée Palace, and when we meet, Pinault is wearing a single-breasted, tailor-made navy-blue suit, black moccasins very well polished, a blue striped shirt with elegant gold-and-lapis-lazuli cufflinks, and a navy-blue tie. In line with his simple good taste, his office is minimalist. With him are his assistant and Jean-Jacques Aillagon once again. I ask him if he feels he has changed since he was the son of a wood merchant in Brittany; now, of course, he is one of the richest men in the world, whose fortune Forbes estimates at $13 billion. He replies:

"I left my village to join a small city, then I left my region to come to Paris, and now I have become a citizen of the world—but still I am as thirsty for and as curious about what surrounds me." Although today he is a very rich and powerful man, he says he never forgets where he came from and the many humiliations he had to face in his life: "I learned from the humiliation never to humiliate other people." In others, enduring humiliation often turns into inflicting humiliation—not Pinault, though. His admiration for Warren Buffett, as humble as a billionaire can be, seems fitting, too. Is it true that he never has any regrets? "I do not live in a state of nostalgia—nostalgia makes you sad. I wanted to get out of my social class; I wanted to have money to be my own boss and not dependent on anyone."

But he does obviously regrets the fact that he did not attend university; instead, he went to work in the wood trade, in his father's lumber mill, and then was a soldier in Algeria. Later, when his timber business expanded, he instinctively understood one of the entrepreneur's maxims and hired people he considered better than himself. He works hard, too, starting his day at 5:00 a.m. and often by 7:00 a.m. taking meetings. "If you want to make the difference, there is only one way, to work very hard: I had no tennis, no golf, no skiing in my life." Nevertheless, although he is clever, tough, and diligent, he also credits good fortune. Time and again during our interview he says you need "to have baraka," an Arab word that means "luck."

Which was the first deal, I ask him, that made him look beyond local timber—that made him see the wood for the trees, so to speak? At the end of the seventies, he says, instead of being happy with his local success, his home, his Mercedes, and his house by the sea, Pinault decided to move to Paris and enter the world of big business, buying and selling new companies. It was the eighties that saw him leave wood work, although his improved fortune and new friends didn't make him happy, and he did not allow himself much of a social life: "I did not want to drown myself in a sterile social life—you lose too much time. What is important in business is your business surface."

Jacques Chirac became a close friend of Pinault's over the years, and Pinault knows the new president, François Hollande [elected in 2012]: "He is an open man and you can talk to him. It is important for politicians to engage with businessmen." Engagement with businessmen has not been Hollande's strong suit; see the row with Lakshmi Mittal over closing furnaces in north-eastern France and the rout of French industrialists over the seventy-five percent rate of income tax. Unlike his erstwhile foe Bernard Arnault, who applied (and was rejected) for Belgian citizenship, Pinault says that whatever measures the government takes, he prefers to stay in France. He does not want to leave the country that gave him the opportunity he has so successfully seized. "In any case," he says, "France cannot have a tax system so different from other European countries forever."

I LEARNED FROM THE

humiliation

NEVER TO HUMILIATE OTHER PEOPLE.

But going back to his life and business, I ask him how he became a globe-striding businessman. He started locally, buying the Printemps chain of department stores, the mail-order company La Redoute, and the retail company FNAC in the early nineties. But soon he realized it was the rest of the world that was most promising: "I understood globalization, and I believed in the growth prospects of globally known brands. When my oldest son François-Henri, who is now the chairman of PPR, was in California, I realized he was quite interested in the fashion business. I understood that we had to move on. When, at the end of the nineties, we had the opportunity to buy Gucci, I didn't hesitate for one second. I moved on. Then came Saint Laurent, Alexander McQueen, Stella McCartney, Bottega Veneta, Boucheron, Brioni, Puma . . . PPR sold Printemps and is in the process of selling La Redoute and FNAC. Once these have been sold, the group would have ninety-five percent of its revenues coming from outside France—from Asia, America."

What about Christie's? "Artemis, my personal holding, bought Christie's in 1998. It was an extraordinary brand that was going through a bad period. Now it is a great business." It was under Pinault's ownership that preceding years of corruption—a cartel between Christie's and Sotheby's that saw the owner of the latter go to jail for a year—were exposed. Since the bloodletting, Christie's has been buoyed by the global art-market boom: last November, for example, it set a record for a postwar and contemporary auction by making four hundred and twelve million dollars."

And Château Latour, another legendary name he has bought? "I come from a world of farmers, I am a country boy and I wanted to invest in a property in the countryside; in other words, I wanted to own some land." (One of the best and most renowned vineyards is a very particular—and very expensive—piece of land.) "Through friends at Lazard, Antoine Bernheim, and then Bruno Roger, I understood that the owners of Château Latour were considering selling it. I reacted quickly and bought Latour without visiting it. Although it is a fantastic first growth, I did not think that it would have become such a great investment. At the time vineyards were making no money. Again I had baraka."

Not everything always goes well, of course. What is his attitude when things go wrong or something does not go the way he wants? Pinault's model is Winston Churchill, who said "Never surrender," and that for him is valid in professional and in private life. He regrets that he devoted little time to his children when they were young, but now they are very close to him. François-Henri, who has a degree in economics, is his successor; his second son, Dominique, is a lawyer with his own activities; and his daughter,

Laurence, works at Théâtre Marigny, the theater near the Champs-Élysées, which he also owns. François-Henri trained for fifteen years in the group and was very carefully watched to see if he was capable of running it.

When Pinault speaks, his blue eyes are very lively and he is surprisingly energetic, considering that he only arrived from Los Angeles that morning. (He does concede that you sleep better on a private plane.) He still gets anxious about business, even on vacation, so he spends most of his time on the phone, but he has a home in Saint-Tropez, a home in Dinard, in Brittany (a house in the country like all the "French bourgeois," he says), one in London, and an apartment in New York. In Venice, even though he owns two extraordinary buildings—the Palazzo Grassi, which he took over from the Agnelli family, and Punta della Dogana—used for showing his collection of contemporary art, he stays in a hotel, usually the Cipriani or the Gritti Palace.

Taking a lesson from Talleyrand about the importance of food, how good food and good wines create a pleasant atmosphere and make any kind of meeting or conversation easier, in Paris he has a very good chef. His wife, Maryvonne, who was an antiques dealer in Rennes, has maybe the most important collection of eighteenth-century furniture in all of France. There are also beautiful objects and paintings by Picabia, Picasso, and the Old Masters of the sixteenth and seventeenth centuries. Of late it is his art collection that has pushed Pinault into the public eye. In 2005 he bought the Palazzo Grassi to house some of his 2,500 artworks—currently he is showing Jeff Koons and Thomas Houseago—and in 2007, after a long, public, and bitter battle with the Guggenheim Foundation, he bought Punta della Dogana for the more monumental works of art in his collection. The architectural project there is by Tadao Ando.

Pinault thinks that "Italy is more fun" than other countries. "The Italians live well, they are well dressed, and the women are pretty," he says. He enjoys its art, too, collecting works of Maurizio Cattelan and Rudolf Stingel. He started his collection by buying a small painting by Paul Sérusier representing a Breton woman in the courtyard of a farm; the woman looked like his grandmother, he says. Then he started collecting art of the twentieth century, from Mondrian to Man Ray. As he says this, he pauses the conversation for a moment and goes into the room next to his office to take a photograph of a Man Ray that he has just bought in an auction. He quickly understood that it was interesting to follow contemporary art and artists: In 2007 he bought a very important installation of Sigmar Polke paintings, and he owns works by Subodh Gupta,

Paul McCarthy, Bruce Nauman, Donald Judd, and Robert Ryman. More of his collection will be shown in temporary exhibitions, starting with France this year, then Berlin.

We move on to a discussion about the global economy. He thinks Europe has to defend itself and consider itself as an entity. While the southern European countries go through a tough period, the Germans have to understand that for them the French, Spanish, Italians, and Greeks are important commercial partners, important clients, and so it is in their interest that these countries get out of the crisis soon. He believes in Europe: "There is no choice other than Europe. It will succeed for the next generations."

The Middle East? "The situation is as always very unstable." China? "In spite of a small slowdown, China remains the great power of the future. The road is traced, even if the U.S. and the dollar are far from being dead. Likewise, Brazil is now an emerging power with interesting prospects. Africa, too, will make it, since it has all the commodities, but it will take time, they come from very far."

What is the main danger facing us today? "The big danger is the return of populism. The system is tired, even if democracy is still the best system." Pinault insists on the fact that we have to think that as Europeans we are 400 million people living in a politically stable area for the time being. About France, he concedes a loss of speed, but is confident about the future, given the capacity of his country to overcome difficult times and the direction taken by François Hollande's government to tackle the economy's structural problems.

I ask him if he is an optimist. "No, I am an active pessimist. But you still need a little bit of blue sky."

Paris

February 14, 2013

Originally published in *Spear's Magazine*

~

MICHELANGELO PISTOLETTO

ARTIST

In 2015 the world celebrates the seventieth anniversary of the United Nations. The creation of the United Nations and the adoption of its charter were major achievements at a time of war and upheaval, and the organization has worked tirelessly to fulfill the promises of the charter, with many remarkable successes. Still, seventy years later, humankind continues to struggle with conflicts, hunger, illnesses, and other development-related challenges in a fast-changing and globalized world.

Pistoletto, in Geneva on October 24th you will attend a very important day for the Third Paradise Symbol, and the Rebirth movement?

The Rebirth symbol embodies the purpose and mission of the UN: finding balance between diverging ideas, creating a new world of harmony through a dialogue of opposites, bringing diversity together, providing inspiration for alternative ways of governance and politics, and promoting inclusive and sustainable development. The United Nations is committed to address the challenges it faces in more effective ways and adapt to changes by modernizing its policies and practices while staying true to its ideals and principles. Hence the idea of using the symbol of rebirth to convey the intention of the United Nations to embrace this new path for diplomacy to undertake a renaissance and symbolically commit to a new start.

Where can the sculpture of *Rebirth* be found?

The sculpture of *Rebirth* is placed in the Ariana Park at the Palais des Nations. It will be a reminder to staff, delegates, and visitors of the need to "meet in the middle," to bridge distances and find harmony.

What does your installation symbolize?

The sculpture represents all UN member states united in the *Rebirth* symbol. The stones will be left rough, and be approximately 50 centimeters in height, length, and width. One stone from each country is included in the sculpture, and the name of the country is engraved on the stone. The sculpture will be inaugurated during a ceremony in Geneva on October 24, 2015, with the participation of representatives of all UN Member States and of civil society. Representatives of youth, the new generation, will also be invited from all UN countries as "ambassadors" of "rebirth" and new beginnings. The inauguration of the *Rebirth* sculpture will be accompanied by a series of art events and performances, as well as talks on the themes of rebirth and infinity.

Can you describe the meaning of your Third Paradise symbol?

Someone once defined me as a concept worker, and this is the only definition: It stems from a reconfiguration of the mathematical infinity sign. Three circles are drawn: the two opposite circles represent the world of nature and the technological world, developed by humans through a process that has now reached global proportions; the middle circle is the conjunction of the two and represents the generative womb of a new world, the Third Paradise, the Rebirth. This new world is the ideal place where the technological world and nature meet in harmony, and it is reached through the efforts of humans working together to bridge differences, find sustainable development, promote peace, and create dialogue.

What is going to happen in Cuba in November?

On November 24, 2015, the first Rebirth Forum will open in Cuba. The forum will mark the beginning of a permanent workshop of art and politics in Cuba that will be developed in line with the seventeen Sustainable Development Goals declared by the UN. With this forum, Rebirth is opening a workshop of art and politics in Havana that, starting out from specific local characteristics and needs, will push the different tensions and conflicts toward resolution in a real balance, and one that can be extended to every other part of the planet.

What will the first Rebirth Forum comprise?

The forum brings together faculty members of Cuban universities, representatives of national and local public institutions, and members of Cittadellarte. The forum is being held under the auspices of the United Nations. The program consists of an initial exposition of the Rebirth project followed by speeches from the participants and will continue with sessions of discussion and exchange of ideas. The United Nations list of Sustainable Development Goals forms the main plank of the subjects that will be tackled and will be considered as the basis for a possible commitment to development in the future through a collaboration between the Rebirth Embassy and the government and citizens of Cuba.

art & POLITICS

ARE, IN FACT,

2 elements

THAT CAN BE

united

TO PRODUCE A

3rd element,

ONE THAT CONSTITUTES
A COMPLETELY NEW REALITY
FOR WHICH THE
WHOLE WORLD IS WAITING.

Do you believe in a strong link between what is happening in Cuba today and the Rebirth movement?

For sixty years Cuba has been at the center of the world's attention as a focal point and mirror of the social, economic, political, and cultural conflict that divided the world into the two camps of the Cold War. Throughout that time the world has been in the grip of opposing forces, and we are well aware that the underlying reasons for that conflict have not yet been resolved. At a moment in which we are seeing a resumption of relations with the United States, Cuba assumes a crucial position in the world on account of the direction that this evolution might take. Today there is an urgent need to develop a new balance to take the place of the previous conflict.

What does the future of the Rebirth movement hold?

The Rebirth Permanent Workshop of Art and Politics in Cuba will maintain a connection and cooperation with university and government institutions and a constant interaction with the University of Ideas at Cittadellarte, promoting collaborations with Cuban and foreign artists on the island. A second meeting of the forum is planned for the fall of 2016 in order to compare notes on the progress of the Workshop and to update the program, in connection with the network of other Rebirth Embassies in the world.

How do you maintain and develop all these interactions with Cittadellarte?

Cittadellarte–Fondazione Pistoletto is a great laboratory, a generator of creative energy that triggers unprecedented processes of development in diverse fields of culture, production, economics, and politics. The activities of Cittadellarte pursue a basic objective: to take artistic interventions on a practical level into every sector of civil society in order to make responsible and fruitful contribution to addressing the profound changes of our age.

Why did you found Cittadellarte?

I founded Cittadellarte with the aim of placing art at the center of human activities—economics, politics, culture, education—and promoting environmentally friendly and sustainable development through an artistic approach.

Why do you think art and politics should work together?

At this moment of momentous change in society worldwide, an activity in which art and politics work together has become essential in order to develop a prospect of sustainability on a global scale. Art and politics are, in fact, two elements that can be united to produce a third element, one that constitutes a completely new reality for which the whole world is waiting.

Biella

October 14, 2015

~

ZAC POSEN

FASHION DESIGNER

Zachary E. "Zac" Posen is walking around his new atelier in the Upper East Side of New York, one block away from the St. Regis Hotel or the newly opened, very chic Polo Bar. The spaces are extremely minimalist. On display all around one can see his latest collections, including the astonishing red dress that Naomi Campbell was wearing at the conclusion of Zac's last show, in Grand Central Station in New York. The dress somehow has a material that reminds him of a Jeff Koons piece. Zac Posen is smiling. He wears a three-piece suit in beige Cheviot, which he designed, a lilac button-down shirt, and a knit, pale-blue tie by Brooks Brothers. We sit in his office. Zac does not spend much time at his desk. He would rather go around his office atelier, switching from the creative rooms, where dresses are made and created, to the marketing, PR, and business rooms.

Zac, what has changed in your life since you set up your first atelier in your parents' living room in 2001?

A lot has changed. When I started I was very naïve and pure, my work was more theatrical. I did not understand how the actual fashion world worked. Now I am much more disciplined and confident. Now I know who I am, as a person and as a brand. I am more comfortable today, being myself rather than trying to fit in. From the business standpoint, I have learned my business.

Have you wanted to be the person you are now since you were a child?

As a child I wanted to be a performer: I trained as a singer, an actor, a dancer, and then it evolved and at sixteen I started to work in the fashion district on Seventh Avenue, and that got me hooked. I had very inspiring girlfriends who were wearing the clothes I was making in my high school time. I am thinking of Lola and Stella Schnabel, who were my muses and my inspiration.

Who did you admire as fashion designers?

Of course my first obsession was Madeleine Vionnet, the true first feminist of fashion, because she embraced the cut and construction of clothing to use movement and sensuality. It was not restricted to glamour. Then I would say I greatly admired Azzedine Alaïa, and I was lucky to be able to research his work in the archives of a friend. 1997 was the height of John Galliano and Alexander McQueen, and the finale of Thierry Mugler's haute couture. All these designers are very theatrical, and I call them "imagineers."

And when did you have your first success?

I've been fortunate enough to have many moments of success throughout my career but I'm still very hopeful that there will be many more to come. Having these hopes and dreams is part of what keeps you driven.

In 2012 you also became a TV star in the program *Project Runway* on Lifetime TV?

I have always interacted with the media, it was part of my desire when I started working in fashion. There was a concern that to be taken seriously you could not be on TV, so I am happy I did not go on TV at age twenty-one. Once I turned thirty I was ready, and *Project Runway* is having its best ratings and I'm very proud that *Project Runway* is now Lifetime's number-one cable network in its Thursday time period with women.

What does it give you to be on TV?

It gives me a direct voice to the consumer, and it gives the public an emotion behind the person, and one can teach them about fashion. Just in America the program has millions of viewers per episode. Therefore it gives an experience, so that partners, licensing partners, feel that there is broad enough recognition to grow their business. This is what it takes to build a fashion business globally in today's world, and this is what it takes to sell enough clothing to support my creativity.

What kind of designer do you think you are?

I think I am most known for modern glamour, contemporary romanticism, and in America my role is to continue a great tradition of social dressing.

How would you define luxury?

To me luxury today is defined by rarity. The consumer is getting ever more educated over the Internet, so it becomes more challenging and more expensive for the luxury groups to justify their prices. Keeping our top line with exclusive distribution, and taking our time to grow, made all the other products that actually make the money more valuable.

Recently you also became the creative director for the Brooks Brothers women's brand?

Brooks Brothers is the oldest clothier of the U.S., iconically tied to the way American businessmen are dressed, and their wives. It is the American classic look. For me at this stage it was important to take the challenge to work with a brand that has its own stores worldwide, and also to prove to myself and to the industry that I can make sportswear.

How is it going?

Very well, and tomorrow we style our first collection. It is shoes, bags, scarfs, shirting, outerwear, jewelry, hats, a full world. And this is the beginning.

Is this in competition with brands like J.Crew or Ralph Lauren?

Sure. These are lifestyle brands, and they all look to the original style brand which is Brooks Brothers. They are all going for that chic, classic, American sportswear look.

Is Naomi Campbell your icon?

She has been with me since very early in my career, she is family. There are many other women in my life. They all bring different qualities to the brand.

Is Michelle Obama one of your women?

Yes, and Natalie Portman, Angelina Jolie, Uma Thurman. I also have some very private clients that we never name, for their own discretion.

What kind of woman do you dress?

A creative, glamorous woman, somebody that is comfortable with her femininity, and for me those things are not defined by age, body shape, or race. I like real bodies, and I am not turned on by over skinny, unhealthy bodies.

How is business going?

Good, very solid. On collection we sell what we make, and the secondary line is growing by double every year, and our licensing partners are very happy.

Do you work most of the time?

Wonderfully I am in a relationship with someone who is the creative director and the stylist of the company. I started the company as a family business and feel very lucky that I have such a close relationship with my family, and feel very grateful to have such a great working relationship and trust with my professional and personal partner.

I have a great dialogue and relationship with my management in my company, which is key to success. Art and commerce work together.

Are you a happy man?

Yes, I am happy that I am able to create every day, to collaborate with my employees, to be a positive voice about creativity on TV, to have a wonderful relationship with my partner and my family, to eat great food, and live in New York.

How can you keep so thin?

I eat whatever I want, but basically I drink no alcohol and that saved me. For lunch I eat every day chicken soup and salad, at breakfast coffee, one egg, and orange juice, at dinner whatever I want. However, at home I mostly cook vegetarian, because my partner is vegetarian.

You have three dogs?

I had a poodle named Tina Turner, my boyfriend had a dachshund, and then together we got a third dog, a baby dachshund. It is important, very important, to have a life outside of fashion, a normal life, even if I work twenty-four hours a day, seven days a week.

Why are you so happy to be a New Yorker?

Because I am able to interact with so many interesting people from different disciplines who are here to make it happen. I flourish off the ambition of New York City. I would love to live in other places at some point of my life, you never know, but now I am happy to be here. Since I was young I had been offered opportunities to work in Milan, Paris, Tokyo, but it was not the right time and I wanted to build my brand for myself. Between the different brands, I am currently overseeing sixteen separate seasons of clothing collections a year, plus fur, handbags, eyewear, fine jewelry, and hosiery.

So you never rest?

Yes, I read, I go to the theater, to the opera, and I go to the movies all the time. But if I really want to have relief I go to my parents' vegetable garden. The best place for me is nature and to be in a garden. I don't go to the gym, it is not relaxing, but I am dancing around all day and that is my way to stay fit.

New York

April 1, 2015

~

MIUCCIA PRADA

FASHION DESIGNER

Miuccia Prada is a unique woman and for her fashion is a statement that combines past, present, and future. Her style is unique, very feminine, and at the same time controversial, because she has an idea of beauty and fashion that is at once both classic and also profoundly modern. It does not matter if we are talking about her new collection or one she proposed ten years ago, she understands that, even if art, and fashion are not the same thing, fashion needs to be inspired by art, because art anticipates as a metaphor what is really happening or will soon happen in the world. So as much as she is looking at the future she is rooted in her past collections and in her tradition.
Prada is somehow a philosopher of taste, which is not necessarily good taste but what people sometimes don't even know that they are looking for. Like most artists today she is a citizen of the world, but she needs to live in Milan, the city were she was born and grew up, because there she has her home, her family, and her identity, and she does not want to lose it. She is proud to be Italian, an Italian artisan who dresses all kinds of women and all kinds of men, all over the world.

Miuccia Prada, Christmas is approaching and how are sales going?

We are now in a phase of rethinking everything. It is not true that people are not buying. They are not buying so much just for the sake of buying, but only when they are really motivated to do so.

What are you doing about this?

In our New York store, every season we present a Vintage collection, a show of our previous productions—not in the sense of our being a museum, but rather in the sense of styles that are important today because now they are out of production. This is an idea that has greatly tickled the fancy of Americans, who loved it. There are some stores in the world which we call epicenters; they are special, experimental, designed by great architects. And it is also part of a unique sales system, so that, for example, in the evening we also show movies or hold other events.

Is the only store like this the one in New York?

That one is the first of a series. The second is under construction in Tokyo and will be opened in 2003. At the beginning of 2004 we will open another one in Los Angeles.

And in Europe?

They are being planned, but they will be different. While those in New York, Tokyo, and Los Angeles are hugely demanding and expensive, in Europe they will be just as interesting but less costly. It is possible that there may also be one opening in Beijing.

How is the market generally speaking? Are you still expanding? And what about the Chinese?

For special projects I have made some caftans that allude to the traditional story of Prada: They have all been bought by a sheikh who is creating a super trendy fashion sales outlet. However, as regards China, it is the market that everyone thinks will work more than any other. Because they have a great curiosity and a different spirit from the Japanese who are more puritanical. The Chinese are big spenders and have a great passion for objects and for clothes.

And they love counterfeiting. . . .

Because it is the only means of access that they have, but they have a great amount of money to become consumers. In our New York store for a few months we will project on our screens a series of films about China.

When it comes to Prada's fashion direction, where is it going?

What I feel is necessary is the recovery of beauty, which is not being nostalgic. It's the beauty that comes after the ugly and the trashy.

Are you thinking of a more feminine woman?

I am speaking especially about aesthetic forms. Speaking of beauty one usually thinks about the haute couture of a Dior. But then the world switched to blue jeans and a dirty T-shirt. We would now like to create a sense of greater dignity: To regain and revive the knowledge of quality. I am currently working on fabrics that were made on looms that these days nobody operates.

You are speaking about tailoring then?

Also. The tailoring of a fabric that is no longer made, to use specific beautiful materials to make wearable clothes. It also interests me to rediscover the kind of work that most people simply do not know about any longer. It is a heritage that should not be passed up. I have worked extensively within European culture, maybe today this is not enough any longer.

Prada has also sought this elegance in sailing boats?

Sometimes the elegance of a hull does not coincide with the speed of the vessel. Therefore when it comes to boats it is not always beauty that holds the right key.

One of your passions is contemporary art. With your husband, seven years ago, you created a foundation, which is more and more active . . .

Until three or four years ago my attention to art was in a kind of historical and cultural way: We mounted exhibitions of artists from the generation of the sixties. More recently we have worked closely with contemporary artists, where there are no texts or studies or cataloges, we have come to understand that we can only come to know them by familiarizing oneself with them and cultivating the same interests. For me this is a necessity of my own personal life and it's something which is very real.

Does contemporary art have similarities with fashion?

They both have the same social inquisitiveness and reflect the dramas, the joys, the pleasures of life as it is lived today.

Do you think that Italy is a country that lacks culture?

No, because it has deep cultural roots, but it rather lacks when it comes to being bang up to date. It is not just our problem. With the foundation I tackle also the problem of thought. To try to understand all the complexity of today.

How do you see Italy?

It's still fantastic, perhaps the best country in which to live, where art, beauty, and the quality of life are higher. Perhaps it lacks curiosity about the present time and engagement with what is happening in the rest of the world. I'm talking about film, art, architecture. There are isolated instances of superb quality, but not generally throughout the environment.

To use the jargon of economic policy, is what you are saying that there is not a "country plan?"

Yes, that is the exactly case. The best artists are always traveling the world, but when you are in Italy you simply do not find an available ambience of writers, filmmakers, or musicians. So a center of excellence has not been created.

Where in the world is it different to this?

In London, in New York . . . .

THE SAME OLD

FRIENDS—THE FAMILY, THE HOME—

THESE ARE ALL THE ADDITIONAL

ANCHORS OF OUR SALVATION.

And yet you insist on living in Milan.

I do not know if I insist, but it is the house in which I was born.

Do roots count?

For me they count a lot: The enormous complexity of countries is our root and the point that keeps you in balance. To have roots is like an anchor of reassurance; an almost practical tool that enables one to maintain one's equilibrium.

And the family?

That, too. The same old friends—the family, the home—these are all the additional anchors of our salvation.

And the black suit?

It has its own value, it is very important, as the blouse is just as much! Such clothes provide reassurance. The endless process of frantically looking for the new, the constant anxiety of trying to understand the complexity that is all around. Exactly the same mechanism works with clothes. As one needs roots and family, so one also needs black suits and blue blouses.

In the windows of Prada you also see many traditional suitcases. Yet one does not use the old accoutrements of travel so much any more?

If we want to talk about fashion, a classic is the fashion of today, understanding it also as a cultural privilege; and perhaps it is even necessary to have a beautiful leather suitcase. At the end of the day at Prada this is how we started, in 1913, with leather goods and luxury items: it was our hallmark.

Are you always working so much?

I work at my own pace. In the morning I go to the office late; if it is necessary I work a lot, if not, then I don't.

Are you very much involved with your children?

I would say yes. Unless you are talking about the computer environment that I find interesting but which I really do not know.

You find it scary?

No, I'm just not capable, or rather I haven't tried it all out properly yet.

So are all your designs drawn by hand?

I do not design as such, I tell a story to my designers and my assistants.

You have created a new watch. Why only one model?

It is one of my husband's initiatives, a limited edition to celebrate the America's Cup. It's enough to begin to address the timekeeping problem.

Is fashion today still so important or does it need to downsize a bit, is it in crisis?

It's not in crisis: It is one of the young people's strongest obsessions. Fashion affects people in an almost agonizing way; it's as if it holds an exaggerated interest. Fashion is tied up with everything that represents physical appearance, and health, it is part of the quest for eternal youth that holds us all in its spell.

Milan
December 8, 2002

~

We would now like to create a sense of greater dignity: To regain and revive the knowledge of quality.

TIMOTHY RADCLIFFE

DOMINICAN FRIAR

Timothy Radcliffe OP is a Dominican friar and served as master of the Dominicans, the Order of Preachers, for nine years. He inspires people in his addresses and retreats in all corners of the globe, and is one of the best-loved Christian spiritual teachers of our times.

Father Radcliffe, Pope Francis has recently named you "consultor" of the Pontifical Council for Justice and Peace. What does it mean to you?

I am grateful. The work of the Pontifical Council is very important. It's a way to support the Pope, who has put this at the heart of his mission. Most people were named by Pope Benedict, but I was named later, a bit out of the blue.

Does this imply you will move to Rome?

I accepted because I am able to continue to preach and lecture around the world while based in Oxford. Whenever the Council needs me I can go to Rome, to offer whatever support I can.

As a Dominican Father, what is your relationship to the Pope?

We feel a deep link, as he is the center of unity. Pope Francis is a man for whom I have enormous admiration, so I am very happy to give him any support.

How often have you met him?

I met him in Buenos Aires when he was archbishop, and then had a long conversation eighteen months ago in the Vatican. Then a third time, in December, I was present for a meeting of the Pontifical Council for Interreligious Dialogue. We had a meeting of Christians (Catholics and Anglicans), Muslims (Shia and Sunni), and an Argentinian rabbi who is a close friend of the Pope.

Do you support the Pope because of his agenda for change? Are there many changes afoot?

I have supported all the popes, but I love the new freedom that he is breathing into the church. Pope Francis believes that the Holy Spirit is poured upon us, and we do not know where it may take us. He realized in a retreat, reflecting on his term as a Jesuit Provincial, that he had been a bit too controlling. You have to trust people. The Spirit is given to each of us. I think the Pope is not trying to push his personal agenda, he is trying to encourage free and open discussion at all levels of the church.

What did you find in your six months of sabbatical when you left your role as master of the Dominican Order?

The purpose of the six months was to reflect on the meaning of "virtue." I was once in Slovakia with a Polish brother, and he said that for Saint Thomas Aquinas the whole point of Christian life was to share God's joy and God's freedom. I found this a fascinating thought that I wished to explore. Often people think that morality is about rules you must obey. The pursuit of virtue is about growing strong and joyful in God's friendship. This is a new way, and also an old way, of seeing the moral life. It was the medieval tradition as found in Aquinas.

What are your major concerns today?

I would say the crisis in the Middle East, which is why I went to Baghdad, which used to be a great center for Islam, Christianity, and Judaism. Now there are no more Jews left in Baghdad, who had been there for twenty-five hundred years. They arrived in the Babylonian exile five hundred years before Christ, and now they are gone. The Christians, too, are disappearing, only ten percent of what they were. I stayed in the center of Baghdad, where there was a thriving Christian community, and now there is almost nobody left. So many states are in crisis: Libya, Syria, Iraq, and Yemen. This has generated a vast movement of people seeking a home in which they can survive. I think it is the great crisis of our time.

What is going to happen?

I don't know. These migrants are exploited. Networks of traffickers are making money from them and then abandoning them. They queue to come to Europe and there are thousands waiting in Calais to cross to England. Faced with this vast tragedy we have, as Pope Francis said, lost the ability to weep.

Do you think Europe will become a Muslim world?

No, I don't believe so. I think there is a real crisis of faith for young Muslims in Europe and in the Middle East. I think the new generation in France and the UK have just the same struggle with faith as young Christians do.

Why?

It is complex. Because they face secularism and because they experience their own religion as not liberating. Many young Muslims find their faith shaken by the brutality of ISIS and the conflict between Shia and Sunni.

Are people less religious?

People are less religious, certainly in England, one of the most secular societies.

Why is England like this?

In some ways, our society is marked by fundamentalism. There is a scientific fundamentalism, which thinks that everything can be explained by science. The church has nothing against science as long as it does not make totalitarian claims! Then there is market fundamentalism, which reduces human beings to *homo economicus*, people seen as consumers and producers, functions of the market. Religious fundamentalism is a response to these. I think many young people are searching for a vision of humanity which preserves a sense of our beauty and dignity. We have lots of young university students coming to Mass here, so I am not pessimistic at all.

And do they want to join the Order?

We have an increase in vocations in the Dominican Order. Here at Blackfriars we have twenty-eight brothers and an average age of about thirty-five. Religious life is not finished!

Is the Catholic church changing?

I think the big change is that often there have been divisions in the church between progressive and conservative, now we are getting beyond that. The new generation usually transcends that polarization, which is alien to Catholicism. We are breathing an air which is fresher. When I look at our young Friars here, you cannot describe them as either conservative or progressive, they want to find what is best. I don't like these categories, for example when people say to me, "Oh, you are very progressive." I do not wish to be confined by any box!

Is the Catholic church still strong?

Yes and no. It is true that in Western Europe many fewer people are attending Mass every week, and yet religion is more than ever a point of reference. I think if you look at the Pope's Encyclical on Ecology, it is very interesting that many people are saying, "If anybody can get the world to face the ecological crisis it is the Catholic church." Politicians lack the conviction. Much industry lacks the motivation. Maybe it is only the Pope who can achieve something. So that is a significant strength.

The church has been under siege, with both financial and sexual problems?

And a loss of credibility. Certainly the whole sexual abuse crisis has been absolutely terrible, but I hope and pray that the church is becoming the safest place in the world for children now. We were the first into the crisis, but now it has hit the BBC, government, schools, NHS—you see it very widespread. So I hope the church, with all its humiliation and self-reflection, can now help society to be a better place for children.

And the Pope was very important in this?

He has been very strong and has made powerful moves. We must admit that Pope Benedict began to make important steps. Often we contrast Francis and Benedict too much. There is more continuity between them than is generally admitted.

Is it strange to have two Popes?

Well, we will get used to it. It think it was very courageous of Pope Benedict to resign.

Why?

Because there was huge pressure on John Paul II not to resign. He wanted to, but the pressure on him was not to. Benedict was very clever, he didn't tell anybody. If he had tried to tell anybody they would have stopped him.

You go around the world to preach. What are people looking for?

They look for hope. The big challenge of our time is to recover hope. Many young people are unemployed; the economic and political crisis all over the Muslim world, our uncertainty about the future of the planet—the most important thing is for people to hope. There is a Eucharistic Congress in the Philippines in January 2016 which will take the theme of hope.

Have people lost hope? The hope of what?

Happiness; the hope of finding meaning. People distrust institutions. Politicians think about the next election, journalists about the next edition, companies the next financial year. We live with a very short-term awareness. The church should embody the long memory of humanity and its long-term aspirations.

Is this because of the Internet and technical progress?

I think it's one element, connected with a detachment from the rhythm of nature. Everything has to be instantaneous. In England this is the "Now Generation." Christianity teaches us to hope by reminding we can dare to hope for a future, even if it comes slowly.

Is there a nervousness?

The English expression is, "Let us eat, drink, and be merry, for tomorrow we die." Which means we have to enjoy life, because tomorrow we may not be. Life is longer, we now know this world was created thirteen billion years ago and humanity four hundred thousand years ago, and each of us is living much longer, so on one hand we have a sense of enormous time, but on the other we want to live for now. It's the paradox of our culture.

How can we find our spirituality?

We have instant access to information but there is a crisis of superficiality, the attention span is very limited. The Superior General of the Jesuits, Adolfo Nicolás, talked of "the globalization of superficiality." We must dare to ask the complex questions which take time to reflect upon. And we must dare to ask these questions in collaboration with those young people who are wrestling with them, whether in literature, art or poetry.

Should religion be simple?

God is utterly simple. So simple that we cannot understand Him. I think the life of religion should make us stronger and more coherent. But it is difficult to become truly simple.

How can you be happy in such a terrible world?

Because I meet wonderful people all the time and I live the contemplative life. I went to Baghdad. It's not easy in Baghdad, but I met extraordinary people and had a very happy time there. I see great beauty wherever I go. There is a lot of terrible suffering, but people meet suffering with great courage. I used to go to Rwanda during the crisis, once every year. I wanted to give hope, but I found they gave me hope.

Is God a necessity for humans?

People often ask if God is relevant for our lives. God is more than that. Everything is relevant in so much as it leads us to God, who is the point and meaning of everything. I think that everyone has some sense of an ultimate meaning, even if they do not call this God.

What is the purpose of religion?

For a Christian, it is that we are made for happiness, which is God. God is pure happiness and that's what we are made for. Religion is the invitation to share God's happiness. Religion is not about being good. You are good, not because it is required, but because it's wonderful, a joy. The French writer [Georges] Bernanos said the only happiness is to be a saint. To enter the religious world is to move from living in black and white to living in color.

Have you ever had a crisis in faith?

I wouldn't say I had doubts about God's existence. I have had periods of being bored by religion, when I thought God seemed absent, when everything became gray.

What did you do when it all became flat?

You carry on and say your prayers. I once fell in love with a woman and then it was very difficult, because I could imagine a life with her. We remain friends, but I had to say, "I am somebody called to this life, this is the life for me."

Are you very supportive of gay people?

I think that we should give thanks for the gifts of gay people. I think each person has to find their own way to love. God is present in every love. Personally I do not believe in gay marriage, but that is a long topic. But I do believe gay people are a blessing. Gay people have a lot to give us, and we should welcome their gifts.

As a friar you can't marry? Or have a sex life?

As friars or monks we have the possibility of fantastic friendship with people, friendship is absolutely the center of our lives. Chastity frees us for deep intimacy with people.

Are you tired of all this obsessive sexual interest?

There is a curious obsession with sex while at the same time our society often trivializes it, as if it were merely a recreation. We must welcome people whatever paths they have taken. We must find a way for people who are divorced and remarried to come home to the Eucharist, even if this involves a clear reflection on what happened. We must respect and honor the complexity of people's lives, and the complex paths by which they come to God. The temptation is to reduce religion to morality, and reduce morality to sex. I think that's very limiting.

Does education make for less racism and hate?

In Baghdad the Dominicans founded the Baghdad Academy of Human Sciences, with five hundred pupils, seventy percent of whom are Muslims. We teach anthropology, psychology, philosophy, and the scientific study of religion, because the best opposition to fundamentalism is education. The enemy is not religion. The enemy is reductionism, fundamentalism. Saint Dominic sent the friars to universities to study, to Bologna, Paris, Oxford.

Are people frightened in the Middle East?

It's dangerous, but it is their home. I would not say frightened. They live from day to day. One brother of our Order had just arrived in Baghdad from France and he said, "I have never been so happy in my life."

Why?

Because he gives himself. The only happiness is to give oneself.

And faith?

When you meet a young person, the question is not do they have faith, the question is what do they believe in? Everybody believes something. You have to start with the belief they have and then walk with them as they search. We hope that this will lead them to Christ.

As a priest do you find yourself useful?

Last night I had to go to Bristol as a man has cancer and is dying. I had dinner with him and his wife so we could talk, so he could face this cancer. Afterward, I talked with a confused young man for an hour who searches for some meaning to his life. Now the next thing I have to do after this interview is go on a soup run, to visit the homeless, to feed them. I do not know whether I am useful! But the world is filled with people with whom I hope to share a small word of hope. But my life is not just helping people. I also have a wonderful life, a very happy life. Sometimes this joy is found with people who are in difficulties. I don't think you have real joy if you run away from suffering. Often I have the joy of friends, and great literature! I have the joy of nature in its profusion.

What do you think about possessions and money, the main preoccupation and ambition of the contemporary world?

We must not be enslaved by it. As a child I grew up in a family most people would consider wealthy. We had fourteen bedrooms in a big house. But my parents did not think that money was the important thing. My wealthy relatives living in stately homes were not happier. As a child I very quickly saw money does not make you happy. My friends thought I was mad, giving up a wealthy background to become a poor Dominican, but it was not because I wanted less, it was because I wanted more. If that makes sense.

As master of the Order of Preachers, the worldwide father general of the Dominican Order, you were a man of real power. You have gone from being a sort of a pope to being a brother. How was that compared to now?

You only have power so as to empower other people. So, it could be a power over other people, but that would be an abuse. Your power is given to you to make them strong. If you use power to make people weak and to dominate them, you would be very unhappy. In the Dominican Order the highest authority is the General Chapter, the parliament of the Order. When I went to Rome I met a Cardinal who said, "You are the supreme authority in the Order." I said, "No, I am not. The brethren, the brothers, are the supreme authority." Now I am just a brother, but then as master I was also a brother, and so the change is not so dramatic. My only obligation is to go to all the General Chapters until I die or go mad!

But you don't become someone like that unless you are gifted?

It was an election. The brothers interview you in a five day process, and then they vote.

Is the Order doing well?

One in six brothers are in formation, which is very high. So yes, the Order is doing well.

And will you stay in Oxford?

It is for the English provincial and his Council to decide. I am happy here in this very lively community with wonderful young brothers. It's a beautiful city, with the stimulation of a great university, and only one hour from Heathrow!

Oxford
June 12, 2015

~

JOHN RICHARDSON

ART HISTORIAN

The wind is blowing on a very cold New York winter day when I arrive in the downtown Fifth Avenue building where I am expected. I have come to interview the art historian Sir John Richardson, who has just turned ninety-two years old. The lift takes me up to his apartment and we enter into one salon, and then there is another one and another one; with English furniture, modern paintings, Old Masters, drawings, photographs, objets.

There is a strange colorful cardboard puppet representing Donald Trump, given to him by Annette de la Renta for his birthday; a photograph with President Clinton; and art books and art magazines everywhere. There is a book on Guernica, and a portrait of Richardson by Lucian Freud, and one by Andy Warhol, and plenty of other drawings. The English furniture is from the nineteenth and eighteenth centuries, and there are wonderful curtains and bookshelves. The floors are wood parquet with carpets, and a lot of light comes in through the windows.

His bedroom is very similar to all the salons, and John Richardson—who has just had his coffee and is dressed in an Austrian type of jacket, a plaid flannel shirt, and red suede loafers—says, "I would prefer to go into my study." He takes me to another large salon-like room, not very different from the others, where one of his assistants is typing on the computer. He was able to buy this very large apartment many, many years ago, when New York was a much cheaper place to live. We sit on the couch and start the interview.

John, you have spent your entire life in the world of art?

Yes, I went to the Slade School of Fine Art, but during the war the school moved to Oxford. Being in Oxford killed two birds with one stone, as I happened to get this strange rheumatic fever and, thank God, I did not go to the army. Back in London, to make money I helped do the windows of Harrods, and once I fell asleep in one of those windows. I also designed textiles to keep me going—this was during the Blitz. When I realized I could not be as good an artist as I wished, that I could not be a Picasso, I wrote a lot for the *New Statesman*, which was a left wing and intellectual newspaper at the time.

What did you write?

I wrote art criticism, and I did reviews on the ballet and opera. I was launched on a sort of journalistic life, but one day I went to a party and met Douglas Cooper. He was one of the main people tracking art stolen by the Germans. He could speak German in Berlin slang or Austrian German or any other way; he was great at languages. He was a key interrogator of Germans during the war. Douglas was a very aggressive person.

Did he start his art collection when you met him?

He started in 1932. He was well off, because his grandfather made a fortune in Australia. He wanted to make the best possible collection of Picasso, Léger, Juan Gris, and Braque. After the First War the great art dealer Daniel-Henry Kahnweiler's stock had been confiscated by the government in France, and divided into four lots that were auctioned around 1921. But all Kahnweiler's stock was not entirely sold, and a lot was still on the market. At that time Douglas became friends of all these artists. Sadly Juan Gris died in 1927.

Did you meet all these artists, too?

With Douglas we went to Provence in the south of France and saw some extraordinary columns around sort of a ruined neglected château. We investigated and found out that it was for sale. I said to him, "Give me that château for Christmas." Of course, he bought it for himself. Picasso was a friend of Douglas's, and he came to see us. The château was half way between Nîmes and Arles. Often we had lunch with Picasso and then went to the bullfight, and then we came back to the château; Jean Cocteau was with us. We had dinner in the garden and got gypsies from the Camargue to dance. This was in the fifties. We were regularly going to see Picasso, and I had the idea that I wanted to write about him. He was very generous to me. He sensed somehow that I was going to write about him. He had a very strange understanding of his work. When I decided to write about him, originally it was going to be about a specific part of his life, his portraiture, about the people he met, going back to the early years.

Were you less interested in his late work?

I was fascinated by his latest work. I remember that before Christmas he said to Douglas, "I want to show you some drawings I did yesterday of Jacqueline." This was 1955 or 1956. He asked us, "Which do you like best?" I personally chose the strongest simple one; Douglas chose the most elaborate and apparently glamourous, that he thought was the most expensive. Picasso said, "Okay, these are your Christmas presents." Then he said, "I don't think Douglas's is ornate enough," and he continued to paint, more and more on the painting, until eventually he ruined it.

ANDY FOR ME
WAS LIKE A CHARACTER IN
A RUSSIAN NOVEL. THE BOY IN THE VILLAGE WHO
HAS SOME SACRED QUALITY. HE NEVER
GETS HURT. THEY WALK THROUGH ANY
KIND OF TROUBLE WITHOUT BEING TOUCHED.

When did you start writing about him?

I wrote a book on his watercolors for Holbein-Verlag, the Swiss publisher, in 1956. Picasso liked that. Later on he wanted to buy Douglas's château in exchange for a lot of paintings, and Douglas said no. But I had discovered that the Château de Vauvenargues, near to Aix-en-Provence, was for sale, and I suggested to Picasso, who had come to see a bullfight, that he stop to see it after. And he did, and he bought the château.

Why did you stop living in France?

At that time, I got bored of being with Douglas in the French countryside. It was like living with Gargantua. I came to America and knew all the dealers and museum directors in New York because they had come to Douglas's in the south of France. Nine dealers who got on with each other asked me to curate a show in nine different galleries, covering Picasso's work: drawings, cubist, and different phases of his life. And that took place in the summer. In those days people could wander from a gallery to another after having dinner. It was an enjoyable way to pass one's evening and get to know Picasso.

Did you fall in love with New York?

Yes, and decided to live here. There were not many opportunities in London. All the action was in New York. The energy was so marvelous at that time. Douglas tried to blackmail me, he got to the authorities when I came back and I was stopped, not allowed into the country. Douglas denounced me as being homosexual, which was forbidden at the time. I denied this and a lawyer got me out of it.

You started Christie's in the United States, in New York?

Yes, I did. I had never worked in an auction house, but I got the job by unwittingly outing one of the Christie's directors. The recent revolution in Cuba had provided the communist regime with a mass of looted works of art. In the greatest secrecy, Christie's had sent a director to spy out the land. One of my closest friends, a foreign correspondent, told me he had spotted the Christie's man emerging from a Cuban warehouse. "What on earth were you doing in Havana," I asked the director after his return. He was amazed that I was so well informed. Christie's offered me the job of representing the firm in America. It was enormous fun setting up the first great auction house in New York. However, after a few years I came to loathe the business of art and reverted to my first love, writing—above all about Picasso, who had become a close friend when I lived in the south of France.

At the same time you were a friend of Andy Warhol, and you even became an actor in one of his movies?

Yes. In those days Andy was amazing. None of us could imagine that his paintings would be worth millions and millions and millions, like Picasso.

Were you impressed by him?

Andy for me was like a character in a Russian novel. The boy in the village who has some sacred quality. He never gets hurt. They walk through any kind of trouble without being touched. I realized that Andy went to Mass every single day of his life. I realized his Catholicism. He had this quality of being utterly innocent in the middle of the worst perversion, but he was untouched by it. He walked through life and made a huge amount of work. He had his partner, Fred Hughes, who made the connections and the sales, and he could not have had anybody better.

What about your obsession with Picasso?

I flew to be with him on his eightieth birthday. I was staying at a friend's in Cap Ferrat when someone told me that Douglas had been stabbed near Nîmes, so I went to look after him. I nursed him in hospital for a week. Picasso came over a bit later.

Did Picasso speak French with you?

Yes, he didn't speak English. He spoke French with a Spanish accent.

Are you now writing the fourth volume of his biography?

Yes, I am up to 1939, and I want to go through the war. Nobody knows all the details.

What happened during the war?

Max Jacob was taken to the concentration camps. He was able to send messages to Cocteau who did all he could, but failed. Cocteau during the war was helpful, but he was a collaborator. Picasso was passionately anti-war and anti-German. He was so vulnerable since 1937. He was in trouble because of Guernica, but the Germans treated him decently because Hitler's architect, Albert Speer, was an admirer of Picasso. But I am just about to start the war and I am not yet fluent with it. One of the points with which I have a problem is why did he paint three very large portraits of the Corsican black market art dealer Fabiani. I am surprised to see that, because Fabiani was selling stolen Jewish paintings and doing all sorts of terrible things. But Fabiani was doing this because he was providing money to support a Resistance newspaper. At the end of the war he was arrested, but because of the paper they saved him. Most of the war Picasso spent in Paris in his house on rue des Grands-Augustins with Dora Maar, and also with his Spanish secretary Jaime Sabartés, who deeply disliked Dora Maar.

THE DIFFICULTY WITH PICASSO IS THAT THERE WERE TWO EXTREMES.

HE COULD BE EXTREMELY CRUEL TO WOMEN, AND COMPLICATED.

AT THE SAME TIME HE COULD BE THE KINDEST, MOST GENEROUS, GOD-FEARING MAN.

When are you going to finish the next book?

I have two choices. Do I finish it in 1940, or do I take it over the war years—and then I can take it up to 1944.

And what happened after 1944?

Picasso became passionately in love with de Gaulle, and some Gaullists asked him to dinner. He went to the dinner and when he came back Dora Maar told me that he said, "C'est une bande de cons" ["They're a bunch of stupid jerks"]. And then, the following day, he signed with the Communist Party.

You have had a sort of double life, yours and Picasso's.

I like him and I am still obsessed by him.

Is it true that he was a monster?

He was so kind. He was not a monster. The difficulty with Picasso is that there were two extremes. He could be extremely cruel to women, and complicated. At the same time he could be the kindest, most generous, God-fearing man. He was not at all ungenerous. He was immensely intelligent.

Did he realize who he was?

Yes, he did. The more I dig I find another aspect of him.

As an artist?

Yes, and also as a human being. You never know which way he is going to jump. He had this extraordinary nature. He came from a family that, going back in the generations, had many priests, and also a hermit. Picasso is quite capable of saying terrible things about the Catholic Church, but his Catholicism was a secret that he never divulged. Jacqueline once said to me, "Il est plus catholique que le pape" ["He is more Catholic than the Pope."].

Who were his masters?

Spanish painters: Velazquez and Goya. And also Cézanne.

And after all these years, what do you feel?

The more I find, the more I dig, the greater he becomes. As does the depth of my feelings and understanding. Of course Picasso had weaknesses like anybody else, but I should say more faults than weaknesses and it is very difficult to separate his life from his work. What is difficult is that whatever you say, the opposite is equally true.

Are there any Picasso's around nowadays?

There are no Miros or Légers around. Very thin pickings. I don't think there are great artists today, but I have very little knowledge of what happens in Asia or in Africa, and I am too concentrated on Picasso.

Did you have other friends among great artists, like Francis Bacon and Lucian Freud?

Yes, I remember that Francis was broke and lived with his blind nanny. He suggested that he put an ad in the *Times* to say that he was looking for a protector, and the blind nanny found a certain gentleman. But then Francis stole some money and he was fired. The gentleman was a remote cousin of Douglas's, but as Douglas couldn't care much about relatives and he liked trouble he became a sort of protector of Francis. I was a friend of his, and a passionate admirer. I certainly think he is a great artist, as much as Lucian Freud, who is totally different. I admire them equally.

Did you know Bacon very well?

Yes, and I was behind the scenes. He drank too much at the end of his life and he went to pieces. He was fun. He was naughty. But I think that his late pictures are of no interest. Lucian on the contrary never dips, and I think somehow that it was much more gratifying to spend time with Lucian. I must say that I knew Lucian well. We had known each other since our teens and I must say that I am enormously fond of Lucian. Lucian was a great admirer of Picasso, more than Francis.

Now you are ninety-two, how do you feel?

I still feel the same. My mind is still very straight. I am alone, but I have the most wonderful three people working with me, writing with me, doing an enormous amount of research. I must say that I still work every day, even weekends.

New York
February 11, 2016

~

ABY ROSEN

ENTREPRENEUR

The interview with Aby Rosen took place on the island of Saint Barthélemy, where he was finishing his winter holidays with his family. In his living room, a sort of Japanese wood house composed of various pavilions, we sat on large white canvas couches, surrounded by white windows, facing a beautiful beach on a turquoise sea. Aby Rosen runs RFR, one of the largest real estate companies in the U.S., with his partner Michael Fuchs, who is, like him, a Jewish German from Frankfurt. "I have known him since nursery school," says Aby. "He is my best friend."

How old are you?

I am fifty-three years old. I was born in 1960 in Frankfurt. It has been a long run growing up in Frankfurt, being a Jew when only one percent of the population was Jewish. My father was Polish and was kept in Auschwitz until April 1945. My mother was born in Brussels in 1935, and in 1940 she was brought by my grandfather to a non-Jewish family of farmers, very simple people, and lived with them until 1945. Later she became a painter, an art where she could express her fury.

How was it to grow up in Germany fifteen years after the war ended?

We were too young to realize what had happened. It was later we realized what it meant, what had happened. It was hard to recognize such a trying environment. For myself, I thought it was nice to be special, different. My father made money and we felt financially secure. I realized I was positive, friendly, outspoken, driven.

But how did you start your professional success?

My father had a heart attack and therefore retired from work when I was eighteen. I was in law school then and I worked in my father's real estate business. He gave me the keys.

Why did you go to the States?

I didn't want to be a lawyer. I always liked America: it was smart, new, innovative. New York is a town you choose, not because it is beautiful but because it suits you.

How old were you?

I was twenty-seven. I took a loan from my father. I wanted to be independent.

So what did you do?

I bought an empty building on the corner of 44th Street and Lexington Avenue, a fantastic location. I hired a very good architect and we did a very good job. I spent too much money, to turn the building into a great building. Normally, if you have a great location, you would not usually upgrade the building. But I was smart to make it aesthetically very nice and lease it to McDonald's, and it became the nicest McDonald's in the city. From then on I understood how much real-estate and architecture were connected. You also have a premium for great architecture.

Since then do you own some very significant buildings?

Yes. I own the Seagram Building by Mies van der Rohe and then Philip Johnson. And Lever House. Built in 1954, it was the first glass building in the world. In one year I bought two of the best pieces of real estate ever. I have built fifteen buildings, renovated more than thirty, and altogether I own seventy-one buildings.

All in New York City?

No, also in Miami and Las Vegas—and a big portfolio of real estate in Germany.

You also have hotels?

Yes, the W South Beach in Miami, the Paramount in Times Square, the Gramercy Park Hotel.

Art has a lot to do with your work?

I realized that art and architecture have a strong relationship and I started to put art in all the buildings, plazas, rented apartments. . . . We commissioned lots of artists' work. We buy art for our spaces and also help our tenants to put together collections.

What kind of art?

Progressive artists as well as established ones.

You are yourself an art collector?

I have eight to nine hundred paintings. From Warhol, Twombly, Basquiat, Koons, Ed Ruscha, Damien Hirst, Richard Prince. . . I love sculpture because it is a form, you can place it anywhere you want. With a painting it stays on the wall and doesn't change the shape of the room. Sculpture is a form in the room.

Are you very close to Israel?

We had big ambitions to build in Israel but eighteen years later we have only built the W hotel in Tel Aviv—Jaffa. I was disappointed not to do much but it was too competitive. Israelis are very tough and not very internationally-oriented. But the W hotel will be beautiful, in a historical building.

Now, after so much success and so many years, do you feel German or American?

100% American. I have an American wife, American children. I feel gratitude towards America, who enabled my success. I have to be appreciative, and it is my home.

And how do you feel when you go to Germany?

I feel like a visitor. I know that I am coming and leaving. Germany was my home for the first twenty-seven years of my life, but I don't have a cultural relationship with the country. When you embrace the culture, that is when you decide this is your home.

Culture is also language. What is your language?

My language is English, even if I speak German to some of my old friends.

Are you sure that Germany had no impact on your culture?

It had a long, strong impact. I studied the classics in German and I still like some of the German books. Some German movies of the sixties and seventies are hysterically funny. We grew up only with the classical music of Brahms, Wagner, Beethoven, operas . . . . Everything was German.

So what is the difference between Germany and the U.S.A.?

Americans and Germans are similar when it comes to being proud, nationalistic. To have pride, the desire to be precise, to be a leader, leadership is the same. Maybe the U.S. is a continuation of what Germany was. The desire to succeed was huge in me. I don't know if it was because I was a Jewish outsider or just a German who was looking forward.

And as a Jew how do you feel?

Not as religious as before. Religion was an important part of me because Jewish history is linked to their religion. I love the fact that my father used to say, "Maybe Auschwitz was God's will." It is a cheap excuse but helped him. America is the place where I was able to express myself. I enjoy life, I love it.

How is the real estate business?

Real estate is always good. As a business it gets better with low interest rates. If interest rates are high it's bad for business. If they put up rates, business will slow down. But everyone needs a home, a second home, an office. Housing is what we think about all the time, that is why it is always a business.

Are you sometimes afraid?

In 2008 I was really afraid, for two or three months. If everything failed it was very dangerous for the system.

Do you think art prices and real estate prices are in a bubble?

No, art is demand and supply. The demand is gigantically strong. It has become a commodity, an asset like stocks and real estate.

But what about art itself?

It is an asset and people want to buy, for investing, for pleasure, for documenting (like the museums). Art is the reflection of what is going on and by acquiring it you own your segment of the time, like a photograph. Today people who make money are more and more sophisticated. There is so much money! There are so many billionaires and millionaires everywhere.

What about your future?

I think that one has to have a conviction and a plan. Time is your enemy if you are not decisive. Time is also a healer when you make a mistake. My program is very similar and simple. I continue to do what I do: create good housing, good spaces, and use art for longevity, for long term things. I would like to use great architects, work with landscapers. Landscape architects have to be recognized. I look for commercial success. I am a capitalist but if I can do it with good architects, good landscapers, good artists, and create longevity this makes me happy. I would like to be remembered as someone who had a good eye. A good eye means a good judgment.

And what is the definition of your work?

I make good things better.

Saint Barthélemy
January 7, 2014

~

ISABELLA ROSSELLINI

ACTRESS

Inspired by silent movies, Isabella Rossellini has made a series of funny films for the Internet under the titles of *Green Porno* and *Mammas*. She has developed *Green Porno* into a new art form, a one-woman stage show that she has taken around the world and is currently performing in Australia [in 2014]. In love with animals since she was a little girl, she went to university to study animal behavior. Her passion for conservation has become part of her career, and she does it with humor. Isabella is amazed by the diversity of animal mating behavior on the planet and finds the thousands of ways there are to make love, to form bonds and to propagate the species in the animal kingdom hilarious. *In Green Porno* the actress transforms herself into mating animals, ranging from dolphins and deer to snails, songbirds, and earthworms. Her great interest in animals and their conservation comes through clearly in the following extracts from my archive interview, which was originally published in *Vanity Fair* in January 1991.

She lives in a two-floor apartment in an old house in SoHo, the favorite Manhattan neighborhood for New York's artists. Isabella Rossellini is not yet home when I arrive, and so I wait for her in a big room with light wooden flooring, a rustic table, and a few chairs. This room is at the same time the kitchen, the living room and the hall. Everything is extremely clean and organized. I am sad for her, because I know her relationship with movie director David Lynch, with whom she had been together for six years, has just ended and that they broke up during his shooting of the film *Blue Velvet*.

I hear a rattle of keys, the front door opens, it's Isabella. She's smaller than I remember her to be. Her hair is cut short, and she wears gray pants, a white shirt and black suede shoes. We take a tour of the apartment. I see her wrought-iron bed, a little study with its desk on which sits a typewriter, and the new bathroom that, as she comments with a smile, "Is as big as a movie star's!" Next to her own room is her daughter Elettra's bedroom. Elettra is named after her grandmother, Roberto Rossellini's mother. It's as clean and well organized as the rest of the apartment.

I inherited a taste for order and cleanliness from my mother [Ingrid Bergman] and my Swedish family. I love order, in my daily life as well. When I'm in New York I wake up at six in the morning, come to the kitchen, and make a cappuccino. Coffee and cappuccino are the two Italian things that I can't live without. Then I read the newspapers until seven o'clock. At seven I wake Elettra up, help her get dressed, prepare her breakfast, walk her to school, and come back home where my phone calls then begin. The most difficult thing in my life is organizing my "schedule," allocating my time. I divide myself between my work as a model for Lancôme, which includes photo shoots, travel around the world, and the promotion of their perfumes, and my work as an actress. I just got back from three months in Russia, where I shot a film with Giorgio Ferrara.

What did you think about Russia?

Most of all, it scared me. I had this feeling that something nasty was about to happen, and then, while I was there by myself in the hotel, I had a phone call from David Lynch in the middle of the night telling me that everything was over. You can imagine how bad that made me feel. I am a big *mamma* that becomes very emotionally attached, and if it was left solely up to me I would never end a relationship. So, when I wasn't working I spent some very sad days sitting in my room, since it was raining outside, and I forced myself to read some books.

Sometimes Isabella smiles and the expression of her eyes becomes more tender, more feminine. Several times she repeats the idea that women are frailer than men, and adds:

Men need free spaces, to be left alone, hopefully to live an adventure or two. Women are different. When they are in love they are faithful to a single man.

Don't you think that your extremely busy life and always working could have contributed to the break up with David Lynch?

No, I don't actually think it was a problem of closeness or distance. Ours was a long distance relationship, we spoke for hours on the phone. . . .

Isabella constantly returns the topic of our conversation to discussions about family. She says that she is more of a sidekick than a star. Even today, despite her success in film and her Lancôme contract, Isabella doesn't feel like a star and doesn't behave at all like one. In fact, both for me and for others who have known her for many years, she has remained totally straightforward and natural.

I TRAVEL ALL OVER
THE WORLD,
BUT MOST OF THE TIME THE
O
N
L
Y
PEOPLE I SEE ARE
A STYLIST
AND
A MAKE-UP ARTIST . . .

I have always lived among superstars, first with my parents, then with Martin Scorsese and David Lynch, people that were virtually incapable of thinking about anything but their jobs. For them love is, in a certain sense, subordinate to work. I have not been lucky in love. I always look for men who are difficult geniuses that in some way remind me of my own family. Then, after a few years, they leave me and I don't understand why. I always take it badly. Some time ago I saw Martin and he told me that, when we met, it was very important for him to think that he was in a relationship with Roberto Rossellini's daughter! Now that I'm financially independent, I'm happy because I don't want to be dependent on the men with whom I live. These great genius types often don't deal well with contingent responsibilities. Martin and David are alike, they think up great ideas, they think about the problems of the world. I recall seeing David cry while he watched a TV show about children in Nicaragua. The men of my life are visionaries, a bit like my father. I feel extremely inspired by them, overawed in their presence, because when I'm on my own I don't think about these things, I'm much more preoccupied by daily life.

The fact that she has made a lot of money amuses Isabella and she tells me what she has done with it as if she is sharing a cooking recipe. The first money that she earned from Lancôme enabled her to buy this apartment. Then she listened to the voice of her own common sense and decided that she would divide her capital into three parts and that she would have three different people invest it for her, in competition with each other.

This strategy turned out to be rather sensible, and I have to say that I'm happy with my investments.

Isabella assumes an expression that on one hand makes her look identical to her mother and on the other likens her to a young girl that has been up to some kind of naughtiness. Then she adds:

If I hadn't had enough money to be able to live comfortably with my daughter, I don't know how I would have been able to bear being left by a man at the age of thirty-eight, after six years of being together with David. There is just no doubt that money helps. I have seen some other friends of mine that have been left by their husbands who have found younger women. In many cases they've had to change their lives, some have ended up in tiny, horrible houses. It's not easy for a woman to grow old. That's why I respect my work so much, why I like it, even though being on the road a lot becomes a heavy burden at the end of the day.

Do you read many books?

Yes, mostly biology books, books about animals. I've always had a great interest in biology, and I think that when I'm older I will dedicate myself to study and research. These days, whenever I travel, I always spend time in little-known places where they have animal reserves for endangered species.

How on earth did you develop that interest?

I was a lousy student at school, but I always liked biology a lot, and history as well. They are passions inherited from my father. He seldom talked about movies and didn't go and watch them. He would stay in bed, reading for hours, and then when he was with us, with his children, he talked to us about books, about ideas. He liked reading history and keeping up to date with scientific advances. Deep down he was an Italian patriarch who was very attached to his family. He died when I was only twenty-two, but I remember that he was very jealous. He was jealous of the boys with whom I spent the evenings: I always had to be back home early.

And your mother?

My mother was an actress in the purest sense of the word. She liked movies, the world of cinema, she loved going out with her actor colleagues. She wasn't strict at all. We only ever saw each other frequently during the years when she was ill.

Isabella, do you feel just a little bit Swedish, or are you only Italian?

I've lived in the U.S. for twenty years, and at the end of the day this is now my country. I'm happy to be in New York, where I have my apartment, my daughter, and so many excellent friends. This is a country where you are free to make your dreams come true. You can think of doing something, try it out, and often you can succeed. Even if it's true that during these months we're going through a big crisis, and that for years there have been problems of extreme poverty. But I think that these are in many ways the best of times for New York and for this country. Moments of hope. This is a tough country, a country of pioneers, and it's precisely during the tough times that you learn to live better, because there's a new spirit, people roll up their sleeves and search for something new. I certainly didn't like the eighties so much, with all their emphasis on money and the yuppie mentality. Perhaps a little bit of my rebellious feminist past has stuck with me.

What do you do when you are not working? Do you have loads of friends?

I do usually lead the high life, but more for reasons to do with charity or my work. Otherwise, Elettra and I remain here or go to Long Island, to our country house.

Isabella has made us coffee. She has small hands that are in contrast to her large and determined personality. She rests them on the table and moves them nervously.

I travel all over the world, but most of the time the only people I see are a stylist and a make-up artist, and we spend hours and hours alone together in the hotel bathrooms where they help me get ready for the photo shoots. Speaking about makeup, I remember that once when I was shooting with Mastroianni, I saw him one morning while they were putting on his makeup. He was fast asleep and let himself be worked on without so much as a flinch!

I have always liked the world of fashion better than the movies. It's more fun, it has less intellectual pretensions than the world of film making. For some years now one very important person in my life has been Howard Gilman, an industrialist who created a foundation in Florida where they have a farm for endangered animals, and scientists from all over the world live there. Misha Baryshnikov, with whom I go there a lot at weekends, introduced me to him. I really think that I will dedicate my old age to that field, even if my primary ambition now is maximizing my success in movies. When making my last few films it has very much felt to me that I am on the right track.

Isabella is very attached to Rome, where she spent her teenage years with her sister, Ingrid, who these days teaches at Columbia University in New York, and their brother, Robertino, who lives in Monte Carlo. But she no longer wants to live in Italy, as she doesn't feel that she is taken seriously there. She feels that she has to double her kindness, her punctuality, her professional capacity, so as not to be constantly reminded of how extraordinary her parents were. Isabella has talked very openly with me. And if she speaks with the kindness and the fluency of somebody who is used to being interviewed, I also sense that at heart she is extremely shy. She has told me all that is needed. She walks me to the front door. It's rush hour, and she's worried that I won't be able to find a cab. Her parting remark is:

Deep inside I'll always be the Italian *mamma*, to which she adds, I worry about everything.

New York

January 1991

Originally Published in *Vanity Fair*

~

JACOB ROTHSCHILD

INVESTMENT BANKER

Jacob Rothschild, how do you manage to deal with so many different philanthropic organizations, with your own collection, with your art foundation and the one in Israel, and at the same time be a businessman?

In fact, I commit a lot of time to all this, but these are things that interest me very much indeed and I never want to say no.

As a young man, what did you want to do?

At Oxford I studied to great benefit, and I could have stayed on and become a history professor. The philosopher Isaiah Berlin also encouraged me to consider if it would be best for me to remain at the university.

And then, as opposed to all that, what actually happened?

I was put under pressure to join the family bank, of which I was a minority shareholder, and I worked there for twenty years. My mother belonged to the Strachey family, all of whom occupied themselves solely with art and literature, and therefore she was part of the famous cultural circle known as the "Bloomsbury Set." My father likewise was very taken up with the arts.

But wasn't there also a bit of mythology around the Rothschild name?

Yes, certainly. When I left the bank, I had to make an enormous effort to create a new company of my own. Anyhow, it was proposed, again by the philosopher Berlin, that I should act as Chairman of the National Gallery in London. I was appointed by the government at the time when the new Sainsbury Wing was being built and I did that job for eight years. Then, for another five years, I became Chairman of the Heritage Lottery Fund, which donates large sums to support the arts and museums.

At a certain point you began to take care of Waddesdon Manor, a house which was donated to the National Trust by your family, a place visited by over three hundred thousand people a year.

I was left with this responsibility when my cousin Dorothy Rothschild and I became very involved with all the related restoration.

So do you now live at Waddesdon House?

No, I live in another house nearby, but I am actively involved with managing it all. As well as the gardens and the great house itself, there are some two thousand five hundred works of art of great value. And recently we have also purchased two wonderful paintings by Giovanni Paolo Panini from a noble French family.

You have money available to make new acquisitions?

Yes. We have a fund that allows us to buy works of art, and we are also the owners of the Château Lafite winery.

Did you ever imagine that Lafite would become such an important business?

Absolutely not. For a hundred and fify years, the company had never paid any dividends and it is only recently, thanks to the fact that the Chinese are buying hundreds of thousands of bottles, that it has it become a very big business.

Is the Rothschild family very united?

Let's say that we are all very close, but also that we all compete with each other. For example, Château Lafite is a competitor of Château Mouton, which belongs to another branch of the family. And my cousin Benjamin's banks compete with those of the French Rothschilds, and so it goes on.

And are you not also competing with them?

No, because I am independent. I work in a company, of which I am the largest shareholder, which is actually an investment fund.

Do you find your investment work satisfying?

Very much so, because I have had to manage the money for the family, but also for about ten thousand shareholders: I like to take care of them very well, and to treat their interests as my own.

And how are you doing in these choppy waters?

We have just acquired thirty-eight percent of the Rockefeller business, one which is fairly similar to our own, which deals with "money management." In many instances we work together with them.

How does it seem to you that the world is going?

Of course, austerity does not help, I think that in the next ten years there will be slow growth and that the real danger comes from political situations. I am thinking of China, the Middle East, America, and also, of course, Europe. Which is perhaps the most complicated situation of all.

And what's going on in England?

It is in an ambivalent position with Europe, with whom it has many contacts and business, and it is also ambivalent because it oscillates between Europe and the United States.

How do you invest?

In things that are, in all honesty, very boring. The best thing you can do is to invest in large, established companies. And then every so often you look for opportunities in the world of Silicon Valley, where there are small companies that can represent outstanding opportunities.

And art?

I buy art all the time. I started my own collection many years ago.

What do you think about the situation in Israel today?

We are strong supporters of Israel, but not politically, as the foundation. We have worked a lot to help bring about the integration of the Arab-Palestinian population.

What is the situation of Jews in England?

It is excellent. We are active in many community related fields and are much loved and respected, although there is just a little bit of anti-Semitism that still exists.

When you are not working what are your distractions?

I love spending time with my eight grandchildren and my four children, with whom I do very simple things, like going to football games.

London
October 28, 2012

~

I like to take care of them

very well, and to treat their

interests as my own.

STERLING RUBY

ARTIST

The American artist Sterling Ruby works in a large variety of media, including ceramics, painting, drawing, collage, sculpture, and video. Proclaimed as one of the most interesting artists to emerge in the twentieth century and recently as Calvin Klein's latest muse, Ruby's work examines the psychological space where individual expression confronts social constraint. MIX PIZ is the title of his show at the Vito Schnabel Gallery in St. Moritz, Switzerland.

Sterling, when did you start making art and where did you grow up?

I drew as a kid in Baltimore, where we lived until I was nine. Then we moved to New Freedom in Pennsylvania. My mother was Dutch, my father American.

How did you become an artist?

I started working in construction right after high school. I got a labor job in Washington D.C. But then, around age twenty, I got so depressed that my mother said, "You have to do something with your life that you like." So at twenty-one, I started art school in Lancaster, Pennsylvania, drawing figures and still lifes. It was a very foundational art school, we only read Gardner's *Art Through the Ages*. After I graduated, I worked in a sporting goods shop.

When did you understand that you were an artist?

Very early. When I was a child my mother used to take me to visit relatives and we would take day trips to see paintings by Bosch, Rubens, and Van Gogh, the Dutch masters. I didn't think that to be an artist could be a career. After four years at art school in Pennsylvania, I still didn't have a degree. A few years after that, I moved to Chicago, and I finished my BA degree. There I also studied philosophy and psychology, and then everything changed. I started to understand that there was a possibility to be an artist for life, or as a life.

Where did you show your first works?

In Chicago. It was easy to show. There were all of these artist-run spaces, all very DIY, there wasn't the idea of dealer-artist or collector relationships at the time. We did shows in apartments and garages.

It then became a career?

I wouldn't have called it a career, not yet anyway. To go back to the school in Pennsylvania, they had a very small library and they had a copy of the *Helter Skelter* catalogue of the exhibition from MOCA in Los Angeles. This book was very significant for me. It completely shifted my understanding of what art could be. After Chicago I went to L.A. to get my MFA. The desire to go to L.A. was mostly because of *Helter Skelter*.

Did you live in L.A. since then?

I have never felt that comfortable in a big city, but I felt okay there because it didn't look like a real city. I found that the work that had been made in Los Angeles in the eighties and ninties was more pathological than in New York.

What happened to you?

In school I was working with artists. Everybody was showing in L.A. I became an exhibiting artist. I wasn't very successful. I was doing photography, sculpture, painting, ceramics. I didn't have real success until 2005 when I was in my early thirties. I had a couple of shows in Los Angeles and in Europe. Shortly after that I had a show in L.A. at MOCA. The curators were Paul Schimmel and Philipp Kaiser, a Swiss curator.

And then something changed in your life?

I had a lot of debt to pay, but after 2005 I saw a light at the end of the tunnel.

What was your art about?

I had this idea that my work was operating between expression and repression, and I wanted my work to represent both. I saw my work as an intermediary between law and crime, old and new, future versus past. I wanted the work to be a balance of these things.

How did it come out?

This is how my head works. My personality and behavior, it was about two polar extremes. I started to think that the work was a representation of my bipolar personality. The relationship between expression and repression was me.

Did you take a lot of drugs?

Well, yes, I did, mostly ecstasy, before I went to Chicago, and then I stopped . . . cold turkey.

I like big dogs.
I prefer them over small ones.
I know a lot about cats.
I might even love cats more than dogs.
My favorite cats are Russian Blue and Bengal cats.
The content of my work can come from anywhere I suppose.

Has your work changed much over the years?

I make a good bit of work even if things have changed. I see a lineage from everything I have been doing. There are artists who are known for a repetitive kind of gesture, like Bacon or Still, whom I admire greatly, but I have to work with multiple mediums. I am not criticizing the singular gesture, but I couldn't just make one kind of painting, one gesture.

Do you have a specific color that you love?

Red is my favorite color. I just opened a show in St. Moritz, MIX PIZ. There is an all-red painting in the show. I did all of the work for the show thinking of this region, the Engadin. I was thinking about the eternal return of Nietzsche, the landscape, the physical act of hiking and walking. In the show, I represent hiking and walking in an abstract way, just the sun and the moon and mountaintops, an inspiration that is very far from Los Angeles, where I live.

You seem to be in love with Los Angeles?

I am, but it also has significant problems, like homelessness and earthquakes.

You thought of moving somewhere else?

I have three kids. I am heavily invested there. I would love to live in the mountains, but it is not realistic right now.

So the city is not good for you?

I don't feel comfortable in the congestion of a city. In L.A. you spend a large part of your day in the car, by yourself. That is good for me because I like the solitude, the space to think. You can't get that feeling in New York, or Paris, or Hong Kong.

Color is very important for you?

Yes it is, and I like the representation and symbolism of colors, like flag colors.

Did you have teachers, models, professors?

I always looked at the Bauhaus as the most significant historical movement. I love Russian Constructivism. I love Vasily Kandinsky, I like Paul Klee, Bernhard Schemmel, Marcel Breuer. They represent a nonhierarchy.

This has to do with your Dutch roots?

Most of my childhood I saw people working. My mother, grandmother, and my aunt were sewing. I felt comfortable when men and women had tasks. I felt pretty comfortable with sewing and woodwork. When I was in California I had a lot of teachers. I was the teaching assistant for Mike Kelley, some of my other teachers were artists Diana Thater and Richard Hawkins, and theorists Sylvère Lotringer and Dr. Laurence Rickels.

Is there somehow an "L.A. school?"

Not so much now. Most artists in the late nineties/early two thousands were teaching. There were four colleges where important artists were teaching: UCLA, CalArts, ArtCenter, where I went, and USC. Nowadays artists don't teach so much anymore.

Do you have to produce a lot of work?

I enjoy doing a lot of shows. It helps me to move through new ideas and new series.

What are you working on at the moment?

A ceramic survey for the Des Moines Art Center, a show at the Nasher Sculpture Center in Dallas, and a survey that will include painting, sculpture, and collage presented by the Institute of Contemporary Art, Miami, and the Institute of Contemporary Art, Boston.

What is the material that you most like to work with?

I don't like one material in particular. I switch from one thing to another because I am restless.

What influences your work?

It can be anything. I like cinema from Salvador Dalí and Luis Buñuel . . . to Blade Runner. We can talk about this movie industry, such a big industry that one person cannot work without a team, but there are still auteurs that do things on their own. We can talk about dogs like the one you just asked me to draw for you. I like big dogs. I prefer them over small ones. I know a lot about cats. I might even love cats more than dogs. My favorite cats are Russian Blue and Bengal cats. The content of my work can come from anywhere I suppose.

How do you work?

I have a nine-to-five, Monday-to-Friday routine when I am in L.A., and on the weekend I work at home. All the drawings and collages are done at home. I like the difference between the very big space of the studio and the team, versus the house where it is just me working in a small space. I like that my kids are there and sometimes if I leave my work on the table for too long it becomes their work.

St. Moritz
April 2, 2017

~

I cannot think of another thing
that represents

autonomy

as well as being an artist.

FREDERICK SEIDEL

POET

Why is *Widening Income Inequality* the title of your new collection of poems, published by Farrar, Straus and Giroux?

The title is used with some considerable irony. It is a very common phrase, used by politicians and economists, and this is considered an essential, crucial problem in American society. The distance between the very rich and the very poor is far greater than ever before, and represents a danger to American society, never mind that it is serious social unfairness.

What is the book about?

I have no idea. It is about poems in many different forms, mostly rhymed, often in regular meter, some not. Very often in poems where the meter is regular, it is my pleasure to interrupt it. The point of poems is the music of the poems, not the so-called meanings. Music and energy are important, the sound and the thrust of the poems.

Is there a *fil rouge* in your poems, a guiding thread made up of some recurring matters?

Much of the action of the poems takes place in New York, in the Upper West Side, Broadway. My poems are acquainted with cities, look at cities, talk about cities; and through the cities look at the world.

Are there feelings in the poems?

In some sense the poems are feelings. Poems are poems. That is what they want to be.

One of these poems is called "Polio Days?"

Polio is something that reminds of a tragic condition of the past. It disappeared with the advent of the vaccine, but that did not help the people who were stricken before the vaccine, trapped to their iron lungs.

How do you compose your poems?

Sometimes they come with the form of an idea, or sometimes on the form of a line already formed that gives life to the rest of the poem. But it is important to remember that, as interesting as the subject may be, the work of the thing is to be a poem. If you think of the poem as a work, something you create, it becomes something outside you. That is how it has to get through, as an object you created, separate from yourself.

Do you write and rewrite?

Endlessly. Changing words, a word, changing the shape of the stanza, a line break. It does happen, but it is rare that a line comes from the start the way it is going to end up being. Mostly when something appears fully formed in your head it is not going to last. You put it down on a page and it will soon be altered. There are gifts that come and stay as they are, but that is exceptional.

How do you work?

Many hours every day, and I require a very great deal of time to do the work in. I want gallons of time to do the work. It gives you the opportunity to hear it, to smell it over, to meditate, to listen to what you are writing. You work and you work, and then comes a moment when the poem abandons you, the poem is finished. What has not been sufficiently emphasized is how important the sound is, the sound the language is making.

Do you write one poem at a time?

Yes, but there may be poems on my desktop that I have tentatively finished that are sitting there. You return for further scrutiny.

Do you read poetry?

Yes, I read a great deal of poetry in my time. As you know, I was very powerfully influenced by Ezra Pound and T. S. Eliot, who I got to know, and later by Robert Lowell. These are the masters I revered, but there have been many poets through the ages, writing in many languages, that have influenced my work. Eugenio Montale is an example of a poet in another language whose work delights me.

What is the role, the place, of the poet in American society today?

I have no idea because I do not participate in the way other poets do. I don't teach, I don't give readings, I don't belong to poetry societies. I do my work and send it out to be published.

I

salute

CRAFTSMANSHIP

of all kinds,

and elegance.

You publish quite a lot, in the *New York Review of Books*, the *London Review of Books* and the *Paris Review*?

Yes, before the poems are gathered into a book and published by Farrar, Straus and Giroux.

Your poems have a lot of politics in them. Are you following the just started presidential campaign?

Eagerly, intensely, with horror, with amusement. I am passionate about politics, I enjoy it. So of course some of that gets into my poems.

You also have a passion for motorcycles and clothes. Motorcycles are often in your poems, for instance in the poem "Montauk," but very rarely clothes?

I don't consider clothes a futility. I admire the serious craft of making beautiful clothes. I salute craftsmanship of all kinds, and elegance. And the idea of elegance includes certain motorcycles, which have the additional attractiveness of going fast.

Why not cars, or planes?

I love airplanes and aerobatics, and I love very fast cars.

Why very fast?

I also like to fly low and slow in an airplane. But the sensation of speed is a lovely one, also in the poems.

You said that most of the poems locate themselves in New York, but you never forgot your hometown, St. Louis?

You could say the city I grew up in, St. Louis, Missouri, does appear in the poems. But New York is my place. It is where I live and my mind lives.

Why do you love New York so much?

I love it because of its power, its vitality, its variety. Its nonstop vitality. Its colorful, nonstop vitality.

New York
February 14, 2016

~

ROBERT SILVERS

EDITOR

Robert B. Silvers is the editor of the *New York Review of Books*. The offices of the *New York Review of Books* in the West Village are in a large, very simple, open space. Robert Silvers works at a desk piled high with books, with other editors and assistants around him. When it gets too late—after 2 a.m.—he sometimes sleeps in a monastic room next to his office. The night before our meeting he worked until two and then resumed at around ten in the morning. He opens with:

I have worked seven days a week for fifty-one years, since the first issue of the *Review* that Barbara Epstein and I cofounded with our friends in 1963. You see, there is an infinite amount of work. We have to publish fifteen to twenty reviews every two weeks. We have writers all over the world.
In every issue there is a piece on fiction, one or two on history, something on science, something on American political life, art criticism, and a poem. By the way, I am just now expecting a long reportage from Ukraine.

Bob Silvers, as his friends and writers call him, is eighty-five. He looks and acts exactly like he did thirty years ago, and has the same passion and drive for his craft of editing that he calls a "métier."

What is your work as editor?
To look at the incoming books and to send some out to review.

Who is reviewing them?
The best people, the best in the world for the specific book in question.

How do you know who is the best?
You have to consider that over fifty years we have published sixteen thousand articles. We are always looking for new young people.

How many of you are at the *Review*?

I have four assistants and three senior editors who read manuscripts and galleys and check facts. All our reviewers are outside, since the beginning. Every review is commissioned. I personally edit every article and there is nothing I have not carefully gone through.

But what is editing?

You think of each article as having a voice. The voice has to be clear. Then there must be style and imagination. You have to hear the voice. Clarity is the goal. You make suggestions and you send the text to the author.

How can you manage fifteen to twenty pieces every two weeks?

Some pieces are done and ready in advance, some have to be edited at the last minute. An issue has to be shaped and, as I said, there should be history, political events, poetry, novels, what is happening in our political future.

Do you sometimes publish special issues?

Yes, in June we will publish a special issue on art. For instance, we have a big piece on the Italian Futurism show now at the Guggenheim Museum. One of our regular contributors on modern art should be writing about the Sigmar Polke exhibition at the MoMA.

Do you think that there are fewer books translated in America today?

Yes, less than in the sixties. It is probably an economic matter. America is quite isolated from Europe. But many European writers today have an eye on America. Yes, there are fewer translations from French, Italian, German. But today in America one of the most popular and followed writers is the Danish Knausgård, who writes very long and detailed stories about his own family; he is particularly fascinating.

Did you discover many writers?

Some writers became more known because of the *Review*. We were one of the first to publish the work of Oliver Sacks—his early stories of neurological abnormality—and now his books are widely read.

You helped writers like Primo Levi and Milan Kundera to become well known in America?

We published marvelous articles about them when they were not as well known here at the time. I remember that in 1977 Václav Havel was among the leading intellectuals during the Prague revolt. I knew that Tom Stoppard was Czech so I got his number from Harold Pinter. I called him and asked him, "Can you go to Prague and report?" He answered, "I have been waiting for this call for fifteen years!"

You published a play by Harold Pinter in the *Review*?

Yes, a wonderful short play, *One for the Road.*

Who are the most famous writers that you have published?

I particularly liked Isaiah Berlin. We admired his mind range: philosophy, politics, British history. He wrote for us on de Maistre, Turgenev, Machiavelli. He became a sort of shadow editor and he meant a lot to us. It was a privilege to have someone with that kind of intelligence and moral integrity willing to help us. To go back to your question, from the very beginning we published: W. H. Auden, Norman Mailer, Bill Styron, Jimmy Baldwin, Mary McCarthy, Gore Vidal, Philip Roth. . . .

Have you always been an editor?

From 1954 to 1959 I was in Paris as an editor of the *Paris Review.* Then I was hired by *Harper's.* Elizabeth Hardwick, Robert Lowell's wife, wrote an article for me on book reviewing called, "The Decline of Book Reviews." She said that *The New York Times* was becoming trivial and made it clear something else was needed. In 1962 there was a huge strike at *The New York Times* lasting for months. Jason Epstein, editor of Random House, said that it was the only time in history that one could publish a new book review without putting up a penny, because all the publishers still needed to advertise their books. We just had to have a plausible project. When Jason proposed this, I left *Harper's* and asked Jason's wife Barbara to join me. We called many people: Gore, Norman, Bill, Mary, and others. Because of the strike at *The New York Times* we sold one hundred thousand copies of the first issue.

And today?

We sell one hundred and fifty thousand copies and we have our *New York Review of Books* blog. The brilliant editor is Hugh Eakin, and many of our contributors write short pieces for the blog. We also started the *London Review of Books* and asked Karl Miller to edit it. Now we only own one third of it. In the 1980s we sold the *Review* to Rea S. Hederman, who has been our publisher since then and he helps the *Review* a great deal in its advertising, promotion, distribution, and development—but Rea has never interfered with our editorial work and I am totally free.

Barbara Epstein died in 2006, do you miss her greatly?

Yes, I do. We had a lot of fun working together every day and we collaborated on everything. She was a charming, very intelligent girl.

I edit with a PENCIL and PAPER, but I use the INTERNET.

Do you think that an editor should never write?

It depends. Some of us have been very good writers, like Cyril Connolly. Or there are people like me that consider editing a "métier." As an editor what you care about is to create a marvelous journal.

Do you sometimes reject pieces?

We do. I consider that some things are not good enough. Occasionally you have to say, "Look, I am so sorry." It is crucial to sustain a quality of a certain level. I believe in beautiful writing. Clarity is the fundamental thing. Good English is a question of voice. You want to avoid clichés, bad metaphors. You want a certain quality of language, and not to descend into the vulgarity of loose, sloppy, thoughtless, non-authentic popular usage.

What makes a brilliant writer?

A distinctive original voice, intelligence, originality of view.

Do you think that people are reading less?

We are on the verge of a new mentality. In the digital world, "tweets" have one hundred and forty characters, sentences are very short. The new quick communication has an effect on language. There is no criticism of the digital world itself, no critical voice, yet there is a tremendous amount of reading and writing on the Internet. Forms are changing.

Are you becoming digital yourself?

I edit with a pencil and paper, but I use the Internet.

How do you read?

I read a lot, at some times quickly, at others every page carefully. Sometimes it is good to go straight to the conclusion because often it is in those last pages that a writer makes his or her most intense effort.

Have you published many poems in the *Review*?

Poems come in and we know most of the poets. We just published a poem by Fred Seidel.

How can you still be so faithful to the *Review* after so many years?

It is the most fantastic opportunity for an editor. We have had complete editorial freedom from the first issue. I think of Donna Tartt, who just won the Pulitzer Prize and has had good reviews everywhere. But our reviewer had criticisms of a book that seems full of clichés. Our task is to have our own opinion. So the very reason to continue is the rare opportunity to be free.

What about politics?

We have tried to make intelligent criticism of Obama and of the fierce, unfair attacks on him. We have been both favorable to him and critical of him. We criticized the fruitless, futile, and expensive war in Iraq. But we have been critical of American wars since Vietnam.

Are we going back to a Cold War?

The European position vis-à-vis Eastern Ukraine is weak. Putin wants to create a Eurasian group. He wants to reunite the Old Empire, with Russian dominion.

We end our conversation. Robert Silvers has to go back to work at his desk and he gives me a copy of the first issue of the *Review*. I look at the names of some of the contributors: Norman Mailer, Mary McCarthy, William Styron, Gore Vidal, Robert Penn Warren, Elizabeth Hardwick, Jason Epstein, Alfred Kazin, Irving Howe. . . . When I leave, I think he is a very rare man, and of what John Richardson wrote in his article in *Vanity Fair* in 2007: "Jason Epstein's assessment of Silvers as 'the most brilliant editor of a magazine ever to have worked in this country,' has been shared by virtually all of us who have been published by Robert Silvers."

New York
April 17, 2014

~

SUSAN SONTAG

WRITER

Susan Sontag, in your latest book, you write that the United States is a country where one can always start over in life. Is that true?

It's definitely a myth, but because people believe in it, it ends up being possible. This is people's fantasy when they come to America, a land of new horizons. It's a more profound idea than finding one's fortunes in America. Moreover, the characters in my book found success in Europe and come to America where they have a worse life, but with the hope of starting over. In America, you can be a grandmother and take parachuting lessons and everyone will tell you, "Good for you!" There's no sense of being ridiculous.

Is this freedom?

No, I don't know. I love the theater and actors. I wanted to write a book with a protagonist who was a great actor, and then I planned on writing a book on a foreigner. So I created a story about a great Polish actor.

Do you consider yourself a foreigner in America?

Yes, but I am cosmopolitan by nature. As a child, I loved to read travel books and I liked to feel like I was somewhere else. My parents even lived abroad. I always wanted to be far away. Yet when I am in Europe—and I've lived half of my adult life on the Old Continent—I see myself as American. I see it in my interest in constantly fixing and improving things. Perhaps my European friends are more cynical and, all in all, not being cynical is very American. I live in New York, a city full of foreigners.

Does being Jewish also make you feel cosmopolitan?

I don't think so. Maybe a sociologist would say that. And I come from generations of atheists. I would be a nationalist if I came from a small country.

What can you tell me about Bush's America?

The Supreme Court just carried out a coup d'état, and the court should be above taking sides politically. Yet two people should have stepped down because they were part of Bush's electoral campaign. But what America do we see? Isolationist and more focused on money than ever before. Ideas of social justice no longer have support in this country. Two businessmen from the Texas oil industry were just elected president and vice president and one of them is the son of President George Bush who used him to vindicate himself.

What will happen in the intellectual world?

I don't know. I believe Gore should have won. I don't understand how he lost and how he could have run such a terrible campaign. People are furious and today certainly cut off from politics. Gore won in Florida, but they stopped counting votes. I think we will see apathy in America.

What will you do?

Nothing, like all of the rest of the people. Well, I will certainly continue to talk, be active, and write. I certainly won't leave the country. But I have clearly said what I think.

What is your life like?

Being a writer means alternating periods of complete solitude and putting oneself in another's shoes with periods of active participation. I am convinced that the so-called writings that will remain must be written in solitude. *In America* is a book I am very proud of. I wrote it in isolation. Far away. You might find it funny, but I wrote a lot of it in Bari, where I lived for a long period, at the home of my translator, who is also a friend. I love that city, and I spend two months a year there. I was in Bari a year and a half ago when the war broke out in Kosovo, and I could hear the planes going by overhead. I also wrote a part of the book in New York. It took a lot of time. I also spent a few years in Sarajevo and then I had cancer. I was really ill, but now I am getting treatment. I am doing tests and am in remission. If it lasts long enough, I will be cured.

Why do you choose always to wear black?

Because I live in downtown Manhattan, and I think one dresses this way because it is attractive and affordable.

When you travel what do you look for?

I want to be as in touch with reality as possible. I like realities that are not my own. I don't have a lot of money, but I have great respect for most of the people on the planet. It's too easy to live in one's own small privileged bubble. If you aren't careful, as you get older, you can go back to being more like a child. I, however, want to travel and to see things. I have traveled and spent a lot of time in the Balkans. I just came back from Sarajevo where I saw a lot of friends. I go there often.

Is friendship the driver in your life?

Passion, loved ones, and contact with others especially. . . .

What about love?

Sure, she laughs. that's one type of passion.

Do you like being an American writer?

I don't particularly love being American. It might sound snobbish. I am an American writer, of course, but many foreigner writers are more important in my mind. Take Calvino and Tabucchi, who are certainly better than many American writers. I am happy to merely be a writer.

Do you write every day?

I would like to. My friend Alberto Moravia wrote every day. I asked him once, "But what happens if, while you are writing something important, you are called to breakfast?" He told me that he would stop and start again the next morning. I, on the other hand, write intensely, but I do it in bursts. I don't feel like I have to do it every day, but I admire those that do. I have written fifteen books, and I could have written forty, but I believe in what you leave behind and in the judgement of posterity. I don't think it's important to write a lot of books. And then I love to read.

What do you prefer to read?

A lot of history. A lot of poetry. And I reread a lot.

Do you think women are extraordinary in this historic period?

The situation has improved for privileged women in the rich parts of the world. But elsewhere—if I think about Congo, Peru, or Afghanistan—it's a completely different story. . . .

Has Susan Sontag changed a lot?

I am wiser, and I am perhaps a better writer.

Are you courageous?

I don't think I should make those kinds of judgements about myself. It's not for me to say. I think it would be crass.

What would you like to do?
I would certainly like to continue to write and read a lot.

New York

Jan 28, 2001

~

I am happy to merely be a writer.

PAOLO SORRENTINO

DIRECTOR

For the first time you have made a television serial, *The Young Pope* produced by Sky Atlantic, HBO, and Canal+. It has had great success in Italy and all over the world. How different did you find doing this from shooting the films you have made like *The Consequences of Love* [*Le conseguenze dell'amore*, 2004], *Il Divo* [2008], and *The Great Beauty* [*La grande bellezza*, 2013]? Does a series correspond to a movie that lasts ten hours? Is making a TV series a new way for you to explore cinema?

The difference is in the physical fatigue! It means working for seven months instead of for two. It means being concentrated every day for seven months and keeping the very long continuity of ten episodes with many characters. As well as the physical fatigue, you also have to maintain the psychological intensity. In this work one cannot self-indulge. You have to keep concentrated. Otherwise it's the same thing, using the same instruments as for a film. I never ask myself what the difference is between TV and cinema. I work with the same people in the same way. The only real difference is in the writing. The process of making a TV series is like writing a long novel, whereas film is more like a short story. In filmmaking you need to have the ability to proceed by synthesis, whereas a TV serial is like writing a long nineteenth-century novel.

Do you think today's TV series have replaced the cinema?

No, the paradox is that nowadays a TV series makes it possible to create a work of art, which the cinema doesn't anymore. What used to be authorial cinema in the old days, nowadays you can do that on TV. Anyhow I consider any cinematographic fruition to be cinema. When you watch a film on your computer there is such an exclusive relationship between you and the film that it has more or less has same principles as the cinema itself. The only difference is that by going to the cinema you have the collective ritual of being in a theater.

Do you think that cinema theater is finished?

What is finished is the uncomfortable, hostile, cold place you used to go to watch films. Nowadays the cinema theater is a comfortable place where people get together, and the movie house survives as a modern stadium. In other words, you are comfortable and there are all sorts of different amenities. In London for instance, and in other cities, there are theaters that are very comfortable. The natural destiny of theaters is that they have to be competitive with home viewing, and therefore a cinema has to be as comfortable as a home with the difference that you have a pleasant exchange with others. But we don't see queues of people waiting to enter a theater and chatting about films any more.

Is it true that you are at the moment preparing a second series of *The Young Pope*?

I wrote a second series, yes, and at the same time I am thinking about making a new film.

When is the new series of *The Young Pope* coming out?

I think it will be ready in 2018, but I can't talk about it. The only thing I can say is that I will not be the only director. I will share the making of the next series with another director.

And what about the film?

I am tentatively approaching ideas for a new film, but I don't yet know which one I will choose.

You shot many prestigious award-winning films using the same actor, Toni Servillo, as your protagonist, and then this changed and you worked with foreign actors. Is that very different?

The main difference is in the language. In general, I have worked with actors who have great intelligence and they put themselves at my disposal to work with me. Great actors have many great qualities. As I said, the real difference is in the language.

How do you feel when you work in the English language?

Of course I am better in Italian, and it is more tiring and takes greater concentration, but English is a more musical language and the musicality of the dialogue is better in English.

From now on will you therefore work only in English?

No, I never thought about whether to work in Italian or in English. It depends on the

MY PRIORITY

is to

ESTABLISH

the image

INTO WHICH

I let some actors

F

A

L

L.

film. It happens by chance, since it is the idea that I have to realize that brings me to a specific country, language, or actor.

Is there a leitmotiv that runs through your work?

There is a leitmotiv of the dominant sentiments to which I am affectionate. For instance, melancholy, nostalgia, and the relationship with solitude. These are the dominant themes that traverse all my films.

How did the idea of making *The Young Pope* come to you?

I thought a lot about the Vatican and the life of a pope. I have always found this fascinating, and I found it fascinating to tell this story. Obviously the story of the Vatican and the pope had been told many times, but not in an intimate way, and I made a particular and extended research into a scandal in the Vatican and this is what the American public especially were looking for. I wanted to tell the story of a Vatican where a person works and tries to guide Catholics spiritually. There is a strange contradiction between the miniscule Vatican State and being the spiritual guide of more than a billion souls. This must be an incredibly arduous job, and I wanted to recount the story of a pope in his daily life, of the man that lives inside the cassock. The pope is a man like any other man.

What was the reaction of the church to *The Young Pope*?

They didn't react. A silence descended. I don't know if this means that they are intelligent and they don't want to get involved with controversial arguments and therefore they let it go.

Are you a friend of Nanni Moretti? Because Nanni did a film on more or less the same subject called *We Have a Pope* [*Habemus Papam*, 2011]?

Yes, we know each other well. His was a very beautiful film, but he dealt with the opposite argument. In other words he talked about a pope who takes a step back and renounces the job. My pope on the other hand is a very active pope who wants to absolutely take onboard the responsibility of his position.

Do you think Jude Law makes a good pope?

It went very well. It has been said that it is the best role that he ever made in his life.

In your life there is a parallel career since you are also a writer. You published your third book last Christmas [of 2016], and the title is *Gli Aspetti Irrelevanti* [*The Irrelevant Aspects*]?

It is a novel composed of twenty-three portraits that tell the life stories of twenty-three characters, and the book is illustrated with photographs by Jacopo Benassi. It is a choral novel that reminds me of the characters of *The Great Beauty*. To be honest I believe I am more a writer than a director. I am much more at ease with writing, because from the age of twenty to the age of thirty I only wrote screenplays. I like to make cinema, it's a great activity, but whenever I have some time I also write books.

What is the difference between writing a film and writing a book?

A book allows you absolute total freedom. All that has to happen is there on the page. But for the cinema you know that what you write will then have to deal with other realities. Writing for the cinema has obstacles and barriers, but when a novel is finished the publisher publishes it. The screenplay is only the first step in cinema, even if it is obviously fundamental and the fortunes of a film start with a good screenplay.

Do you write your own screenplays?

The first four films I wrote by myself, and then I did two with Umberto Cantarello, including *The Young Pope*, where some episodes are written by me and some by Cantarello.

Why did you choose Sean Penn as the protagonist of *This Must be the Place* [2011] and Jude Law as the protagonist of *The Young Pope*?

I met Sean Penn in Cannes when I showed *Il Divo*. He told me that he liked the film very much and he told me that he was keen to make a film with me. As he is one of my favorite American actors, I immediately started to write the script. Jude Law is the actor who emerged from the character itself.

Do you think about the character or the actor first?

First I think about the character.

Do you enjoy working with actors?

I am not the kind of director who particularly empathizes with actors, and this is the reason why I always try to find intelligent actors. My fascination is primarily for the image. My priority is to establish the images into which I let some actors fall. The first part of the image comes when you write the script, and then there are many other elements, which come by making the film.

Is making a film like conducting a symphony?

The métier of director is similar and proximate to the role of a conductor of an orchestra. You have to make all the instruments speak together, and in the case of a film this means the actors, the lighting, the musical score, and the dialogue.

SUCCESS

DIDN'T

CHANGE

ME,

AND

I

HAVE

NEVER

MADE

BIG

CHANGES

IN

MY

LIFE

.

Is it a difficult métier?

Yes, very difficult, but very pleasing. It is tiring and long, and then you have to wait a long time before you see the results. You need a lot of patience, but if you have the chance to make cinema and are able to do the work it is the most delightful job.

Are you happy?

Yes, I am very happy, because the work itself is great fun. Working on a film is a real buzz and gratifying. To be able to put together such a complex machine from nothing is a great joy.

What is the indispensable quality of a cinema director?

To be gifted with a good intuition. Cinema has to be made quickly and you have to make quick decisions and therefore you have to make your decisions trusting your intuition.

Is total dedication another necessary quality?

Yes, you can also make a film with partial dedication, but it's not the same thing.

How does this affect your personal life?

I am immersed in my work from seven in the morning to seven at night, but then I have dinner with my wife, or my children, or my friends.

Is Rome a good city for you to live in?

It's very good because of its royal indolence. It gives me a necessary calm because, being a dying city, it is wanting in temptation. If I was in London or New York I would stay out and about much more than I needed to be.

Have you been changed by having so much success?

Success didn't change me, and I have never made big changes in my life. I am married to the same wife and I live in the same house. I am a self-contained person and I read very little of whatever it is they write about me. I have the same life that I had twenty years ago, and that's a very good way to put boundaries on temptations. I didn't change my life, and I still have the same dream that I had as an adolescent: "To Make a Film." When I was a young man I was afraid that my dream could not be realized. Now I know that I can realize it, and this gives me the necessary serenity to write a novel or make a film.

Do you also want to become a great novelist?

I still have to become a great director! I feel like someone who has just learned the métier. Other people are great directors, people like Fellini, Scorsese, Bergman, people who have made much more important movies. I am only forty-six years old and therefore I am moderately young, and I still think I am yet to realize my great film; and this is a kind of pressure that stimulates me for the future.

When a film of yours is released do you suffer from stress?

I am not afraid. I forgot to tell you that what is also very important in the work of a director is not to be too anxious. You need to be unprejudiced and take risks. I never forget that I have the privilege of dealing in a great game.

What do audiences need?

People have a great need to be consoled in their own solitude, and the cinema helps. Cinema, through strange and mysterious convergences, alleviates the pain that comes from solitude and that lives inside each one of us.

Do you go to the cinema much?

I used to go a lot when I was a young man. Now I don't see so many films because I live in films all day and at night I prefer to do something else.

Do you read?

Yes, I read a lot, novels, essays, and often things for my work. The novel that struck me like a lightning bolt is the *Voyages au bout de la nuit* [*Journey to the End of the Night*] by Louis-Ferdinand Céline. I read that when I was twenty-two years old, and I am still lit up by it.

What else lights you up?

New York when I was a young man, and football, which is one of my great passions. Football in general, even though I am a supporter of Napoli. Obviously my children are another great passion.

Are you a good father?

I think so, and I care a great deal about my children. When they are not in school, if they can they come and stay with me, wherever I am working.

Rome
February 21, 2017

~

MARIO VARGAS LLOSA

WRITER

The Peruvian writer Mario Vargas Llosa, in Italy to present his new book *The Notebooks of Don Rigoberto*, wanders through the streets of Rome and enters a bookstore, remarking:

It seems as if only women buy books. I have counted some eighteen people in this bookshop, and only two of them are men.

How would you define yourself?

I am a liberal and I do not want to be mistaken as being on the right. Liberalism is the defense of liberty.

And in the U.S.A., which side would you vote for?

As far as the economy is concerned, I would say that I would be a Republican, and from the social and institutional point of view I am more a Democrat. For sure, liberalism is in favor of private enterprise and against state-controlled industry, this is its tradition.

What do you think about a Europe that is going towards the left?

I do not think that's true. Blair's victory in England has nothing to do with Jospin's victory in France. In England, the breakthrough of the *laboristi* towards liberalism is secure. While in France the left is more statist, more populist.

And Italy?

Italy is "crafty." Italy has found a subtle and civilized way to privatize its industries. Italian politics seem to be more decorative than anything else, even theatrical, and the essential issues have become separated from political life.

Is Italy a modern country?

Yes, of course. It's more France that has a terrible identity crisis, because they do not agree that they should become modern.

And Europe?

I think it's in crisis. The European Union will, probably, become held back.

And South America?

It's going better, with the exception of Cuba and Peru. There is more civilization and more democracy. I always cite Bolivia as an example: It was the most chaotic country, with a tradition of dictatorships and of being ungovernable. Now it is a model of democracy and has a liberal economy.

And literature?

It has a space that cannot be replaced by television, but the competition is enormous. TV is superficial and creates passive attitudes. It rules out the imagination.

Do you use a computer?

Yes, but I write my first drafts in longhand.

Do you write every day?

Every day; literature from Monday to Saturday, journalism on Sundays. Journalism is a way of keeping one foot in life and being grounded in reality. A writer must not become completely isolated in a world that is purely mental.

What point is Latin American literature now at?

There aren't any major figures like Borges, Cortázar, or Márquez, but on the other hand there are lots of writers and poets.

Why do so many women write these days?

These are the women who read, who go to the theater, who attend conferences, who occupy themselves with the culture. This is a worldwide phenomenon.

Does the modern male appear to you to be weak?

No, but he takes care of practical things and thinks that culture is a luxury.

Today there is a big turning back to spirituality throughout the world.

Yes, it's true: globalization has created insecurity. The disappearance of borders and the crisis of ideologies makes people look for support and therefore you can see how this is favorable to the resurgence of religion.

nostalgia

IS GOOD MATERIAL FOR WRITERS.

What do you think is the reality of today's world?

That despite the enormous problems, humanity has never had a better existence than today. We have never had better tools to fight poverty, violence, disease, and create a civilization under the sign of freedom and the rule of law. I do not feel like being pessimistic, and Karl Popper said this a few weeks before he died.

Why do you live in London?

London is a great city to work in, and for writing; anonymity is guaranteed, the English are the most discrete people in the world, and then the weather is always bad and therefore you need to stay at home.

So you are a masochist?

No, but in London there aren't all the irresistible temptations of Rome, Milan, Turin, Madrid, and Paris.

Do you work all day?

All morning at home, and in the afternoon in the libraries of the British Museum.

What are you reading?

All and many more. For example, a dialogue between Jean-François Revel and his son, and Tabucchi.

And what are you writing?

I started on an old project, it's a novel set in the Dominican Republic under Trujillo.

Who is your favorite writer?

For the moderns, Faulkner and Borges; and then Flaubert, Cervantes, Shakespeare, Montaigne, and Dante.

Rome
August 6, 1997

~

GIANNI VERSACE

FASHION DESIGNER

So many years have passed since I went to interview Gianni Versace in June 1993, but I still remember him very well. He was a clever man, a talented man. He was not pretentious and really friendly. I saw him again a couple of years later on a boat in Turkey. He was the same: simple, friendly.

When I heard about his death in Miami in 1997 I was sad for him and also felt sorry, even if I cannot say that we were friends, because he was gone forever and we would not be able to talk any more. It has been a real loss for fashion. Versace was a free spirit and he brought something new. I know that his sister, Donatella, is doing very well, they were very close and loved and respected each other so much. I am moved to read Gianni's words again after so long. . . .

Gianni Versace, forty-six, works and lives in an ancient palace on Via Gesu in Milan. His apartment is on the first floor, the door is opened by a rather po-faced, middle-aged servant. We pass through living rooms with floors of inlaid wood, libraries full of old books; there are comfortable sofas, splendid objects, two paintings by Paladino, one by de Chirico. Through a glass door you can see the kind of terrace full of flowers that you would find overlooking the Mediterranean Sea.

How do you live, Gianni Versace?

I live as I please.

How about your work?

My work is very important for me. If I did not feel I was leading from the front I would quit right away.

What is your family background?

Mine is a middle-class family from Calabria. My mother was of Dutch origin and was a seamstress, while the Versaces were landowners. I spent the first twenty years of my life in Calabria, after that I came to Milan. These days I divide my time between Milan, Miami, and Lake Como.

I live as I please.

How did your explosive success come about?
It comes from where I want to be, from what I want to accomplish. I understand people and I have a good business sense. And then we work together as a family: my sister and my brother are both very good indeed.

What's your opinion of the eighties?
They were marvellous. I have never been a socialist as they would have liked you to believe, and precious few of my clients had any problems with the authorities.

And how do you think the nineties are and will be?
Perhaps a bit difficult in Italy, but easier abroad. I think that with us you will see the need to work harder, for higher quality, with fewer distractions and more focus.

What is your life like?
My life is completely down to earth; I only go out when it is necessary for my work. The rest of the time I stay at home and read lots of newspapers and loads of books. A good chunk of the stuff one sees on CNN TV disgusts me.

What clothes do you wear yourself?
When I was forty-three I hated jeans. Now it's as if I only ever wear jeans, and I always wear them in black or very dark blue. But what matters is how we are in ourselves, not the clothes we wear.

Who are the men who you consider to be elegant?
Oscar Wilde and Jean Cocteau and André Malraux. In a certain sense one can even say that Moravia had his own sense of style. But the intellectuals of today are less involved with fashion.

Who are the cleverest people you have met?
I would say Richard Avedon, who is an extraordinarily cultured man. I also think Guy Béjart is a great choreographer and he has read everything, even Arabic literature.

And among women?
I like women who work. I am thinking of Tina Brown, the editor of *The New Yorker*, and of my sister Donatella. Of course, through my work I live surrounded by the beauty of women like Claudia Schiffer, who is very much an ingénue, Linda Evangelista, and Kate Moss.

When do you think about work?

By now it is part of my life cycle. I cannot distinguish myself from my work. It is always there, as necessary to me as drinking water. It's something completely natural. I have never forced myself to try to do anything in my entire life. For example, I wake up, I sit down at a table, and I wait to see what idea comes to me. I never see my clients, unless I would enjoy doing so. I always sell a high-quality product and I eat alone or with whoever I want to.

Do you consider yourself lucky?

Yes, although for me it comes to the same thing—that I am my own person and I like myself.

Do you have a good relationship with your colleagues?

With some of them. I think of Issey Miyake, of Yoji Yamamoto, and of Karl Lagerfeld, who I consider my teacher.

What's going on in fashion today?

Power to the people in the United States. Otherwise, lots of very snob items at extremely high prices, like the traditional Chanel or Hermès.

And the avant-garde?

Even they are, for the most part, quite traditional.

Who do you like to see most from among all your clients?

Lady Di or Alba Parietti. But I am not a snob in that sense, I am the same person for them all.

Milan
June, 1993

~

GORE VIDAL

WRITER

Interview with an angry writer. Gore Vidal opens with:

The Attorney General [referring to Special Prosecutor Ken Starr, a former federal Solicitor General] is nothing but a puppet. Let me tell you about this massive conspiracy.

Gore Vidal, you followed President Clinton's speech on TV at your house in Ravello. What do you think about it?

In a few words, the president was furious with Starr and his questions, which—this is certain—have nothing to do with politics, but are part of a conspiracy to destroy Clinton. That he was enraged was shown only in Clinton's deliberately slow manner. His three lawyers have prudently advised him not to put himself on a collision course with Starr.

How does the president come out of this situation?

The American people are satisfied with Clinton's presidency. Curiously, the mass media despise the people so much that they consider them even more stupid than the mass media is itself. Every single man in the United States has sympathy for Clinton, a human being who is similar to himself in terms of sexual behavior; and every single woman understands Monica's behavior. This explains Clinton's curious, almost starlike popularity, despite the theater of the absurd that has been constructed around his life.

What are the chances of impeachment?

Clinton has real enemies for other reasons. First of all, many rich Americans are joined together by their pathological hatred for black people. And Clinton is a white champion of the blacks. There's more: in 1993, Clinton tried to provide Americans with a national healthcare service, something that all civilized countries in the First World have, without realizing that he had declared war against the so-called 'ruling class' of the United States, the one that represents the great financial groups. Today, a third of the money spent in medical cures in our extremely costly and inadequate healthcare system goes to insurance companies; for them it is a source of enormous profit. And the corporations have immediately joined forces against him, allocating—so they say—half a billion dollars for TV advertisements against the healthcare plan, which they make out to be a "Communist plan."

Is there a risk of an economic crisis?

The stock market is in turmoil, and we might be heading towards a Japanese scenario. But economic situations are beyond the real power of a president. The great financial groups that control every aspect of our lives, and particularly the mass media, will face up to and deal with a crisis as and when it happens. Let's hope that there will be a strike before they achieve their dream, which is the total privatization of the national health service, in order to steal the money that citizens have already paid for their pensions.

Is Vice President Al Gore going to succeed Clinton?

I do not think that Clinton will be impeached because then Gore would have two years of presidency in which to prepare himself for the 2000 elections. And if he were to win them, it would signal the end of the Republican right.

Will Americans forget the Lewinsky affair quickly, or will the storm continue?

If Elizabeth Taylor had a romantic crisis and married her Japanese gardener tomorrow, Monica Lewinsky would immediately be consigned to the oblivion in which Joan of Arc and Charlotte Corday live in the mind of the American public today. Prime Minister Prodi hopes that the Lewinsky affair won't have serious consequences and that Clinton will remain strong, because this is important for the power balance of the world.

Your prediction?

Clinton will carry on as before. He is against war, which distinguishes him from other presidents, but like all other presidents, he doesn't have real internal power. It is the American corporations that rule. Nothing will change, and Prodi can sleep peacefully.

Rome
August 19, 1998

~

MONICA VITTI

ACTRESS

Do you feel more like an actress or a director?

Actress, absolutely. Also because it's a different type of work. *Secret Scandal* [*Scandalo segreto*, 1989] was something all mine, and so I directed it. But that's not my job. I only want to act.

What are the most important films for you?

Most definitely the Antonioni films and then the comedies, like, for example, *The Girl with the Pistol* [*La ragazza con la pistola*, 1968, directed by Mario Monicelli]. Making people laugh is a wonderful thing. Discovering how to make people laugh is like discovering you are the king's daughter.

What do you think about the new Italian cinema?

I think very positively of it. What's new in Italian cinema is that it doesn't seem like any other kind of cinema. It's a new wave, a different way to tell stories, and I like it quite a lot. The actors are good. Today there's acceptance even for those who don't have a good voice. The big directors used to dub everything. Now they no longer do.

Would you work with the new directors?

Yes. They are extraordinary. I've just seen [Francesca] Archibugi's new film, and I think she's very good. But there's a whole group of good ones. They seem lighter, less tied to the traditional rules.

Are there new divas?

Perhaps there are no divas, but that's an advantage. There are so many very good young actresses—Margherita Buy and Valeria Golino. I personally have never been a diva. I've never been dubbed. That's what is new today. You no longer dub.

Do you think actors should take on politics?

It's not an obligation. If one wants to, he should. You need to feel the necessity. You need to know politics. But to really take it on, you need to dedicate your life to it. I would prefer to do many other types of jobs before that.

Do you think it's right that Marcello Mastroianni complained about what is happening in Italy right as he was receiving an award from Minister of Culture Jack Lang?

I don't know the details of what happened. But what comes to mind, seeing as how I've also received awards, is that actors at one time were relegated to the other side of the wall and today are being consecrated. We've come a long way.

For you, is love passion?

No. Love is love. For me, it's a necessity. I couldn't live without it. Love is a physical and mental condition that is in the blood and hormones. There are those that don't know and can't love. There are those that have fun with it and need it. I need it. I'm passionate.

What is the cinema?

It's a game, freedom. A great invention. We should take flowers to the person that invented it. It's a gift to go see. I always go. And I watch television like everyone else, but not passively. I am choosy. *Il rosso e il nero*, for example [the 1997 film directed by Jean-Daniel Verhaeghe, based on Stendhal's novel *The Red and the Black*], or Costanzo's show [the *Maurizio Costanzo Show*, Italy's longest-running television talk show], but I am not a habitual watcher.

Is it difficult for a beautiful woman to grow older?

I don't know if I'm beautiful. I was the least beautiful in my family. I was always different. Too tall, too thin, and I wore glasses from the time I was a little girl. My hair was important, and perhaps my eyes and legs weren't bad. Fortunately, it's not a problem for me. Of course, it is sad to get old because we are heading toward the end. But it's gone well for me up to now. My physique, and my desires haven't changed.

How would you describe yourself?

If I'm forced with a gun to my head to describe myself, I will comply, and start like this: a true blonde, a true astigmatic, truly passionate, a true glutton, a true friend, truly curious, and . . . .

Would you like to be different from how you've described yourself?

Perhaps I will be different tomorrow.

Rome
April 19, 1993

~

MARCO VOENA

CONNOISSEUR & ART DEALER

The art dealer Marco Voena is interviewed in London on the eve of the opening of the ground-breaking exhibition *Beyond Caravaggio* at the National Gallery, which will be followed by an exhibition at Robilant+Voena Gallery, *In Pursuit of Caravaggio*.

Marco, you are originally from Turin. How did you come to be interested in paintings?

My approach was unanticipated. It began when, at the age of eighteen, I had to prepare a speech for a school visit to the Uffizi in Florence. I was intrigued by the mystery and symbolism of the story, and meaning behind a painting. As I studied the famous portrait of the Duke of Urbino by Piero della Francesca in the Uffizi for the presentation to my class, I wondered why the portrait was in profile. It fascinated me to learn that the Duke only had one eye. Obviously, the most flattering way for the artist to portray him was to paint him in profile. It's a very simple example of how learning and research reveal layers of meaning. It is what inspires me to study, research, and understand a picture.

Who was your inspiration?

The great Italian Renaissance connoisseur Bernard Berenson was my inspiration. His biography sat at my bedside table throughout the beginning of my career. Ironically, he was not a fan of the baroque.

Did you study art history?

I completed a PhD at the University of Turin in the history of art. While I was there I had the opportunity to study with extraordinary Italian art historians, including Andreina Griseri, Giovanni Romano, and Enrico Castelnuovo.

Where and when did you buy your first painting?

While I was at university I bought an unattributed painting for my father in an art gallery in Turin. It was my first discovery. When I saw the picture it struck me that it was similar to the work of the Sienese painter Bernardino Mei, whose paintings I had seen in an exhibition in Siena a few years prior. When I found the signature "BM" on the lower right side, I knew that my instinct was spot on. And then, while researching it, I found it documented in a guide to Sienese paintings written by Ettore Romagnoli. It was a heady moment for me as a young man in his early twenties.

How did you realize that you wanted to become an art dealer?

By instinct. I originally wanted to be a connoisseur and a collector, but I could not collect on the level of the legendary art collectors like Baron Thyssen, whose collection in Lugano I visited often as a young adult with my mother. I understood that the only way I could possess the greatest masterpieces was to become a dealer. The only distinction between a dealer and a collector is that for the dealer ownership is temporary. You own a masterpiece for one minute, one hour, one day, or one year. You can't own it for eternity. In a way, it's a Casanovian approach to collecting.

How did you begin your career as a dealer?

In 1984, at the age of twenty-three, I bought my first painting at auction to sell at Sotheby's London. It was a signed landscape by the Baroque painter Salvatore Rosa. A few years later I opened my first art gallery in Turin. I expanded to Milan in 1994, in 2005 I opened a space in London with Edmondo di Robilant, and in 2014 in St. Moritz. Interestingly, many years later I bought back the Salvatore Rosa landscape for my private collection as a reminder of how it all began.

Did you start by being interested in baroque paintings?

Not particularly. At the beginning I was equally interested in Italian, French, and Spanish Old Masters, from Gothic through to Neoclassicism.

Do you consider yourself a specialist in Italian artists?

Now I have come to specialize in Italian art. As an Italian, I can't help but wave the Italian flag.

What attracted you so much to the Italian baroque, a period in which Caravaggio seems to be the star?

It is the ambiguity of the art of the baroque and of Caravaggio that I love. I don't like anything fundamental, because life is not fundamental—it is a great poem, and Caravaggio understood that. In many ways it is for the same reason that people respond to Basquiat, who is the "Caravaggio" of today. Both artists straddled the light

I TRUST MY INSTINCT AND MY EXPERIENCE. CONNOISSEURSHIP IS UNDERAPPRECIATED TODAY, BUT IT IS VERY IMPORTANT.

and the dark sides of the human condition. They were both extreme. It is what enabled both of them to give nobility to different aspects of street life, and in doing this, their art exposed deeper artistic truths than the art of their contemporaries. They touched people more universally. But I want to clarify something. I do not believe Caravaggio's art is baroque. I believe that Caravaggio instigated the baroque. It is an important distinction. The baroque period in Rome began in the 1630s. This is explained well in a famous essay by Giuliano Briganti, "La Nascita del Barocco," in Pietro da Cortona o Della Pittura Barocca. The baroque was also inspired by another great artist who is often overlooked in this discussion, Annibale Carracci. His fresco cycle in Palazzo Farnese in Rome presented a new modernity that was vastly separate from Mannerism. Caravaggio and Carracci opened the door to the baroque together.

Did you become interested in the *Caravaggesque* at the beginning of your career?

Yes, in 1990 I bought a painting of the Holy Family by Bartolomeo Cavarozzi at auction in New York. I sold it to the Istituto San Paolo. This acquisition was the first time that a financial institution in Italy invested in art, in a manner similar to the British Rail Pension Fund collection.

Can you tell me about another of your discoveries?

In 1992, while riding in a taxi from my hotel to the airport at the close of a trip to New York City, I bid on the phone for a painting that I had just viewed at Sotheby's. It was a portrait of a man, attributed to Carracciolo, the greatest of the Caravaggisti in Naples. After purchasing the painting I brought it to Turin to have it cleaned. I was shocked by the results. It had all the hallmarks of a Caravaggio. I asked Mina Gregori, one of the great specialists on Caravaggio, to view the painting. She, too, believed that it was by the master. But I needed an academic consensus to be definitive. I sent the painting to New York to show it to Keith Christiansen, curator of paintings at the Metropolitan Museum of Art, who also agreed. Finally, I showed it to Sir Denis Mahon, who was also confident that it was by Caravaggio.

How do you establish that a painting is the original and not a copy?

I trust my instinct and my experience. Connoisseurship is underappreciated today, but it is very important. When I hold a picture in my hand, the fine details help me understand if it's painted by one artist or by another artist, if it is a copy or an original. It comes down to intuition and knowledge.

Do you sometimes make mistakes?

Of course I make mistakes, but never with the important artists, as I am hyper-vigilant when acquiring these works. I do, however, make mistakes with lesser-known artists whose oeuvres I am not as familiar with. This is how one continues to learn.

Who do you consult when you have a doubt about an Old Master painting?

I still consult Keith Christiansen at the Metropolitan Museum of Art. In this field, he is one of the best art historians and connoisseurs. Early in my career I used to consult Sir Denis Mahon, who revived interest in the baroque. He did this in a similar way to how Roberto Longhi revived interest in Caravaggio around 1925–1930. Longhi was a great expert of Italian culture, who was well versed in Gothic, Renaissance, and baroque art, but the only two artists who impressed him were Piero della Francesca and Caravaggio.

As a young man from Turin, how did it feel the first time you sold a painting to the Met? What does it mean for an art dealer to sell to such museums?

I was not brought up in a family of art dealers (my father was a doctor, my grandfather was an industrialist), so the realization that I am now in a position to offer works that are chosen by curators to hang on the walls of the world's great museums is an enormous honor. It is also extremely motivating. To have a painting currently on view in the *Beyond Caravaggio* exhibition at the National Gallery of London, a temple to Old Master art, is as humbling today as it was when I first sold a painting to a museum.

Are you driven by your passion for art?

Absolutely. If you don't have passion it is impossible. Art serves as an antidepressant for me. I'm never depressed. When I need to find my balance, I pick up the cataloge of an exhibition or I go to a museum. With a passion for art you are never alone. You always have some friends in the form of paintings and sculptures to visit.

You also think in terms of business, and at the moment it seems that Old Masters are out of fashion?

Fashion, of course, is up and down. Old Masters aren't out of popularity everywhere in the world, because societies change and evolve. Collectors from China, Malaysia, the Middle East, and Africa are creating new collections, and their tastes don't follow Western trends. For Western Europeans and Americans, right now it is easier for us to feel and to understand contemporary and modern art, because when things are perceived as bourgeois they go out of taste. And you can't classify "the Old Masters" as a group when discussing trends, because they span from Gothic Art to Neoclassicism. Besides, anything truly great is never out of style. As for Caravaggio and his world, I doubt that he will go out of fashion as he did in the past. He has become a brand, like Picasso. He is now rightly recognized as one of the iconic artists, a star.

Nowadays do people prefer to buy at auctions or in galleries?

This preference changes all the time. People who want excitement tend to prefer bidding in an auction, but some people prefer the quiet of a gallery. When doing business with a dealer the pressure and immediacy of buying is missing, and auctions give this kind of adrenaline. You have to win against somebody in a short moment, and if you fail to win that work of art the moment of regret can be long. Some people also prefer to buy at art fairs. Buying at a fair is in between buying at an auction and a gallery because, although you purchase from a dealer, the decision needs to be made in a short amount of time.

Are Old Masters now mainly bought by museums or by private collectors?

Recently, the buyers for Old Masters have tended to be museums or foundations rather than private collectors. There are fewer Old Masters collectors than before, but the collectors who are around buy with great passion. What is interesting is that the collectors are not buying for speculation, but for their own satisfaction, unlike modern and contemporary collectors. A friend of mine Leone, for example, has bought around two hundred and fifty Roman and Neapolitan baroque pictures over the past forty years, and has not sold one! I feel fortunate to have shared my love for the *Caravaggesque* with extraordinary private collectors such as Luigi Koelliker. The relationship between a dealer and a true collector can be profound.

Do realized auction prices set the pricing for the Old Master market?

I'm against the idea that the price one painting makes on a single day should be used as the price for everything by that artist going forward. This concept comes from America. It is like the stock exchange of art. An auction price for a painting relates only to that day, that hour, that moment, for that painting. It in no way relates to the price of another painting on another day. It's not the same.

Is a work by Caravaggio priceless?

No, it's not priceless; that doesn't mean anything. In the eighties a Caravaggio was bought by the Kimbell Art Museum for twenty million dollars. There is a range for top-level Old Master paintings by big names with important provenances; it is thirty to eighty million dollars, not more.

How many paintings by Caravaggio are known?

More or less sixty, and I would venture around five to ten are still in private collections.

Why do people collect?

People collect for many different reasons: some for social climbing or upgrading, some for a hobby, some for fantasy. Collecting can be a great escape for people who have difficult work lives or for people who live far away from cities with great museums like Paris, Rome, or London. Art is a way to step out of routine. As I said before, it is an antidepressant. It gives life to everybody when there is something missing. We can collect and feel free. Art is a key part of our everyday lives and, just as you have to eat every day, I say that you also need a meal of aesthetics every day.

Are collectors from the younger generation interested in Old Masters?

I am an optimist when it comes to the younger generation, but in a way I don't think about whether or not they are interested. I try to convey the power and importance of art. So my primary concern as a dealer of Old Masters is to try to find part of our art historical past that is lost. Everything we find from the past is important to our present and our future.

What motivated the British aristocracy to collect superlative Italian works of art?

These aristocratic families in the seventeenth and eighteenth centuries became so rich that they could afford to collect anything. They traveled all over Europe on their Grand Tours. When they saw Rome and the palazzos of the princes and the popes, first they wanted to recreate that magnificence, and then they fell in love with the art and the beauty. And it is difficult to challenge the extraordinary beauty that came out of Italy during this time. Economic power comes first, and culture follows. If you can afford it, extreme beauty is what you want to have around you. And beauty is ultimately the same for everybody if they are willing to look for it. When humans create something beautiful, it is astonishing, whether it is a small object, or furniture, or a painting, or a sculpture, or architecture. No one is immune to its allure.

Despite your long lasting interest and knowledge of Caravaggio and the Old Masters, you are also interested in contemporary art?

I like contemporary art. In fact, I bought my first contemporary piece, by Gilbert and George, in 1996. Contemporary artworks are, of course, the Old Masters of the future. Today the great artists of the twentieth century, from Picasso to Fontana, have already become Old Masters. What is difficult about contemporary art is that it takes an enormous amount of attention, because it has not been filtered by the judgments of time.

To truly understand it, one must be an active collector, and constantly watch to determine what is happening and what is coming next. What is wonderful about contemporary art is that the artists are always one step ahead of the rest of us.

Do you see a *fil rouge* between Old Masters and the works of contemporary artists?

Absolutely, because it's always related to the mentality of the Old Masters. Every artist looks to the past.

You seem to be personally very much involved in the design and layout of your exhibitions. Is presentation a very important part of an exhibition?

I believe every detail is important, including the way you display things on the wall, or frame them, whether they are in a public exhibition or on private display. I think a lot about how to exhibit works of art, and I believe I was one of the first to juxtapose works of art from different centuries around a common subject or theme. The first exhibition that I organized of this type was in collaboration with Gian Enzo Sperone in New York City and Milan in 1999, when we combined Italian gold ground paintings with gold paintings by Lucio Fontana. In Fontana, you have the same mystical notions as Italian religious paintings from the forteenth or fifteenth centuries. This concept is what Frieze Masters was built upon.

Do you have the same aim and passion today as you had when you started as a young man?

Absolutely, but it is a bit less romantic than it was before. It used to be more simple, more pure. Today it's more complicated because the art world became a business, and like any business it doesn't always cater to your initial intentions. My intention was to be free to discover, to study, and to buy and to sell, but in a very simple way. It matters most that great works of art still pass through my hands, if only for a minute, an hour, a day, or a year.

Italian Cultural Institute, London
December 25, 2016

~

DIANE VON FÜRSTENBERG

FASHION DESIGNER

An extremely long, black, rented limousine came to pick me up at home to take me to Connecticut, where I'm going to interview Diane von Fürstenberg. In the car is Tatiana, the designer's twenty-year-old daughter, with two friends. With a supple ride, more like that of a boat than an automobile, the limousine crosses Upstate New York and Connecticut. I pretend to take a nap and listen to the kids, who talk about their love interests and their travels. After an hour and a half, we arrive at Cloudwalk, an enormous piece of property that once belonged to the Johnson family and to the orchestra director Leopold Stokowski.

There are five antique, white houses made of wood: one for Diane, one for her children, one for guests, one for the staff, and one for Oliver, her best friend, who has worked with her forever. Diane von Fürstenberg acquired this property twenty-seven years ago, with her first earnings. "I needed nature, space. A house where I could be with my children, my family, my friends," she would later explain.

Diane von Fürstenberg accompanies me to my room, which is in the guesthouse. The furniture is antique, American. The beds are dressed with the most colorful quilts. We had dinner immediately: Diane, her mother, Lili Halfin, Tatiana, and her friends all took their places at the table. The menu? Roasted chicken, American red potatoes, homemade apple pie (which was excellent), red wine from Bordeaux. Diane drinks two glasses of red wine every evening, in addition to water and herbal tea. Every once in a while she smokes a cigarette. When she is at Cloudwalk, she likes to take long walks through the woods at a decisive pace, followed by her many dogs, each of a different breed.

The following morning at ten Diane is punctual for the interview. She wears a close-fitting pair of blue jeans, a dark-blue cashmere sweater over her bare skin, and cowboy boots. Her silhouette is aquiline. Her large black eyes express melancholy, curiosity, and even severity.

Diane is a solitary woman, one gathers from the way she lives. She likes to direct, organize for others, for the people she cares about, but she likes to be alone. She invites me into her studio, where Leopold Stokowski once worked. It is a big room that looks like a large loft. On the walls there are white shelves overflowing with art books, volumes on architecture, and novels. A retractable screen hangs from the ceiling on which the stylist projects new films procured for her by her ex-boyfriend, the producer Berry Diller, who directs Twentieth Century Fox. In the back of the room there is a platform with two identical, very simple desks with drawers on either side. In the drawers the stylist keeps designs for models and precious fabrics she buys when she travels. During the interview Diane never sits still. She'll go from time to time to one of the other houses to verify that the table she prepared for twenty-two people is ready. She'll receive a fax, answer the phone in a variety of languages and speak about work and personal matters with various interlocutors: with her son Alex, with her ex-husband Egon von Fürstenberg, with a gentleman who wanted to meet with her to get her to sign, for his fiancée, a copy of her book on beds that she just compiled. She takes careful note of his address and then responds politely to my first question.

Are you American?

No, I arrived in America when I was twenty-two and I've lived here for twenty-two years. I have two children who were born in America and who consider themselves American. I was born in Belgium and have a Belgian passport.

And your parents?

My father was born in Kishinev, the capital of Moldavia, and his language is Russian. My mother was born in Thessalonica, in Greece, though she has lived in Belgium since she was a child.

What is your first memory?

When my brother was born, I was almost ten. When my mother went to the clinic, I remember that I was afraid I would never see her again.

What is your father like?

Handsome, very affectionate, not severe at all. Present and absent at the same time, preoccupied above all with his work in electronics. My mother on the other hand was always present, severe.

Did you have a happy childhood?

There is always something tormenting about childhood. As a child life seems like an enormous void. There is the anguish of the unknown. My childhood was gray because Belgium is a gray country. I remember that all of my female classmates at school were blonde with straight hair. I was a brunette with curly hair. The month of November was always very long, sad. Sunday afternoons with my family seemed never-ending. And so, ever since I was very little, I wanted to get out and to make a life for myself.

What type of family do you come from?

A Jewish, bourgeois family. My mother had two numbers tattooed on her arm because she had been a prisoner in two concentration camps during the war. Even if she didn't talk about it and she didn't allow it to burden her, those tattoos evoked the horror. During the war in Korea, I remember noticing in my family a great fear of Russia and of communism. I even began to arrange my bed in such a way that I wouldn't be caught off guard by the sudden arrival of the Russians. I read many novels and did lots of dreaming, conjuring up great destinies. But I was desperate and afraid that nothing would ever happen to me. I had a friend, Mireille. We spent a lot of time together and we dreamed of becoming princesses, of living grand passions. My mother must have understood that I wanted to expand my horizons, and so, when I was thirteen she sent me to school in Switzerland, where there were students from all over the world and therefore it was a less banal environment. Then, when I was fifteen, I went to England, which seemed immediately beautiful to me, and that's where my life began. After England I went to Spain for university, where I studied philosophy for a year. I didn't know anyone, just an anticonformist young man who was a self-proclaimed socialist. Spain was still under Francoism. His name was Felipe Gonzàles, and many years later he would go on to become prime minister. After I left Spain, I moved to Geneva, where I met Egon von Fürstenberg, a young man who had just returned from Africa. In Geneva I found a job with an investment firm and I began to make money.

Did you think much about making money?

No. For me life was an adventure. I didn't think about money.

And then?

In 1968 I decided to go to work in Paris. It was the year of the barricades, free love, the war in Vietnam. I worked for a photography agency, and that's how, representing, for example, David Bailey, I made my first contact with the world of fashion. In January 1969 I went to visit Egon in New York. It was my first time in America. When I left I was only planning to stay for two weeks and I ended up staying two months. New York

I'm always writing:

LOVE
IS
LIFE

&

LIFE
IS
LOVE

For me love is life.
Without love there is no life.

was much different than I had imagined: rather old, with a very stimulating bohemian atmosphere. In Europe they waged a cultural revolution without getting anywhere. In New York, on the other hand, I felt a special energy. I decided to get involved in fashion and I went to Como to work with Angelo Ferretti, who had a fabric factory and a printing press. There, I very quickly learned everything I needed to know about fabric, color, and designing.

And then?

Egon returned from America, we got engaged, I discovered that I was pregnant and we were married, July 16, 1969, in Montfort-l'Amaury near Paris.

In seven months you discovered America, decided to throw yourself into fashion, got pregnant, and married. Didn't it all happen a little too fast?

No, from that moment my life acquired a velocity and an intensity that lasted a long time.

What do you mean?

October 15, 1969 I boarded the Raffaello in Genoa because I wanted to make the journey on my own, to be able to reflect in peace on the new life that awaited me. I had become a princess, I was about to become a mother, and I was beginning my career. I therefore had to take things slowly and think things through. That was when I learned that every once in a while you have to detach yourself for a second, take a step back, to see things more clearly. As soon as I arrived in America my existence became a wonderful whirlwind of activity.

How did your success begin?

I was pregnant and I remember that I had a huge Louis Vuitton suitcase full of samples I was to present to *Vogue*, where I went to meet the woman who was considered at the time the empress of fashion, Diana Vreeland. I was extremely scared, very intimidated, when she received me in her office, which was all red. She was surrounded by assistants and all of these absolutely gorgeous models. I began to show her the clothes I had designed. She looked at them and kept exclaiming: "How beautiful!" "How intelligent!" "How beautiful!" Then all of sudden I found myself alone, with the clothes to fold. She had gone and, disconcerted, I asked myself: *And now what? What am I supposed to do now?* Her assistant began to laugh and told me that Mrs. Vreeland had really liked my work. She explained to me that Market Week was about to begin and she suggested that I book a hotel room and sign up for a slot on the Fashion Calendar and hope that I would receive orders. I followed her advice.

And your children?

My marriage suffered as a result of this initial success and so I dedicated myself exclusively to my work and my children. I traveled a lot. I would take early morning flights so that I could get home to be with my children in the evening. I had a lot of energy. The adrenaline flowed. I discovered America and America discovered me. I discovered women as well as myself. Designing and creating for women, I became a woman. Everything, in one way or another, was connected. That was how at the age of twenty-seven I bought Cloudwalk, the house we're in right now.

You said that success ruined your marriage. Do you think that success is incompatible with a normal family life?

No. I think that modern life, the fact that I got married so young, the freedom of the period and the speed with which I found myself faced with so many responsibilities (hundreds of employees, the production of twenty-five thousand pieces of clothing a week) was perhaps a bit much to also have the patience to make a marriage work. But I have to say that even if Egon and I were separated after just a few years, we remained friends and above all closely united in the education of our children and with respect to the family.

Was your success pure chance? Very few Europeans have been able to do so well in the United States . . . .

Success was how I forged my real independence and my children were my salvation.

You didn't answer the question . . . .

I don't know. Success is the result of the desire to succeed, good fortune and certainly sound judgment. I made things that people wanted and needed and I worked a lot: the whole thing produced a chemical reaction and permitted me to live the "American Dream." However, success is double-edged sword. You've got to keep moving forward.

What happened after 1977 and the "wrap dress?"

A line of cosmetics, housewares, and accessories, aimed at women and still in line with my needs and my instincts. I was the first to come up with attractive and sophisticated fashions at a price that any woman could afford.

Have things changed since then?

For ten years, from 1972 to 1982, I worked like crazy creating an empire. My products were achieving a turnover of a more than three hundred fifty billion lira a year. After ten years of this commercial euphoria I needed other things. In 1980 I took a long trip to Asia and I spent a lot of time in Bali. In 1983 I sold my cosmetics line to a

You've got to keep moving forward.
Success is double-edged sword.

NEVER PUT YOUR FEET UP.

large English pharmaceutical company and licensed out other products. At that point I lost, in large part, control of my brand: selling the name was a bit like selling a child. I missed Europe a lot, so I moved to Paris for four or five years, thinking that I had left America behind for good.

Then what happened?

Little by little, I bought my brand back, and now I am ready to start over and do things differently.

What are your plans?

I understand the modern woman who has to do many things, be ready for anything, elegant, and not spend too much. I want to furnish these women with clothes, cosmetics, and accessories.

What does a typical day look like for you?

By now my kids are all grown up and I live alone, shuttling back and forth between my country house, and my apartments in New York and Paris. Unfortunately I waste a lot of time in airplanes. What do I do? I work. I love my friends.I am fascinated by what happens in the world. I think the world will change more in the next five years than it has in the last fifty. We all have to be very careful and flexible. More than ever we must be ready to face every day of our reality.

What difference do you see between the destiny of Europe and that of the United States?

The great difference between Europe and America is the space. Unfortunately in old Europe, a place that has seen so much history and so much progress, there is little space and always more people.

How important is love to you?

I'm always writing: *Love is life* and *Life is love*. For me love is life. Without love there is no life.

You've hardly said anything at all about other people working in the world of fashion . . . .

In fashion the most important creator of the century is Yves Saint Laurent. For example, nothing has influenced fashion more than blue jeans.

1992

Cloudwalk, Connecticut

Originally published in *AMICA* Magazine

~

ALICE WATERS

CHEF

Alice Waters, at what stage of your life do you feel you are?

I am in a very reflective place, because I know I have an incredible opportunity, and I don't want to push to make something happen. I want to go to the place where it can happen because it is right to happen. I don't want to push closed doors.

During your life and work did you have to fight in order to achieve your purposes?

I never did. Because I was looking for the place of pleasure; I was trying to win people over by good taste, by good cooking, and hospitality, by friendship.

Was it difficult in 1971, when you first opened your restaurant Chez Panisse to convince your father to give you ten thousand dollars to start it?

No, he wanted to help me. He always believed in me, and you know I was part of the counterculture of America at the time. I was empowered because I was in Berkeley—that was a center. I thought my restaurant would be successful. It never occurred to me that it might not be.

You were not interested in financial success at the beginning?

No, I was not. I don't think I will ever be.

You were first inspired by the French culture, and then you became very close to Carlo Petrini's Slow-Food movement [a grassroots organization founded by Petrini in 1986].

I think what is really important is that I went to France when I was nineteen. At that time, it was a slow-food culture.

What does this mean, a slow-food culture?

I believe that we are what we eat. When we eat fast food we adopt the value culture of cheap and easy. We are digesting the values of dead food and it changes our values. So we value things differently, and want all our lifestyles fast, cheap, and easy. In France I used to go to the market twice a day. Children were going home for lunch. You waited in line for a half baguette. Students had free passes to museums. One felt that education was important. All of this is slow-food culture in my mind. Then the French changed and became fast food, so I came to Italy.

Is Italy different?

I came thirty years ago. I went to Tuscany, and then I met Carlo Petrini. Chez Panisse has always been a slow-food restaurant, I just did not know it.

Chez Panisse is considered one of the best American restaurants. What is your secret?

I was always looking for taste. When I was in France I always wanted *fraises des bois* [wild strawberries]. I wanted them for Chez Panisse. I was on a search for taste, and then I found the organic farmers who were growing food for flavor.

They say that somehow you invented the American cuisine. What kind of cuisine is it?

I don't think we have invented anything. We just came back to a philosophy of the past that has been part of civilization since the beginning of time. Eating local products, eating seasonally, eating with friends and family, taking care of the land for the future, celebrating the harvest.

We not only live in a world of fast food, but also of diet obsession?

Diet obsession comes from a disconnection from food and nature, and it comes from an indoctrinated addiction to fast food.

Do you believe in dieting?

No.

How should one eat?

We have to find a balance. I think more grains, fresh fruit, vegetables. I am very interested in the Mediterranean diet and the food of the Middle East. I think that we are imprisoned by the fast food culture that tells us it's okay to eat. It is about portion sizes. There is more in fast food, more and cheap is better. It is a strong message.

I BELIEVE THAT WE ARE WHAT WE EAT. WHEN WE EAT FAST FOOD WE ADOPT THE VALUE CULTURE OF CHEAP AND EASY. WE ARE DIGESTING THE VALUES OF DEAD FOOD AND IT CHANGES OUR VALUES.

But what is the slow-food message?

Less and better is more. A reasonable amount, and affordable. When something is cheap, somebody has not been paid, and usually it is the farmer.

What about the ingredients?

I think ingredients and their purity is the most important thing. I want to know what the animal is eating, exactly. No additives, no antibiotics. I want my food to be grown and raised harmoniously. Nature is our mother and teacher.

What about exercise?

Exercise is important, exercise in nature. For instance, I walk every day and sometimes I do a little yoga exercise.

You are at the American Academy in Rome, where you just gave an award to Carlo Petrini. What does he represent for you? Of course you are the vice president of the Slow-Food movement.

He represents a set of values that I think are essential for our survival on the planet. He is uncompromising.

The movement became quite important over the years?

Yes, we are now in one hundred and fifty-six countries; and I think the reason it is so successful is because it is using pleasure to bring people back to their understanding ideas like sustainability and biodiversity by feeding them. I am a Montessori teacher and I believe we learn by doing. There is no real book for this revolution.

That's why you created a restaurant, Chez Panisse, in Berkeley?

I was frustrated with traditional politics and I always wanted to feed peoples' ideas.

You also tried to create as many orchards as possible? For instance, since 2008 you created an orchard at the American Academy.

It is the Rome Sustainable Food Project. It is a group of artists and scholars who eat lunch and dinner here, they eat at long tables together, and the idea of this institution was to exchange ideas, but nobody came because the food was not good. When they finally wanted to change the food, they asked me to do it. I said I was keen to do it all the way or not at all. They said all the way. I found an amazing Italian farmer and an American cook. The farmer interviewed us to know if we were good enough to cook.

Is it a different food from the one you serve at Chez Panisse?

More things in Italy taste better, because they have been testing seeds for three hundred years. Americans have been growing for quantity rather than flavor. We make mozzarella, but it never tastes like in Italy, because of the animals and what they eat.

Is there something that instead is more special in America?

Our bread sometimes in some places, and we have wonderful garlic. I think we are understanding about meat. We are just learning. I think I know a lot about lamb, because we were working on it for over forty years. The best chickens are in Europe, especially in France. We have succeeded with fruits, we have fantastic peaches, plums, oranges, mulberries, lemons, and grapefruit.

You wrote thirteen books. What are they about?

They are really work in progress. They try to explain what we are learning as we continue the restaurant. In the last book I wrote, *The Art of Simple Food II*, I put a manifesto at the beginning. The first line says, "Treasure the Farmer," and there are many techniques on planting a home vegetable garden.

What vegetable garden did you suggest to Michelle Obama for the White House?

I wanted her to make a vegetable garden on the front lawn. She chose the back garden, and she made it with schoolchildren, a beautiful and important idea. We need vegetable gardens in public places. The mayor of Rome gave us permission to make a permanent garden between steps going down to the Forum, but we didn't do it; it was an inspiration of the moment.

And what about the Vatican?

We visited the gardens with Carlo Petrini, and we talked about it, and Pope Francis wants to use Vatican land to feed people, and I hope it will happen.

What is your menu for the big McKim Medal Gala dinner at the American Academy, where Paolo Sorrentino and Carlo Petrini are honored?

All foods that are part of our project at the Academy. We have little fennel cakes; roast asparagus; crostini with wild chard; a special kind of prosciutto; slow roasted almonds; ricotta ravioli with little tomatoes and basil; spring lamb with farro, with pine nuts, raisins; spring salad; baked apricots with honey ice cream.

And wine?

Of course, Italian wine.

Are you still cooking?
I am still cooking at home, but not at Chez Panisse.

Why?
Because I am traveling the world and talking about the ideas of slow-food. I miss cooking in the restaurant, but for twenty years I have been working on the Edible Schoolyard project. We have schools all over the world. Since we started, food has become a major issue in our society.

Did you imagine this?
I always have imagined food to be the answer. The way to solve the problems is through food. Problems of health, poverty, global warming, wars. Edible education is to teach children the essential values of sustainability, nourishment, and communication. I believe that the whole world has to be educated. Every decision we make is a very political decision. If we change the way we eat, we will have tremendous effect. We should all be able to cook. Finding ingredients is eighty-five to ninety percent of cooking, but it is easy to cook.

Rome
June 1, 2015

~

I THINK

ingredients & THEIR purity

IS THE MOST IMPORTANT THING.

WIM WENDERS

FILMMAKER

Wim Wenders inaugurated a photo exhibition called *Images of Planet Earth* in the Quirinal Stables (or Scuderie del Quirinale, also called the Papal Stables) in Rome, 2006. The great director is walking through the enormous spaces of the Quirinale, putting the final touches on the exhibition and deciding where to put the photos, including the largest ones, he's taken around the world. Wenders, who is in a great mood, sits down in a director's chair in the middle of one of the rooms and asks me to sit with him.

When did you discover that you were a photographer?

I always wanted to be a painter, and I learned more from painters than photographers. When I started making films, I conceived them as an extension of paintings. One of my role models, for example, was Andy Warhol, who had started making films as well. I wanted to be a painter, and I thought making films was a step along that path. But then I became a storyteller, and in the mid-1980s, I began to take photographs. For me, my photographs are like painting.

When are you going to pick up the paintbrushes again?

I still do many watercolors. I haven't done an oil on canvas in thirty years, but I travel with watercolors. But I'm too busy to be a painter, because a painter can only be a painter.

So why aren't you only a painter?

Because I want too many things.

Such as?

I want to tell stories, to be an architect, a musician, and a painter. But I use photography as a means for this.

What kind of camera do you use?

For all of my photographs and large panoramic shots, I use a Fuji 6x17. So the negative is really big. For 6x7 shots, I use a camera called Makina. It's a Japanese model, and

Italians always think I'm joking when I talk about it. Actually it was an Austrian brand originally from the 1940s and 1950s, and when the company went out of business, the Japanese bought it.

How many photos do you take before choosing one?

For the exhibition at the Scuderie, which has sixty images, I got out twenty thousand negatives. Actually, this is the first time I've done such a complete show.

Are your works for sale?

Yes. I have a gallery in London called Haunch of Venison, and I have six copies of each image. Some have already been sold. In Rome, I'm showing my personal photographs, which have never been put up for sale. This is the last time I'm showing them. I showed twenty-four of them for the first time in Berlin in 2001 and another twenty-six at the Guggenheim Bilbao, and then China, Australia, and New Zealand.

There are no portraits in your photographs. Only landscapes.

Yes. But there are people here and there that are part of the landscape. Many of my photographs show traces of people or people left behind.

Did you watch the World Cup?

Yes. Actually, Gianluigi Buffon [goalkeeper of the Italian national football/soccer team] could be a character in my next film. He seems like a *"divo,"* but then he's a man with a secret.

What kind of secret?

This could be the plot of the film . . .

You left Los Angeles to return to Berlin. Why?

I lived in the United States for about ten years, but I always kept my German passport. I shot seven or eight films in Los Angeles, in the United States, but now I want to shoot one in German with German actors. The last time I worked in Germany was 1992. I have to say that I left the United States for political reasons as well because I wasn't happy.

And how was your return to Germany?

When I left Germany in 1995, I left because it was an unhappy country. Germans hadn't dealt with the reunification well. Now Germany has a different spirit. After twenty years, it is starting to think like a unified country.

Did the sadness go away?

You can't really say it's a happy place.

The new pope Benedict XVI is German. What does that mean for Germany?

In Germany we knew he was very conservative, but his election was certainly very exciting. At the same time, there are some worries about his very conservative policies. So there are some people who would have preferred a more progressive pope even if he weren't German.

But Germany is the country of philosophy and theology, and this pope is a great intellectual.

Yes, absolutely. He wrote many important theological books. He is an intellectual but a conservative one.

What kind of intellectual are you?

I am Christian, but very liberal. I'm a liberal Christian if this can be considered a category. A Christian on the left.

Aside from the landscapes shown in these works, what other themes interest you most today?

I am always more interested in politics, but on a more global rather than local level. I am very interested in the problems of globalization. The growing inequality between developed countries and poor countries affects me deeply. That gap is enormous and growing ever more. And, unfortunately, politicians are allowing this to happen.

Did the sadness go away? Are you scared of the atomic bomb?

As a child—I was born in 1945—everyone was afraid of the bomb, but today everyone is afraid of terrorism. I believe that today's atomic bomb is the disparity between rich and poor.

What about Islam?

In and of itself, Islam is a peaceful religion. Actually, the damage done in the name of Christianity is incalculable. The Islamic religion doesn't teach hate. It is because there is so much poverty in this world that fundamentalists can become terrorists.

Are you justifying terrorism?

No, but combating terrorism without combating its causes is wrong. The cause is the growing gap between rich and poor.

What is the artist's role?

Making people understand their fellow man. My exhibition at the Scuderie del Quirinale is called *Images From Planet Earth*, but my hope is that the visitor understands that the earth belongs to all of us in the same way.

I sense that there is something you want to add.

Yes. The Australian aboriginals that live in the desert where I shot many photographs are people of extraordinary beliefs. They believe that they belong to the earth and not that the earth belongs to them. I have spent a lot of time in Australia, and this was very important to me.

Where else?

Then I went to Cuba, Japan, Israel, and the United States. We live in a world of images.

Do words still count?

Yes. Words count even more, because images are out of control and we can control them even less.

Would you like to be a poet?

I write a lot, and I published the book *Once*. It was a travel diary along with text, a bit like a series of poems.

Rome

July 13, 2006

~

I WANT TO TELL STORIES, TO BE AN ARCHITECT, A MUSICIAN, AND A PAINTER. BUT I USE PHOTOGRAPHY AS A MEANS FOR THIS.

VIVIENNE WESTWOOD

FASHION DESIGNER

Vivienne Westwood, what state is the fashion industry in?

I make avant-garde things, but I hear from people that there is a crisis, and that it is serious. I don't know how long it will last though. But then there are still many who can spend a lot for clothing. The message I would like to send is to buy less but choose well. And this is how my collection is. I say to create small scarves, use safety pins and old fabrics. If you spend a lot on one thing and you choose well, this is the right way to do it.

How does fashion change and who influences it?

It is influenced by ethics, by how people see the world. Unfortunately, today everyone wears jeans. What I think is important is how one sees the world, hope, and a yearning for the past.

What is your idea of fashion?

Fashion is the passing of time. It has always been about constraint, volumes, and the eternal dilemma between short and long. Take the woman's suit, for example. Today it's not in fashion, but in fifty years, it may be back in vogue. Fashion is eclectic, though it hasn't changed all that much for a while.

What is fashion like today?

It is very confused, but that is a good thing, because that makes it possible to personalize and mix "the ingredients." For example, I've mixed a satin or tulle petticoat with a tweed jacket and a pullover. This is a way to mix summer and winter. My husband says one should be well dressed for every occasion. If you have to go to a funeral, you need to be well dressed for that occasion.

And what about color? Do you love it or hate it?

My clothes tell a story. They bring to mind, for example, Marie Antoinette or Che Guevara. Colors that have something to do with history. For example, I saw a Mantegna exhibition at the Louvre Museum, and the colors influenced my latest collection. One tries to recreate the colors of a painting, but naturally they are different on a fabric. I adore color. I try to be neutral in the beginning, but then the color takes shape and emerges. You can love just one color as well.

Does the way Italians dress clash with your ideas of fashion?

No, but there is a big difference between the mass-market and designer clothing. I find mass-market clothing to be horrible. It is not attractive, and people have never been so poorly dressed. Better to buy used clothing than mass-market clothes that are all the same.

How would you describe your ideal man?

I don't have an ideal man. It depends. I am more interested in ideas. I want to be around people that inspire me. I don't like the type of men that do body building.

Who are your customers?

I don't take part in society life. I am mainly focused on the environment. I know there are many people that wear my clothes. The wedding dress I made for *Sex and the City* certainly made me very famous in the United States. A very curvy woman wears it best. They love my clothing because it highlights their curves. Take Jerry Hall, for example.

What type of designer are you?

I am small, but I have my company, my business. And nobody tells me what to do. I only do things I like. If it is avant-garde, very well then. I know that fashion makes people feel important and feeling important is sexy.

What is your solution for the economic crisis?

It would be nice if people made their own clothes, such as a mini skirt or a scarf out of a towel, for example. But I can't turn back the hands of time, and I don't know what will happen in the future. So what we need to do is to start to think about saving the forests. Not saving a tree means not saving a child, and things will end tragically for the world's population.

And what can fashion do about this?

Fashion often stimulates the imagination. A previous collection of mine had children painted on it, and I have jungles, monkeys, and butterflies on other pieces of mine.

London
January 18, 2009

~

ELIE WIESEL

AUTHOR

The Elie Wiesel Foundation for Humanity fights for human rights and peace and against racism. It organizes lectures, conferences, and annual meetings with other Nobel Prize awardees like Wiesel.

Wiesel arrives in his office followed by a bodyguard. There are several young people working in his foundation, which he runs with his wife, Marion. He is wearing his *Grand-Croix de la Légion d'honneur* decoration on the lapel of his navy-blue corduroy jacket.

Very few people around the world have reached this notably high distinction. We sit in his office with books all around and start speaking about ourselves, our lives, and our thoughts. Then I ask him if he wants to answer some questions for an interview, and he agrees, "As ever," he says to me, smiling.

Are you writing a new book?

I am always writing a new book. I have sixty volumes published and I have forty manuscripts still unpublished.

Do you always write in French?

Longhand in French, and then I type it on my typewriter with two fingers.

When do you write?

I get up at five o'clock and then I write from six on for five hours.

And then you start your active day?

I often come to my Foundation to meet with people. We work on all subjects concerning humanity. I often say to Nobel laureates, "We have received more than anyone. We must give back."

You are a professor of humanities?

Yes, I have a chair at Boston University and in the winter I teach in Florida. I teach history, philosophy, literature, theater, and I never give the same course. I have been teaching for forty years and sometimes the grandchildren of some of my students have become my students!

And what about Israel?

I have never lived in Israel, but it is one of the countries of my life. I could have lived without it, but since it became a country, I cannot live without it. Whenever I open *The New York Times* I read about Israel. It is a miracle, every day a surprise. I don't follow the politics. I don't want to be involved.

Are you sometimes afraid for Israel?

Of course I am afraid.

Is Russia a dictatorship?

Putin is trying to be and not to be a dictator. I cannot say that he is a dictator. He is not Stalin.

Where does he want to go?

Ask him. His predecessors wanted to conquer ideologically. I don't think it is the case now.

There is a lot of talk that America is now weaker. Do you think so?

Economically, it is still the strongest economy in the world. America is still the major power in the world.

But with some weakness?

It is a living, peaceful, democracy.

You supported President Obama?

I never involve myself in local politics. But, since 1979, when Jimmy Carter was elected president, I have met all the presidents and defended all of them. I worked for all of them outside politics. None of them has tried to influence me politically.

And the political situation today?

Has not changed much. We are still a democracy. When I came to America in 1956 racism was still a low in the South. Today it is not. The problem was canceled democratically.

What about Europe?

They are also democracies. Ukraine is a democracy. For me democracy is the only way of life. The opposite is dictatorship or anarchy.

What about China?

I have not been there yet. China is so huge. It is a wealthy nation looking for its own destiny. The rest of the world should make more effort to bring Russia and China closer to America.

But do you consider American foreign policy valid?

I do not think America is isolationist. Ukraine is a recent development. For seventy long years Israel has tried to make peace, but so far did not succeed. Only with Egypt. But I think that peace will come.

But what about the terrorists?

They have to be eliminated. Terrorism is not an option. They have to learn that it is not an option. It is worth the effort. The real problem is Iran, strong because of its oil. The only time I took a position is when Iran wanted to become nuclear. I published a full page in *The New York Times* with my signature. "Iran must not become nuclear." And it worked.

Are we sure?

For the moment anyway.

What about the Arabs?

They don't have a tradition of democracy. The Koran is a great text, but not a democratic one. But the Muslim world is changing, they are learning. They want to be accepted by the rest of the world, but the world does not accept dictatorship.

What about anti-Semitism?

It is as old as the Jewish people. There is not anti-Semitism today as an ideology. The civilized world must think now that anti-Semitism is stupid.

What about the new Pope Francis?

The last two popes are very good. I am sure I will meet the new pope. He is open, warm. I like what he said about Jews and Israel.

What is your identity?

I am a Jew, a human, person, and an American citizen, a writer, a teacher, a witness.

Why do you write in French if you are American?

After the war I lived in France for some years. When I arrived, I only knew how to say "Bonjour," but it became my language. All my books, except the first which I wrote in Yiddish, were written in French. Yiddish was my first language, we spoke it at home. I am an American Jew, French speaking. You cannot write in more than one language. Words don't come out as well. The discovery of myself after the war was in French.

What occupies you at the moment?

Always the same. What is happening to the world. I know that we are going very fast, and I don't know where we are going. The largest progress has been made in science—in the last fifty years we made more progress than in the previous five hundred years.

What about young people?

Young people want to learn, they are thirsty for knowledge, they want to understand and remember. The main thing is to teach them where not to go. Oppression, not to go; dictatorship, not to go; racism and prejudice, absolutely not to go. This is a moral plan.

Yourself, do you feel a happier person?

My god was never happiness, but to understand and be understood.

New York
April 6, 2014

~

ROBERT WILSON

THEATER DIRECTOR

I arrive in the Watermill Center. Bob Wilson is expecting me in his industrial reconverted building where he lives, where he has his offices, where there is a permanent display of works of art, for instance a fantastic collection of chairs from all over the world. Bob is ready for the interview and sips iced tea, dressed in a black T-shirt, and black trousers. Sometimes the interview is interrupted, first by a theater impresario from New Jersey, who comes to talk to him and introduce his family, and then we go downstairs to the dining hall where there are students and their teachers, who are working and performing at the center this summer. The atmosphere is very tranquil and happy all around. He says:

The peace and tranquility here is gold dust. You can watch your own thoughts drift past like in a meditation. . . .

We are at the Watermill Center and you are the founder and the artistic director. Can you describe it?

It is a laboratory for experimentation. There are over five thousand pieces in our art collection, some go back as far as five thousand B.C. When André Malraux was the minister of culture of France, he said that we must retain a balance of interest in protecting the art of the past and the art of our time. We must balance the art of our nation and the art of all nations. We have here in our center this summer the work of one hundred and forty people from twenty-eight different nations. People can live with some awareness of what we did in the past. One of the few things that remains in time is what artists do. Artists for me are the writers and diarists of our time, and if we do not support them, then we do not have them.

You are a Renaissance artist, multi-talented and also an architect yourself. Though you have created this center, was it also with the help of the people who work here?

Yes, I did it along with the participants. We designed the building, the gardens, and the landscaping. All my work is studied here, but we also support other artists. Diversity is our strength.

You are mainly very well known as a theater artist. Eugène Ionesco said that, "Wilson has gone further than Beckett."

Yes. I made a play in 1971 that was performed in seven uninterrupted hours of silence. I played it for five and a half months to twenty-two hundred people every night. It was called *Deafman Glance*.

Are you known for language, movement, and lighting?

Lighting is one of my signatures. Einstein said, "Light is the measure of all things." Without light there is no space. I admire very much the work of the architect Louis Kahn, because he always started with light. It was the beginning of his concept.

You have worked with very famous artists and writers. Did your first breakthrough come with Philip Glass and *Einstein on the Beach*?

Phillip and I were friends, and I knew his music. In the early seventies I made a twelve hour play, from seven in the evening to seven in the morning. He came to see it, and afterward we had breakfast. I asked him, "How do you write music?" and when he explained it to me I understood that we think alike. We have a common sense of time. I have been fortunate to work with many contemporary musicians and composers. For instance, Lou Reed, Laurie Anderson, Gavin Bryars, Jessye Norman, Helmut Lachenman, Luigi Nono, Herbert Gronemeyer, and recently, Rufus Wainwright, who did the music for *The Sonnets of Shakespeare*, Arvo Pärt, who scored *Adam's Passion*, and CocoRosie, who I worked with on *Peter Pan* and *Pushkin's Fairy Tales*.

Is music your passion?

I have also worked with writers, for instance Susan Sontag, William Burroughs, Darryl Pinckney, and many others.

Was it difficult to work with William Burroughs?

It was great, between smoking dope and drinking Coca-Cola vodka. Really great.

Were you discovered by the French poet Louis Aragon at the Nancy Festival in 1971?

Yes, when Jack Lang directed the Festival of Nancy, he invited me to give two performances of my seven hour silent opera, *Deafman Glance*. Aragon came to see it and wrote a letter to André Breton, who had died some years before. He said, "Dear André,

I have seen the most beautiful thing of my life. This is what we had hoped the future would be." Pierre Cardin was also there, and he produced the work in Paris.

You are also painter, a man of culture, and a furniture designer, and you have Paula Cooper as your gallerist and dealer?

In 1965 I was living on Spring Street, long before SoHo became what it is today, and Paula moved nearby. She always believed in me. I was the black sheep. My work did not quite fit with what was happening at the time and hasn't since, but Paula always supported me.

Were you friends with other artists?

Yes. Robert Rauschenberg, John Cage, Jack Smith, Gordon Matta Clark, Lucinda Childs, Donald Judd, Richard Serra, Paul Thek, and many others. For my first play in Paris Andy Warhol gave me five large unsigned drawings. I asked Andy if he would sign them, and he said he would only if they went to a good collection. Dominique de Menil bought them for forty-five thousand dollars; it was a lot of money for Andy's drawings at that time. I asked her if I could buy them back if I ever had forty-five thousand dollars. Dominique was an amazing woman. I was with her when she was invited by President Carter to the White House; she made such a moving speech that Carter was in tears.

Do you consider yourself an American artist?

Yes, I am an American from Texas. But going back to Dominique, she was a big inspiration for me. I loved what she said when the Menil Foundation opened, "I want people to come to my museum and lose their heads. We have to do what no one else is doing."

That is very much you?

Yes, that's what I try to do. I grew up in Texas in a racist community. Houston was also racist and conservative, and Dominique was courageous, and a strong spokeswoman. She helped elect the first black senator from Texas. She also invited Nelson Mandela to speak when he was released from prison. Her collection is a kind of history of man. I lived in Dominique's house in New York for some months. It was just the two of us. It was a great education. She supported my first play when it went to Paris, and took me to the Louvre for the first time. We were walking in a long corridor and I said, "Don't you think these paintings are boring?" and she said, "Yes, but they are necessary because at the end of the corridor you will see a masterpiece." It was *La Giaconda*.

What about your relationship with Marina Abramović?

In 1971 I was at a press conference in Belgrade, and Marina was in the audience. Someone asked me a question and I answered with the word, "Dinosaur." Another question was asked and again I said, "Dinosaur." A woman started to shout after I repeatedly said the word, "Dinosaur." It went on for hours, and I kept saying "Dinosaur." The audience grew unsettled, but Marina said, "Let him speak." We met afterward and she asked me to work with her. We never did. At the end of the sixties, at the Whitney Museum of American Art there was an exhibition of work from the last decade called *Art Against Illusion*.

My work up until that time had been seen in alleys, loft spaces, and museums, and was anti-illusionistic. Seeing this exhibition I began to think, what is wrong with illusion? I started working in traditional proscenium theaters. As time went on, I became more and more interested in the illusion that is created in theaters, by light, makeup, and what is hidden behind the frame.

In 1993 I won the Golden Lion for sculpture at the Venice Biennale. The room was lit as if in another world. Years later Marina asked me to perform with her at the Biennale. I declined, saying I would never sit in a hot basement with her and all the smelly raw meat. Our works could not have been more different.

Eight years ago, she called me and said, "I have to see you." I met her and she asked if I would design her funeral. She had also asked me to make an opera about her life. For her funeral, she wanted three bodies to be buried on the same day, one in Belgrade where she was born, one in Amsterdam where she lived for many years, and one in New York where she currently resides. No one was to know where the real Marina is. I agreed to make an opera about her life, and to start with her funeral. She said, "Great, now I can see what it will be like."

And what about Lady Gaga?

Three years ago I was in New York for a few days and I was extremely busy. I was in the office, and someone told me that Lady Gaga was on the phone. I spoke to her and she asked if we could meet. I said, "Yes, what about tomorrow about two o'clock?" She said yes, and the next day she came with her bodyguards. We talked for about two hours and decided we would do a work together, and exchanged cell phone numbers. A few weeks later I was in Europe and she called. She said, "Bob, I am Gaga. Tell me something about theater." I told her the Broadway formula is to start strong and end big. She thanked me, and said that was all she needed to know. Several weeks later she called again. She said, "Hi Bob, tell me something more about theater." I said the last second is the most important, and next is the first. She thanked me.

Later she asked me if I would help her with her performance for the Video Music

Awards on MTV. As I was busy with work in Europe, I really didn't have so much time. I told her I would help her with the light and some of the scenic elements. She had a great idea, to start in the middle of the audience with four drones in her dress that would lift her up and fly her to the stage in twenty seconds or so. She had been studying the design for months. Later we were told that we were not allowed to do it. She accepted without any argument and moved on.
I came to New York a couple days before the broadcast and saw a run through. She had the idea to start with a close up of her face with a wide white collar. The camera would pull back and reveal her in a white robe. I watched a rehearsal. In two and a half minutes, she managed to change her clothes, shoes, makeup, and hair five times. At the end, the last second, she was nude except for clamshells on her tits and private parts. She is really amazing. She asked me later how she did. I told her she learns fast. Henri Loyrette, the director of the Louvre, had asked me to do an exhibition, and I asked Gaga to be in it. I made portraits of her from classical paintings from the museum's collection. Again, she was truly amazing. She stood or sat for hours with little or no movement. Her interior sense became her exterior expression. There was no change of clothes, no change of makeup, only a deep, inner concentration. It was very touching. Gaga and I are still friends, and together we did a work called *Cheek to Cheek* with Tony Bennett. He told me, "I have worked with Ella Fitzgerald and Barbra Streisand, but Gaga's voice is the best."

What are your next moves?

Next I will be directing Verdi's *La traviata* at the Landestheater in Linz. Also in development is a production of Puccini's *Turandot*, a radio play called *The Tower of Babel*, a performance of the Norse epic, the *Edda*, and an opera about the life of Nicola Tesla, which I am working on with Jim Jarmusch and Tilda Swinton.
I am sorry but now I must stop, because I must prepare for a wedding of my friend Christopher Knowles. He is a genius, and he and I have worked together since he was very young. He sees the world geometrically and mathematically. He changed my life. I enjoyed talking to you, but I must go as I am an hour late.

The Watermill Center, New York.
August 14, 2015

SOMETIMES

IN THE SMALL

THERE IS MORE THAN IN

the big.

Alain Elkann is an Italian writer and journalist. He has written fifteen novels, namely: *Piazza Carignano, Misguided Lives, The French Father, Money Should Stay in the Family,* and *Envy;* translated into many different languages. Additionally, Alain has written three books of short stories, three nonfiction books and several books of interviews with: Chief Rabbi of Rome Elio Toaff, Cardinal Carlo Maria Martini, Prince Hassan bin Talal of Jordan, the Italian writer Alberto Moravia, and the artist Michelangelo Pistoletto. Alain has been a counselor to the Italian cultural ministry, and the Chairman of the Egyptian museum in Turin. Awarded the *Legion d'Honneur* by the French Republic, Elkann presently serves as President of the Foundation for Italian Art and Culture and is a professor at the University of Pennsylvania and the Hebrew University of Jerusalem. He is on the board of the Italian Academy of Columbia Universtiy and the Chairman of the Friends of the Hanbury Gardens, in La Mortola. He has been a regular contributor to *La Stampa* newspaper for over thirty years.

ACKNOWLEDGMENTS

Thank you to Jacqueline, who patiently stands at my side to support and counsel me, every week, week after week.
Thank you to each of the seven editors of *La Stampa,* who have all granted me complete freedom of choice in my interviews published under the banner of "Domenica con" Alain Elkann in their esteemed newspaper every Sunday since 1989. They are Paolo Mieli, Ezio Mauro, Carlo Rossella, Marcello Sorgi, Giulio Anselmi, Mario Calabresi and Maurizio Molinari. Thank you to David Hornsby for his friendship and precious assistance as the manager and editor of our blog alainelkanninterviews.com. He has helped me publish my interviews online since 2014. Thank you to my agent Marco Vigevani who has progressed it with me.

Thank you to Prosper and Martine Assouline, as well as their very professional and attentive staff, who have ensured the publication of this book.

Most of all, I want to say thank you to the so many very special people who have agreed to be interviewed over the years. Only some of you can be in this book, others will hopefully be in another book. All the people who I have interviewed, and who I hope to interview in the future, contribute hugely to making my life special. I am deeply grateful and privileged to meet them to learn so many fascinating things about their lives, their professions and their thought.

An interview is the image of a moment that remains for ever. I love my gallery of portraits.